PARADIGM BUSTERS

BEYOND SCIENCE • LOST HISTORY • ANCIENT WISDOM

edited by

J. DOUGLAS KENYON

With articles by Philip Coppens, Frank Joseph,
Robert M. Schoch Ph.D., Steven Sora, and others

FROM THE ATLANTIS RISING® MAGAZINE LIBRARY

This edition first published in 2015 by
Atlantis Rising®
P.O. Box 441
Livingston, MT 59047
www.atlantisrising.com
1-800-228-8381

Distributed by Red Wheel/Weiser, LLC
With offices at:
665 Third Street, Suite 400
San Francisco, CA 94107
www.redwheelweiser.com

ISBN: 978-1-9906904-0-5

Library of Congress Cataloging-in-Publication Data available upon request

Edited by J. Douglas Kenyon
From the Atlantis Rising® Magazine Library

Cover design and layout by Kathryn Sky-Peck
Text design and layout by Denis Ouellette
Photos and illustrations reprinted from *Atlantis Rising®* magazine

Printed in the United States of America
EBM
10 9 8 7 6 5 4 3 2 1

Contents

Part ONE • *Beyond Science*

Part TWO • *Lost History*

Part THREE • *Ancient Wisdom*

Acknowledgments

This book represents the hard work of several people who sacrificed much to made it happen. In particular, we would like to thank Denis Ouellette, our go-to graphics guy, whose considerable design and production skills account for most of what you now hold in your hands. A special *thank you* is also due to Randy Haragan, for the cover design and concept, and to Darsi Vanatta who proofed the pages.

It goes without saying, of course, that we are especially indebted to the many excellent contributing authors of *Atlantis Rising* magazine who have provided us all with so much outstanding content. (Their other published materials, with respective web sites, are listed in the back, along with a brief bio of each.) For all of these contributors, and others whom we have doubtless forgotten to mention, we are grateful, and hope that all will be pleased with the fruit of their labor.

From the cover: Pharaoh Akhenaten (*"Living Spirit of Aten"*), one of the greatest paradigm busters in history. He overthrew the established Egyptian religion and replaced it with a monotheistic faith dedicated to the worship of Aten. This bas-relief also depicts Nefertiti (wife and co-ruler) with their three children. Ra, the Sun God (Aten), shines down upon them. (Ra is mentioned in Chapters 19 & 25.)

Introduction

The next time some pompous television narrator pronounces, in reference to some scientific issue—the "Big Bang" for instance—that "we know" something, you might consider substituting the phrase "we believe." If you try to do it every time, however, you may find yourself too busy to follow the program.

The "Big Bang"—the idea that the universe emerged from the mother of all explosions billions of years ago—has replaced God, these days (at least among the scientifically 'sophisticated') as the most popular notion of first cause, and is asserted regularly as something, "we now know." The idea, in fact, has become the new orthodoxy, and woe be unto those who would challenge it. But, in fact, the Big Bang is still just a theory, albeit a popular one. It is based on the claim that the universe is expanding; an idea which, in turn, is based on the observation of a shift toward red in the light spectrum of stars which should, it is believed, be interpreted to mean that the stars are moving away from us, thus generating a doppler effect (the same thing that causes a train whistle to change pitch as it approaches and leaves us) which shows up as "redshift."

The distinguished astronomer Halton Arp, however, has shown that there must be other things that can cause such "redshift." Arp's point is buttressed by the discovery in 2005 *between* us and a nearby galaxy (NGC 7319) of a quasar having *greater* redshift, when, according to the theory it should have *less*, thus, essentially falsifying, the redshift-equals-distance orthodoxy, but Arp's case, compelling though it may seem, has not dissuaded mainstream cosmologists from claiming to "know" that the idea of an expanding universe and its corollary the "Big Bang" are *so* (in other words, something we "know").

Belief and *knowledge* are so frequently confused these days that they may often seem indistinguishable, but the difference could not be more important. *Belief* is something common to all of us, and, to get along in this world, we must learn to respect it, but *knowledge* demands something more from us, maybe even obedience.

"Knowledge," it has been said, "is power," and it is clear that those who claim that their *beliefs* are actually *knowledge* think that they should be in charge. Moreover, these *knowers* seem to think that those "dangerous" individuals who question the authority of their *knowledge* should be sanctioned. Arp, for instance, though once having been quite influential in the highest councils of astronomy, found his challenge to the Big Bang had turned him into something of a non-entity and made him *persona non grata* in those same circles—his career virtually terminated.

From the heliocentric solar system, to cold fusion, the same phenomenon plays out over and over in scientific debate, and some, like writer Thomas Kuhn (*The Structure of Scientific Revolutions*) have perceived a recurring pattern in which ideas which are unthinkable to one generation become the orthodoxy of the next.

If we want to be free now, though, from the tyranny which certain elites would seek to impose on us, we will have to learn to do our own thinking. The first step in that process could very well be to remember that many who claim to *know* may only *believe*. And though they may feel quite passionate on the matter, the rest of us will need to hear something much better before enlisting in their cause.

In the articles collected for this book from the bi-monthly magazine, *Atlantis Rising*, we hope to show that many of the *beliefs* of our supposedly advanced society are a long way from *knowledge*—particularly in the areas of modern science, ancient history, and today's conventional *wisdoms*. If, in so doing, a few sacred paradigms are busted, we say, let the chips fall where they may! ∞

J. Douglas Kenyon,
Editor & Publisher,
Atlantis Rising®

Part ONE

Beyond Science

Kung Fu practice

David Blaine at
New York's Lincoln
Center, 2007

Martial Arts and the Laws of Physics

What Is Science to Do When the 'Impossible' Happens?

William B. Stoecker

Are the incredible feats of some martial artists a challenge to the standard model of physics? Is their brick-breaking, for example, evidence that some of them can control a mysterious primal energy? And martial artists are not alone; throughout history people have done things that would seem impossible for mere flesh and blood.

Modern physics is having problems to begin with, resting uneasily on the twin pillars of relativity theory and quantum mechanics. There has

Karate master and
Hollywood icon, Bruce Lee

been a problem all along with reconciling quantum gravity with relativistic gravity, and grand unified theories (GUTs) have tried and generally failed to bridge the gap. The current favorite is string theory, already morphing into membrane theory, which, unfortunately, cannot be tested either to prove or disprove it. Then there are problems like the missing solar neutrinos, the controversy over dark matter and now dark energy as well, the lack of any single and credible explanation for the magnetic fields of celestial bodies, and the problem of explaining all the internal heat of planets, especially the outer planets of our own solar system.

A lot of people believe that the famous Michelson-Morley experiment in the late nineteenth century proved that there is no luminiferous ether, but it is impossible to prove a negative proposition (like proving that God, Santa Claus, or Bigfoot do not exist). Michelson and Morley never made such a claim; they were simply unable to detect an ether, and Michelson, years later, stated that he suspected that there was some kind of ether filling all of space. Einstein also admitted that relativity actually required an ether. And, in recent years, with little publicity, a handful of trained physicists and astronomers have challenged many of the assumptions of the standard model and the big bang.

As stated above, it is not just martial artists who present a challenge. In *Atlantis Rising* (#70), Len Kasten's article "The Superhero Factor" suggested (as many of us have suspected over the years) that some stage magicians, rather than making mere tricks look paranormal, may actually have some paranormal powers, which they pretend are just tricks. Kasten gave the example of David Copperfield, who seemingly levitated over the Grand Canyon, walked through the Great Wall of China, and made the Statue of Liberty disappear. David Blaine supposedly held his breath for 17 minutes (the world record, without breathing oxygen to prepare for the feat, is officially eight minutes and 58 seconds). Blaine also was publicly encased in ice for 63 hours, 42 minutes, and 15 seconds. Magician Criss Angel has repeatedly levitated in public, once floating some 200 feet from one roof to another and, on another occasion, floating for 10 minutes above the Luxor Pyramid in Las Vegas. Once he seemingly walked on water across a swimming pool, with people swimming under and around him. None of this actually proves paranormal abilities, but such acts are extremely difficult to explain.

In addition to magicians and martial artists, others have demonstrated abilities that are exceedingly diffi-cult to explain away. The teleki-netic feats of Uri Geller and Nina Kulagina might be nothing more than stage magic, but what about the apparent levitation performed by medium Daniel Dunglas Hume, reportedly witnessed by several reputable people? Many, many decades ago, the Polish strongman Siegmund Breitbart, it is claimed, bit through steel chains and pounded spikes into wooden beams with his bare hands. If these acts were not somehow faked, it is impossible for human teeth to cut steel, which is much, much harder, stronger, and less brittle than human bone and tooth enamel. And human flesh and blood would be bruised and even lacerated by pounding against the spikes.

Purported levitation of D.D. Home

More recent accounts of incredible feats are better documented. Some have been videotaped and even televised, as on the "Stan Lee's Superhu-mans" program. "Hammerhead" John Ferraro, a wrestler and strong man, can pound nails into wood with his head and has had assistants break a stack of bricks on his head. This is at least stretching the limits of what is possible for unaided flesh and blood.

A Belgian free diver, Patrick Musimu, dived to 685 feet underwater just holding his breath, with no scuba or other breathing gear. To put this in perspective, scuba divers rarely go deeper than 200 feet without special gas mixtures, which require more advanced training. I have been diving for many, many years and have never been deeper than 90 feet. Wim Hof, the Dutch "iceman," stayed one hour, 13 minutes, and 48 seconds in an ice bath.

He also climbed Kilimanjaro in shorts and did a marathon, also while wearing shorts, when the temperature was four degrees below zero Fahrenheit. He practiced "tummo," a discipline developed by Tibetan Buddhist monks of the Kagyu tradition; these monks claim that they harness the kundalini energy, producing internal heat as a kind of by-product and, to test themselves, wrap themselves in wet sheets in cold weather and dry the sheets with the heat they produce. This has been pretty well documented. At first glance, Hof's hour in an ice bath sounds less impressive than David Blaine's incredible 63 hours in ice, but Hof was in a mixture of ice and liquid water, which would conduct his body heat away more rapidly.

Then there are the magnetic people. Miroslav Magula can cause heavy metal objects to stick to his body and claims to be able to control the force; he was studied by Dr. Friedbert Karger at the Max Planck Institute in Germany in 1997. Liew Thow Lin in Malaysia has been videotaped doing the same thing and was studied by Professor Doctor Mohamed Amin Alias at the Malaysian Universiti Teknologi. Lin and was featured on the Discovery Channel's "One Step Beyond."

But martial artists are probably the largest single group of people who demonstrate abilities hard to explain in conventional terms, with the possible exception of Tibetan monks. A few words of explanation are in order. The term "martial arts" means any art of war, including rifle marksmanship or the ability to pilot a fighter jet. But it is generally used in a more narrow sense to refer to unarmed combat or fighting with clubs and sticks and edged weapons. Western martial arts, like boxing and wrestling, tend to be more fluid and improvisational than most of the Far Eastern arts, which emphasize meditation, breathing, and the practice of often complex but rigidly defined movements called "katas." The one exception is Thai kick boxing, which is as fluid and improvisational as Western boxing.

The Oriental martial arts can be roughly divided into those that mainly emphasize punching, hand strikes, and kicking, and those that emphasize throws, locks, and choke holds. The first category includes such arts as karate, Korean Tai Kwan Do, and some forms of Kung Fu. Kung Fu, or Wushu refers to a variety of Chinese martial arts; some forms of kung fu seem to have originated in the famous Shaolin Buddhist monastery as far back as the seventh century. Kung fu seems to be closely related to the disciplines of Tao Yin, Quigong, and Tai Chi Chuan, systems of postures, exercises, and breath control believed to enhance health and mental well-being. Their similarity to hatha yoga is almost certainly more than coincidental.

Other forms of kung fu, and Japanese jiu-jitsu emphasize holds, locks, and throws more than hand strikes or kicks. Jiujitsu practitioners claim to use the opponent's strength against him. In the late nineteenth century Kano Jigoro developed judo from jiu-jitsu; it is somewhat less lethal (and, arguably, less effective for self-defense) and places a greater emphasis on throws. Mitsuyo Maeda brought jiu-jitsu to Brazil in 1914 and taught it to his friend Carlos Gracie. The Gracie family then developed Brazilian jiu-jitsu, which involves a lot of grappling on the ground or mat. Marihei Ueshiba developed, also from jiu-jitsu, aikido, which is less lethal and attempts to redirect attacks rather than meet them head on.

Most of these Oriental martial arts use meditation, certain postures, and breath control as part of their training, and as any Bruce Lee fan will attest, almost all of them claim to develop a mysterious energy source known by many names across the world: chi, ki, mana, prana, kundalini, orgone energy, vril, and odic force. It is believed that this energy fills all of space and can be controlled by the human will. While indigenous shamanic traditions may be one source for this belief, the Hindu practices of India, especially Hatha Yoga, were almost certainly the main influence. Of course, Yoga itself may have first been developed by shamans on the sub-continent, but given the evidence for the extreme antiquity of civilization in India, that would have been many, many thousands of years ago, far back in prehistory. Knowledge of Yoga could have spread directly and, via Buddhism, indirectly.

Not only might this explain the extreme feats of breaking stacks of bricks or concrete blocks or multiple boards at once, but it might be true, as the Shaolin monks claim, that it is the source of their "iron shirt" technique, which makes them seemingly impervious to thrusts from sharp spears and blows to the head with heavy sticks. Trickery can never be entirely ruled out, but these feats have repeatedly been witnessed, video-taped, and televised. Perhaps it is this technique that allows John Ferraro to perform his incredible acts.

If, indeed, the abilities of some martial artists are due to their control of the chi force, there is a need for thoroughly and rigidly controlled experiments. It should be possible to eliminate any fraud and to determine with certainty if certain acts are possible for unaided muscle and bone or not. Also, just as amateur investigators of hauntings use sensitive instruments to detect electric and magnetic fields, researchers studying martial arts should do the same. I strongly suspect that martial artists, channeling chi, may produce such fields as a side effect; this might also explain the magnetic people described earlier. The problem is that few reputable and professional scientists are willing to undertake such experiments; and amateurs, no matter how intelligent, honest, and thorough they may be (like the people who investigate hauntings), are seldom taken seriously. Much is at stake here.

The chi force, if it exists, may very well be the ether, a dynamic ether that could be a source of inexhaustible "free" energy, and which could, perhaps, lead to new medical technologies. But there is even more to it than that: if the human will controls chi, and chi is the ether, perhaps the primal source of all matter and energy, this would seem to undermine the atheist/materialist status quo so popular among all too many scientists today. ❦

2.

Mystery of the Montauk Monster

*Bizarre Discoveries on Long Island
Raise New Concerns about Old,
but Not Forgotten, Dangers*

Steven Sora

In January of 2010 the last of several very unusual creatures was discovered on the beaches near Montauk Point on New York's Long Island. To date, the creatures have not been identified as any known species. They had turned up in July of 2008 and again in 2009. The mostly-local media had a field day with what was dubbed the "Montauk Monster." Opinions varied sharply on just what the creatures were. It was claimed that they could be some kind of bioterror weapon, possibly carrying the H1N1 swine-flu virus or some other form of contagion. Others said it was the corpse of a dog bloated by long exposure in the seawater. Even Jeff Corwin of the Animal Planet weighed in. In his opinion the mutant creature was simply a raccoon.

CNN and Fox News both played down speculation of an unknown creature being discovered, although experts including William Wise of Stony Brook University's Living Marine Resource said it was not anything that had been seen before. The hairless creature was not a sea turtle outside of his shell since Turtles don't have teeth. It wasn't a large raccoon as the legs were too long in proportion to the body. It was not a rodent based on the unusual teeth, and it could not be a dog as the prominent eyeridge and shape of the feet didn't match.

The first monster had washed up in Southold on the island's quiet North Fork. When another washed up in tony East Hampton, Fox News announced "Its baaaack." Then still another made an appearance on the other side of the Sound in Milford, Connecticut. All were described as smelling badly and looking worse, by all accounts hideous in appearance. While the creatures were compared to different animals, there was agreement on the odd physical characteristics shared by all three. The fourth creature was more human-like.

The first three, though, were not anything close to human. In fact, one of the closest comparisons was to an odd animal called the Chupacabra. The name itself means "goat-sucker" as early reported victims were mostly goats. These creatures would, it is said, leave behind the partially eaten remains of their victims. Loren Coleman, the dean of cryptozoological studies with several books on mysterious creatures to his credit, says the Chupacabras had never been seen until they were found in Puerto Rico in 1995, where as many as 150 farm animals and pets were killed. Since then, these four-foot-tall, large-headed animals have been spotted in Mexico, as far south as Colombia and as far north as Maine. In Texas two were reportedly found. One was eventually declared to be a dog with terrible mange. The other was said to have features of a dog, a kangaroo and a rat.

Could These Creatures Have Reached Long Island?

If there are mutant creatures lurking anywhere on eastern Long Island, the first place usually suspected is Plum Island. The relatively small, 840-acre island lies in the Long Island Sound between the eastern end of Long Island and the southern coastline of Connecticut. It started out as a USDA research facility at the end of World War II. The charter called for investigation into curing animal ailments such as hoof and mouth disease. But this was at a time when the American military, it is reported, was importing ex-Nazi scientists under Operation Paperclip. As many as 2000 were allowed into the United States. They were hired, it is alleged, to continue work begun under Hitler, from the building of rockets and weapons, to more ominous bio-terror weapons.

It was in 1954 that the research became less defensive and more offensive. Specifically the study was intended to provide a way of carrying disease to enemy livestock. Dr. Eric Traub was one of the early German researchers whose mission was to see if ticks could be used to spread disease. He had studied in America in the 1930's and belonged to a German-American "club" referred to as Camp Seigfried before the war. The camp was based in Yaphank, 30 miles from Plum Island. He was a Nazi scientist until the end of the war when the Soviets forced him briefly to work for them. He then escaped to the United States. His Paperclip agreement had him working at Fort Detrick and Plum Island.

These two facilities are on the highest level of such biological research outside of the Center for Disease Control in Atlanta. Two independent researchers Steven Nostrum and John Loftus (author of *The Belarus Secret*) made the connection between this ticks-as-weapons research and the outbreak of a new disease in southern Connecticut. In 1975 the disease was named for the place it was first reported, Lyme Connecticut. Eastern Long Island remains the record holder for the highest incidence of Lyme Disease.

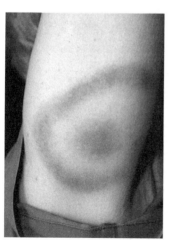

Lyme Disease Target Rash
(CDC)

The victims infected with Lyme Disease suffer from a host of flu-like symptoms including fatigue, headache, joint pains, and sometime, but not always, a target-like rash at the point of infection. Months after infection, even worse problems occur including arthritis, meningitis, inflammation of the heart, and muscle weakness. It is treatable with antibiotics but often misdiagnosed. At its worst, it is an incapacitating disease that causes memory loss, constant pain, paralysis, blindness and even death.

It is transferred to humans through the bite of a tick, mostly the smaller ticks called deer ticks. The tick itself must be infected with Borrelia burgdorferi, a bacteria. The Nazis as well as Japan's infamous Unit 731 studied the Borrelia genus. Why suddenly did this outbreak begin in 1975? Several researchers point to the island two miles from Long Island's North Fork. Several researchers believe that the ticks were not only infected as part of an experiment but purposely released as part of that experiment.

Coincidentally, or not, America entered the 70s under the impression that most diseases had been conquered.

Then, in rapid succession, we discovered Lyme Disease, AIDS, Hantavirus, Legionnaires disease, Hepatitis C, Mad Cow, Lassa fever, and Ebola Virus. Other diseases returned in stronger and more resistant forms. Could research into weapons of bioterror be to blame?

A USDA internal memo circulated in 1978 titled "African Swine Fever" mentioned that Plum Island was experimenting with ticks as a means of transmitting disease. No one seemed to object, as very few had enough concrete information to connect the dots.

The nature of Plum Island's research was already known, however. Cuba would claim that that island's agriculture was under attack. It was most likely a reliable claim, as years later Cuba's Agricultural Research Service is on record asking for a role in our nation's bioterrorism research. In 1999 President Clinton agreed. After all, it is speculated, the winds came from the west and any accidents would simply be blown out to sea.

With the blessing of Congress and the President, Plum Island became the only other laboratory on the level of Ft. Detrick in Maryland. Its mission is the study of zoonotic disease that can be transmitted to humans from animals. These include West Nile disease, Ebola, and Lyme disease. Not everyone was happy.

The top secret nature of the island was not as secret as it was intended to be. In 2001 the New York Times broke the secrecy about "Project Jefferson." This effort by the Department of Defense enlisted Plum Island researchers to study a way to create a vaccine-resistant form of anthrax. Clearly the research was not intended for anything the USDA might have originally envisioned. The government's reaction to being outed was to classify such research and then to turn the facility over to Homeland Security.

With the speculation that disease could escape from an accident on the tiny island, possibly spreading to nearby New York City, any publicity was bad news. One of the worst situations came in 2002 when the union that controlled nearly half of the Plum Island workers staged a walkout. Substitute workers were brought in to insure that decontamination efforts and wastewater treatment would not be compromised. Then the water treatments were compromised. The FBI was brought in to see if this was the result of sabotage. Again the New York Times broke the story and residents of both eastern Long Island and Connecticut were frantic to find out if the air, the water, or their shoreline was contaminated.

The publicity, apparently, brought much more heat than the Government would have preferred. Reporters and freelance researchers attempted to get in on the story. The Government stepped up its guard. Workers on the island would not be permitted to stay overnight and would take a government ferry to and from the island. No one would be allowed either to make contact with the workers or attempt to get close to the island. Even fishermen were warned away. Such defensive measures might work near Area 51, but Long Island is just too populous to keep such a secret.

In 1997 best-selling novelist Nelson DeMille wrote a fictional work about a secret bioterror facility and did not attempt to hide the location. His book was *Plum Island* and a skull and crossbones decorate the cover. The same year *The Poison Plum* by Les Roberts was also published about the facility. So much for Top Secret.

Plum Island was again the source of speculation in 1999 when West Nile Virus hit New York State. It started with the deaths of as many as 10,000 birds, including exotic birds in the Bronx zoo. Then it began to hit horses and cows, killing half the city's cows. The official story was that it was most likely carried from a visitor from Africa to New York City. The problem with blaming it on the global community is that the disease, like Lyme, results from being bitten by a mosquito that carries it—not from a human infecting a mosquito or another human. Also, like Lyme Disease, the symptoms include fever, headaches, body aches, and sometimes a rash. There were 254 cases of West Nile starting in 1999 and 26 deaths as a result. And according to New York State's Department of Health, there may now be over 100 infected mosquito pools, one third on Long Island, two thirds in New York City itself.

The *Wall Street Journal* covered a story about Plum Island in 2002 quoting both scientists and government officials saying the facility should

be closed. Officials seemed un-
concerned about safety but very
concerned over the expanding
budget. When a whistle-blower
came forward regarding the
safety concerns, he was fired. At
the same time, Vermont's Senator
Patrick Leahy publicly ques-
tioned whether the West Nile
Disease was actually caused by
researchers. He had received an
anthrax-laden letter shortly after
the attacks of September 11 and
it was later determined that the
anthrax had come from Fort Detrick, Maryland.

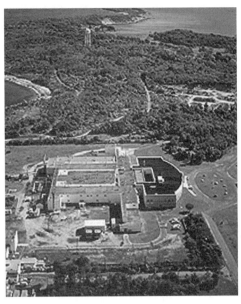

Plum Island Animal Disease
Research Center

In 2004, *Lab 257: The Disturbing Story of the Government's
Secret Plum Island Germ Labora-
tory* was released. The author, New York attorney. Michael Christopher
Carroll, covered Plum Island from its inception with Operation Paperclip.
The "Army Chemical Review" would conclude the book was highly
accurate but deny the link to Lyme Disease. From 1975 to 2010, Lyme
has continued to spread throughout the United States. If the Government
admitted such research, it could present a serious litigation problem.

However, in 2008, a Pakistani woman, possibly linked to Al-Queda,
was arrested. She was carrying notes about a mass casualty attack on Plum
Island. Since only 200 work there, the mass of casualties can only refer
to nearby New York if, indeed, the island's refrigerators, holding everything from Ebola to polio, are crippled.

The recent "Montauk Monster" discoveries may be connected to the
Government's decision to finally close the labs of Plum Island. The new
plan was announced shortly after the last strange creature was washed up
on nearby Long Island's shores. Witnesses said it was humanoid in appearance with elongated fingers. Police were tight-lipped but commented
wryly that it was most likely a neurosurgery patient as indicated by five
holes drilled in the head.

Recently, former wrestler and Minnesota Governor Jesse Ventura, who investigated the story for his series "Conspiracy Theory," announced with a bit of incredulity: The lab and all its contents was actually being moved far from Manhattan, New York, to Manhattan, Kansas.

In September of 2010, the Department of Homeland Security posted a message on its website declaring that the additional space to research animal diseases is needed but is not available, so, they will be moving. The new National Bio and Agro-Defense Facility will replace the Plum Island Animal Disease Center. The message also reiterates that they have never done any research into Lyme Disease. It does, however, mention that the newer facility will be studying Nipah virus, Hendra Virus, African Swine Fever, and Rift Valley Fever as well as a host of others. ❧

Close Encounter
of the Ball Lightning Kind

When a Simple Business Trip
Turns into a Paranormal Adventure

Frank Joseph

Some paranormal events are so extraordinary and inexplicable that they form the outstanding experiences of a lifetime. My own encounter began at daybreak last September 16, when publisher Wayne May and I drove from the offices of his magazine, *Ancient American*, in Colfax, Wisconsin, to an alternative archaeology symposium some 200 miles away.

Before arriving at Marquette, Michigan, where attendees of the Ancient American Preservation Society were meeting the next day, we stopped overnight at a friend's country home little more than an hour's drive from the conference site. Alex, our gracious host, was a Vietnam War veteran, whose bizarre mix of macabre and hilarious recollections kept us up until almost midnight. He also suffers from multiple sclerosis, a chronic, inflammatory disease that attacks various parts of the nervous system leading to muscular disability. Although confined to an automated wheelchair, Alex's mind and spirit are bright and indomitable.

Sometime after 11:00, Wayne and I were shown to our sleeping quarters in a large room on the second floor. A faint drizzle was falling outside, typical of the rainy conditions through which we had passed most of the day during our drive toward Michigan's Upper Peninsula. We doused the lights; the room fell into perfect darkness and silence; and I was soon drifting off to sleep, when I heard a loud "snap!" or "click!" that reminded me of a circuit breaker being thrown.

"What was that?" I asked Wayne, who was lying in his own bed on the far side of the room. He had not yet fallen asleep but happened to be staring unseeing into the night toward the ceiling, thinking about the upcoming conference. The sudden sound brought my mind back to full consciousness, and I opened my eyes.

A nineteenth century engraving depicts a ball lightening event.

Responding to my question, Wayne could only offer, "I don't know." Just then, an intensely bright light exploded, without any additional noise, in our room. The white wall I faced in the darkness lit up in a sheet of intense violet brilliance. I thought at once that an electrical short had shot through the house. But the source of this abrupt incandescence winked on just where Wayne had been staring in the darkness. He was looking directly at a spherical white light the size and shape of a large soft-ball encircled from top to bottom by a broad band of purple neon hanging motionless and without a sound near the ceiling fan. A broad skirt of violet light streamed like an enormous lampshade descending from the orb to illuminate all four walls, leaving the floor and ceiling relatively unlit.

Although the object popped into existence with the abruptness of an exceptionally potent flashbulb, it lingered longer, perhaps two seconds.

It left Wayne blind for a few seconds more until he was able to make out the midnight horizon beyond our rain-streaked windows stabbed with about a dozen lightning strikes. These were followed shortly thereafter by a rolling series of thunderclaps that shook the whole house.

Given the surrounding storm, we assumed our brilliant visitor must have been a meteorological phenomenon of some kind, most likely a form of ball lightning, an atmospheric electrical discharge little understood by science. Most of what is known about ball lightning derives from eyewitness accounts that vary greatly in their descriptions. Reports of color, size, configuration, movement, behavior, or sound all differ in the extreme. The brilliant orbs range from more than 10 feet across down to the dimensions of a pea, with shades of red, green, white, or purple, mostly blue.

According to Brian Dunning, writing for Skeptoid, Critical Analysis of Pop Phenomena (http://skeptoid.com/ episodes/4192, 2010), "Electromagnetic theory makes no prediction that anything like ball lightning need exist. It does predict all known forms of electrical discharge. Some have speculated that ball lightning is a plasma ball, but that theory has been dismissed, because a hot globe of plasma should rise like a hot-air balloon, and that is not what ball lightning does."

Our September 16 encounter did not match this or any other description of ball lightning I was able to locate on the Internet. The orb Wayne saw did not move, nor did its purple band and descending skirt of light resemble anything we could learn about ball lightning, which is invariably characterized as highly mobile, of a single color, and not accompanied by a lampshade-like formation.

Alex wondered if the powerfully charged sphere would have injured, or even killed him, had it appeared instead in his downstairs bedroom, where his sleeping facilities comprise a kind of metal cage he uses to climb in and out of bed. In fact, several documented encounters with ball lightning proved fatal for human observers.

During what was known as "the Great Thunderstorm" of October 21, 1638, four parishioners were killed and some 60 other persons injured by an eight-foot-wide fireball that crashed through the roof of an English church at Widecombe-in-the-Moor, Devon. Large stones crashed to the ground together with huge, wooden beams, while pews were wrecked. The fireball split in two, one half smashing through a window to escape back into the sky, while the other disappeared within the church itself, its ruins almost obscured under a sulfurous pall of thick, dark smoke.

In that unscientific age, the incident was naturally blamed on the Devil. "Later," according to an early twentieth century source (John S. Amery, Joshua Brooking Rowe [1905], Devon Notes and Queries, J. G. Commin, p. viii), "some blamed the entire incident on two people who had been playing cards in the pew during the sermon, thereby incurring God's wrath."

On August 29, 1726, the sloop *Catherine and Mary*, while passing through the Gulf of Florida in a violent thunderstorm, was struck by a fireball that killed a crew member and severed the hand of another man.

Later that same century, "Admiral Chambers on board the *Montague*, November 4, 1749, was taking an observation just before noon … he observed a large ball of blue fire about three miles distant from them. They immediately lowered their topsails, but it came up so fast upon them, that, before they could raise the main tack, they observed the ball rise almost perpendicularly, and not above forty or fifty yards from the main chains, when it went off with an explosion, as great as if a hundred cannons had been discharged at the same time, leaving behind it a strong, sulphurous smell. By this explosion the main topmast was shattered into pieces and the main mast went down to the keel. Five men were knocked down and one of them much bruised. Just before the explosion, the ball seemed to be the size of a large mill-stone." (Norton, Andrews, editor [1813], *The General Repository and Review*, Vol. 3., Cambridge, MA: William Hilliard, p. 157).

Four years later, a Russian scientist, Professor Georg Richmann, was killed near Saint Petersburg as he endeavored to reproduce Benjamin Franklin's kite-and-key experiment of 1752. Ball lightning shot down the string to strike Richmann's forehead, on which it left a red mark, blew his shoes open, and singed his clothes. An engraver he brought along to document his research was knocked unconscious but survived. (Clarke, Ronald W., [1983], Benjamin Franklin, A Biography, NY: Random House, p. 87).

The most aggressive ball lightning attack at sea occurred during a storm in 1809, when HMS Warren Hastings was simultaneously beset by a trio of celestial spheres. A crewman on deck was struck dead by an orb that also engulfed the mainmast in flames. A sailor who tried to retrieve his shipmate's corpse was hit by a second fireball that blew him back and gave him mild burns, while another seaman died after being struck by a third sphere. The entire incident took place in under one minute, although a persistent, sickening small of sulfur hung over the British ship for the rest of the night (Simons, Paul, 17 February 2009, "Weather Eye Charles Darwin, the meteorologist," *The Times*, London).

Wilfred de Fonvielle, the French science writer, told how, "On the tenth of September, 1845 a ball of lightning entered the kitchen of a house in the village of Salagnac in the valley of Correze. This ball rolled across without doing any harm to two women and a young man who were here; but on getting into an adjoining stable it exploded and killed a pig, which happened to be shut up there, and which, knowing nothing about the wonders of thunder and lightning, dared to smell it in the most rude and unbecoming manner" (de Fonvielle, Wilfrid, 1875, Chapter X: Globular Lightning, Thunder and Lightning, translated by T.L. Phipson).Patrick Baird was rendered unconscious by ball lightning that struck Western Australia's Cape Naturaliste Lighthouse, where he was its keeper in July 1907. Apparently, Alex had good cause for concern. He did recall, however, learning of a woman some years ago who was immersed in a specially-made, all-metal bathtub, when lightning shot down either the chimney or, more likely, the vent pipe. Instead of suffering electrocution, she survived. No less miraculously, her multiple sclerosis went into remission. But so little is understood about both the phenomenon and the disease; whatever relationship they may share is unknown.

Globe of fire descending into a room.

Perhaps more than coincidentally, persons afflicted with multiple sclerosis appear to undergo a range of psychic phenomena—particularly out-of-body experiences— mostly beyond the frequency and intensity of others not suffering from such a condition. An out-of-body experience is a sensation of floating outside of one's physical form, often seeing his or her own body from a removed perspective.

It seems clear, however, that the bright orb we encountered last fall was connected somehow to meteorological conditions on the night it appeared near the ceiling and must have been a seldom-seen example of ball lightning. Until recently—in the mid-twentieth century—modern science did not even admit the possibility of such occurrences, strictly relegating them to the realms of fairy tales and liars' clubs.

A 1960 study found that five percent of the U.S. population—some thirteen million Americans—claimed to have witnessed ball lightning, while another inquiry analyzed reports of ten thousand cases (McNally, J. R., 1960, "Preliminary Report on Ball Lightning," *Proceedings of the Second Annual Meeting of the Division of Plasma Physics of the American Physical Society,* Paper J-15 ed., Gatlinburg, and Grigoriev, A. I., 1988, Y. H. Ohtsuki editor, "Statistical Analysis of the Ball Lightning Properties," *Sci-*

On December 12, 1938, during a Mediterranean storm, a passenger aboard the TSS Viceroy of India witnessed a ball of lightning plunge into the sea and later made this painting.

ence of Ball Lightning, Singapore, World Scientific Publishing Co.). Today, the International Committee on Ball Lightning holds regular symposia on the subject in Russia—most recently, 2008, in Kaliningrad—each year.

Forms of ball lightning have been produced under scientifically controlled conditions, but the nature of these experiments is so diverse nothing definite can be concluded from them. German researchers at the Max Planck Institute for Physics, in Munich, discharged a high-voltage capacitor in a tank of water to create a ball lightning-type effect. It has been similarly reproduced by Israeli scientists, Eli Jerby and Vladimir Dikhtyar, who simply placed a lit match in a common, home microwave oven ("Creating the fourth state of matter with microwaves by Halina Stanley," www.scienceinschool.org, 13 August 2009). At sudden, high temperatures, the match flared into a large fireball, above which "plasma balls" floated near the ceiling of the oven chamber.

In the early 1980s, an American physicist created identical phenomena by gradually applying pressure to slabs of granite. Just as the specimens broke and disintegrated, tiny orbs of electric light—mostly deep blue—flew from the rock, as revealed by high-speed cameras.

These experiments prove nothing, save that ball lightning exists and can be reproduced under a variety of circumstances. They seem to have little if anything to do with the stormy or at least rainy conditions during which most instances of ball lightning are reported. To be sure, the encounter we experienced on September 16 lacked most of the known features that characterize ball lightning. Other than its apparent association with that evening's weather conditions, it never moved and left no sulphurous scent.

All my research into the phenomenon uncovered no parallel to its physical appearance—white with an encircling band of purple. No less unparalleled was the distinct "click!" Wayne and I heard some three or four seconds before the brilliant orb popped into existence. If it had been a high concentration of energy, one might have expected electrical systems to be affected in some way. But the ceiling fan near which it materialized functioned normally after the event, while all lights and appliances in the house continued to operate as before.

Was some kind of energetic connection made between an ideal meteorological environment and the multiple sclerosis of our host? Perhaps, because our autumnal encounter with the phenomenon was not Alex's first experience with ball lightning. As a ten-year-old child, he happened to be watching a thunderstorm through the window of his grandparents' home, when he saw a bright globe of blue light shoot from the troubled sky to strike the ground and bounce along their field until it disappeared.

The legacies of such powerful events are only questions defining the limits of what we understand about the infinitely mysterious world in which we live. ♋

Firewalking

*Sometimes Talking the Talk
Is Not Enough*

John White

The flyer I'd received in the mail invited me to a four-hour seminar on firewalking. "Everyone participating will be taught how to walk barefoot on hot coals without burning their feet," it proclaimed. To a long-time investigator of the paranormal like me, it was an irresistible challenge. So I made a deposit toward the $75 registration fee to reserve my place, and eagerly looked forward to the event.

I didn't doubt the reality of firewalking. It has been a well-documented fact for centuries. It is almost always done in a religious context, as part of a ceremony. The phenomenon was recorded as far back as when Pliny the Elder in the first century A.D., told of the practice by an ancient Roman family that performed it at an annual sacrifice to Apollo. Anthropologists have observed it today in India, Greece, Spain, Japan, China,

Bulgaria, Sri Lanka, Tibet, Thailand, Fiji, and Brazil. Then, of course, there is the biblical story of the Hebrews and the fiery furnace.

I'd personally witnessed firewalking in 1974 at a California festival of religious/spiritual/metaphysical organizations; it was done by a Japanese priest, who demonstrated it as part of his sect's worship. Moreover, several years later a friend of mine had spent three days meditating and chanting at a yoga center in Canada as preparation for his own successful firewalk with others at the center. About that time I became friends with Komar the Hindu Fakir, who holds the *Guinness Book of World Records* distinction for having walked on hotter coals than anyone else. Komar (the stage name for Ohio, cheese-maker Vernon Craig) casually strolls over coalbeds wearing Hindu-like clothing and a turban but with no more preparation than perhaps smoking a cigarette and sipping a Coke.

Last of all, I knew that firewalking had been done by thousands of ordinary Americans in the last few years as a veritable craze for it swept the West Coast, thanks to a California teacher named Tolly Burkan, originator of the firewalking movement, and those whom he had trained. Burkan demonstrated it on the Phil Donahue Show in 1984; a student of Burkan's, Tony Robbins, likewise demonstrated firewalking on the Merv Griffin Show. Another friend of mine, a Russian emigre´ and psychic researcher named Larissa Vilenskaya, was writing a book entitled *Firewalking*, which tells of her experiences as a Burkan-trained teacher and as a scientific researcher into the paranormal.

Could it be done? I had no doubt whatsoever. But could it be done by me? That was the question.

Now, I've dealt with fears of many kinds, from physical to metaphysical. As a teenager I had a near-death experience through drowning; I spent four years as a naval officer in anti-submarine warfare and nuclear weapons, with time on the Cuban Blockade and in Vietnam. That's not to brag, but just to say that I've been in some unusual situations where I had to deal with fear, and did. Nevertheless, as I contemplated treading on the coals, I sometimes felt apprehension. After all, their pyrometer-measured temperature would be nearly 1,300° F, higher than the melting point of the cast aluminum used for the engine block in my car. Would I walk or chicken out? Several friends whom I'd told of the firewalk also signed up, and we casually discussed the question, each for himself. My answer: I'll decide when I face the coalbed.

So at 7 p.m. on a bitterly cold evening in January 1985, two dozen people and I met at a private home in West Hartford, Connecticut, for the firewalking seminar. It was the first time for all of us. We'd come for various reasons: curiosity, to deal with fear, to explore our human potential, to say we'd done it, to extend professional counseling and training skills. We were a diverse group: housewives, businessmen, astrologers, holistic health practitioners, karate instructors, an author (me), a dentist, a postal worker, an elementary school teacher, and who knows what else. A reporter and a photographer from the *Hartford Courant* were also present to record the event.

Our instructor was a 32-year-old, slightly-built, bearded Connecticut resident with the self-conferred name of Shoshame (pronounced as three syllables: Show-shah-mee). He told us he took the name five years earlier for spiritual reasons but didn't explain why or what it means. Shoshame's business card identified him as a firewalking instructor, researcher, lecturer, masseur, holistic health practitioner, nutritional and herbal consultant, and a multi-level marketing trainer and distributor of flower pollen, freeze-dried algae, wheatgrass powder, ion generators, and metabolic enzymes. He received his certification from Burkan after completing a three-week training course. Since his first firewalk, he'd been on the coals 17 times.

By 8 o'clock we were ready to build the fire. Bundled up in our coats and gloves, we filed outside in silence to the frigid back yard following Shoshame's instructions to take logs from a nearby woodpile and, one by one, create the pyre. A large area, lit by a spotlight on the house, had been shoveled nearly free of snow. We laid the hardwood logs in a five-foot circle, built it up several feet like a wall, and then filled in the center. When we finished in silence ten minutes later, it was waist-high and solid with half a cord of oak and maple. Next we crumpled sheets of newspaper and stuck them into the pile. Then we formed a circle around it, holding hands, while Shoshame doused it with several gallons of kerosene. He offered a prayer to God and to the spirit of the fire-to-be and then lit the paper. We stood quietly as the flames quickly warmed us. When the fire was well lit, we went back inside single file still maintaining silence.

Now the seminar became more academic. Shoshame resorted to colored pens and a marking board to present some of the key concepts through simple diagrams. His first point used FEAR as an acronym: False Evidence Appearing Real. We are programmed from infancy, he said, to believe that reality works a certain way, and any experiences we have to the contrary are generally dismissed as crazy or hallucinations. We're trained to accept limiting beliefs; we're indoctrinated to remain within conventional boundaries of what's possible and impossible. All our fears come down to 'what if...' What if this or that happens—what if, what if? We go out of our way to place limitations on ourselves by imagining things and by accepting the cultural party line on what reality is all about.

"But what if you walk on those coals tonight?" he asked. "What if you step on 1,300-degree coals and don't get burned? What does that mean about reality? What does that mean about the way you let fear control your life?"

He passed out paper and had us all write down our worst fears and then share them with the group. There were all kinds of fears—fear of height, fear of failure, fear of speaking before an audience, fear of success, fear of rejection, fear of death. "It doesn't matter what kind of fear you have," Shoshame declared. "You can build your own reality; you can change your programming instantly"—he snapped his fingers—"just like that. This seminar isn't about firewalking. It's about overcoming fear. The firewalk is merely symbolic of fear in general. If you can break through that membrane of fear and take that first step onto the coal bed, you can learn to overcome fear and limiting beliefs in every part of your life."

Biblical story of the Hebrew children in the fiery furnace (Gustav Doré)

He paused, then continued. "But the firewalk is purely voluntary. You don't have to walk, and if you choose not to, that's okay. Trust your inner guidance, listen to your inner voice. If it tells you to walk, then walk. If it tells you not to walk, then don't. You don't have to impress anyone. For some people it can take more courage not to walk. But even if you don't go over the coals, you'll have a powerful learning experience. You'll learn how to turn your fear into joy."

By 11 p.m. the wood had burned to embers and we were ready to walk. Outside we went, pant legs rolled up, socks off, shoes loose and ready to be removed instantly. Shoshame had us hold hands and sing a song, over and over, while he raked out the coals to a bed about six feet wide by ten feet long. The heat was intense. When he pulled the rake out and rested it on the ground, it hissed and steamed through the thin cover of snow. With a shovel he patted the embers into a solid mass. It glowed brilliant red-orange in the moonless night, with flames rising from some partly-consumed logs resting along the edges, forming a small alley of fire. At the end of the coal bed where we would step off, Shoshame had the ground soaked with water from a nearby hose, which he would use to douse the embers when the walk was over. We were to step into the wet soil in case any embers clung to our feet. Then we could wipe off our soles on a nearby blanket, return to our place in the circle, and put on our shoes.

Everything was ready. We had been warned inside to walk straight and steady through the coals—no gazelle-like bounds, no running, no mincing steps, no hot dogging. We'd signed a release form that waived "all rights to compensation in case of injury," and there was no doubt in our minds there could be injury because Shoshame had said he'd heard of five cases where people were burned. One case was attributed to loss of concentration when a flashbulb went off in the person's face. Therefore, he'd told us, no one could take pictures except the photographer, and then only of Shoshame.

A firewalking party in 2009

We were ready. I felt clear and calm—no apprehension whatsoever. I'd decided I would go, no matter what. Would I be burned? No way to find out but to walk. Would the coals feel cool, as some firewalkers had experienced, or would they feel warm, even hot, as they had to others? Would they feel like beach sand on a summer day or like peanut shells? These were all part of the description Shoshame had given us.

And then he was walking across the coals. It took perhaps five strides and five seconds. Midway across, the strobe light flashed. He repeated the walk once more at the end of the evening to give the photographer another chance.

Shoshame had hardly gotten off the coalbed before the first participant had his shoes off and was striding magnificently across the embers. The man next to him in the circle followed in rapid succession, and then half a dozen others went, all walking properly as instructed. I stepped out of my shoes and walked to the short line of waiting people. My mind was Zen-like, free from thought and mental chatter, focused clearly on the physical aspects of the event, observing without comment, performing without fear. Because of my years in consciousness research, I can say I wasn't in trance or anything like it. No one else reported being in trance, so far as I heard later. Inasmuch as there was an altered state of consciousness in me, it was simply pristine mental clarity, backed by a willingness— a positive mental attitude—to flow with the experience, no matter what.

Perhaps nine or ten people had crossed the coals and there was now one woman between me and the fire. She walked purposefully up to the coals, hesitated just a moment, and then turned away, almost without breaking stride, returning to her place in the line.

Now it was my turn. Without hesitation or expectation, I walked forward onto the coals. My first step felt quite neutral—neither hot nor cool—except for the crunching sensation and noise as the coals subsided under my weight. The second step was the same. On the third step I felt a slight sensation of heat. The fourth and fifth steps were almost unnoticeable. And then I was off the coalbed, wetting my feet briefly before returning to my place in the circle. My feet felt unharmed as I stood there, watching others walk or not walk. If anything, they began to feel cold and numb from the frozen ground, but I decided to leave my shoes off anyway until I returned to the house.

Shoshame gave a one-minute warning: those who hadn't walked still could, but only if they did so within the next sixty seconds. Five had chosen not to go on the coals; none changed his mind.

Once inside, we shared our thoughts and feelings briefly, after which Shoshame had us write on a notecard. Those who didn't walk wrote, "I can always trust my inner guidance!" We others wrote, "I walk on fire. I can do anything I choose!" We were advised to carry it with us or place it somewhere at home as a constant reminder that we can create our own experience of reality through the infinite potential of our minds. No one was burned; one man had a blister.

The evening ended about midnight with health food beverages and cookies and a feeling of great exhilaration. As I drove home, however, I noticed a slight sensation at two points on my left sole. I hadn't examined my feet closely after the firewalk; they'd seemed okay so I'd just brushed them off and donned my footwear, feeling fine. When I got home, I reexamined them and discovered two slightly reddened spots, each about a quarter of an inch in diameter. Apparently I'd picked up some embers on that third step. But the discoloration was barely visible, and the next day had almost disappeared. There was no pain at any time—only a slight sensation that something wasn't quite right at those points. A few days later a small blister appeared at one spot.

And that was it. To put it in perspective, consider firewalking from the medical-scientific perspective: there is no explanation for it. Shoshame quoted medical authorities who uniformly declare that subjecting human flesh to the conditions of the coalbed would leave the firewalker with CBS–charred bloody stumps. He consulted Bruce Fichandler, a physician's assistant at Yale-New Haven Hospital's burn center for 12 years, who warned that firewalk participants would be seriously burned.

The next day Fichandler told the *Courant*, "I don't know how to explain how they are able to do that. At 1,300 degrees, that ought to burn your feet and burn them good. It would require skin grafting and four to six weeks' hospitalization, depending on how you recovered." Yet an estimated 30,000 people have successfully completed the firewalking seminars.

Some physicists have proposed the Leidenfrost Effect as an explanation. That effect is seen when you sprinkle water on a hot griddle. The water droplets seem to dance around because their surface has vaporized, creating an insulating layer that protects the rest of the drop. The same thing, these physicists say, happens to your feet because of perspiration, so if you don't leave your feet on the coalbed for long—only a second or so—you can get away with it. The only trouble with that explanation is that it doesn't work for well-observed instances, reported by anthropologists, in which firewalkers have remained standing still in the coals for up to 20 seconds. In at least one case observed in Greece, the firewalkers kneeled down in the white-hot coals for several minutes! And speaking personally, I have to say that I don't buy the Leidenfrost Effect explanation either because the sides and arches of my feet were quite dry, so they should have been burned.

Consider firewalking also from a psychological perspective. Making it across the coalbed performs heavy-duty therapy for some participants.

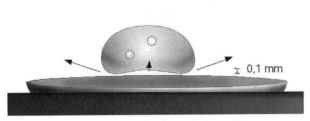

A droplet of water on a hot plate floats
on its own vapor caused by the Leidenfrost effect.

An Arizona woman described it as the equivalent of a four-day *est* seminar in five minutes. A senior editor of Parents magazine said it helped him to do all kinds of things he was afraid of. Shoshame relates firewalking to therapy by saying that even those who choose not to walk receive valuable tools and methods that they can use to overcome all the negative programming, fears, and limiting beliefs in their lives. It fosters personal growth and a sense of responsibility for creating a better world, he says. Who can argue with that?

Do I feel I'm a better person for firewalking? No, not in a moral or spiritual sense—but, yes, in a cognitive sense. There's no substitute for firsthand experience, especially when investigating mysterious phenomena. The power of the human body-mind was shown to me dramatically.

Would I do it again? Absolutely. Would I recommend it to others? Absolutely. But not for purposes of showmanship. And like Shoshame, I warn you not to try it by yourself.

Firewalking is not what I'd do for a living, but it is what anyone can do for better living if fear is limiting him. When fears and belief-based limitations incapacitate you or reduce your happiness, the thing to do is face them. Walk through those fears as if you were walking through fire. Overcome limitations based on belief systems. ✆

According to the Old Testament, the donkey of the prophet Balaam could not only see an angel which Balaam could not, but could talk as well. (Rembrandt Van Rijn, 1626)

What Do Animals Know?

From Balaam's Ass to the Elberfeld Horses,
There Are Mysteries Here

Michael E. Tymn

A few weeks before the Kentucky Derby some 25 years ago, the trainer for one of the leading contenders was interviewed on television and said that his horse was ready for the big race, not only because he was fast and fit but because he was smart and competitive.

I mused over that comment, wondering if some horses are truly smarter than others and if they really care about winning. If they are competitive and not just running hard because of their natural speed or because they are responding to the whip, does that mean that horses have egos? When they win, do they rejoice? When they lose, do they sulk and kick the stable door out of frustration? Is pride or self-esteem driving them, or is it simply that they understand that they might get an extra lump of sugar or a carrot by finishing ahead of the other horses? I further wondered if there is a positive correlation between intelligence and winning.

As I was writing for a daily newspaper at the time, I decided to explore the subject in my sports column. I hoped to get the answers to my questions "straight from the horse's mouth," so to speak. Therefore, I called Calumet Farm in Lexington, Kentucky, then one of the leading thoroughbred stables in the country. They had produced the likes of the mighty Citation and the stretch-running Whirlaway, two of the all-time greats in the "sport of kings." I don't remember the name of the head trainer I interviewed, but I do recall his telling me that horses indeed vary considerably in intelligence and that the better horses are the smarter ones and those who have a will to win.

It wasn't clear to me whether being smart and having the will to win went hand in hand, and I couldn't get a clear-cut answer as to how he knew those things; but I gathered it was simply intuitive on his part, something you come to understand by working with horses for many years. There was no indication that horses were subject to any kind of IQ or motivational testing before being groomed as top athletes.

In spite of the fact that the Calumet trainer seemed to know what he was talking about, I remained very skeptical. I remembered the Biblical story of Balaam's Ass in which Balaam, a prophet on a mission to put a curse on Israel, was deterred by his mule, which stubbornly refused to transport Balaam; and when beaten by Balaam, the animal spoke to him and reprimanded him, apparently as directed by God. However, I was not inclined to take the story of a talking donkey seriously any more than I could believe in a serpent talking to Eve.

In researching the matter of horse intelligence, I came upon the Elberfeld horses of Germany. My boggle threshold was exceeded when I read that the Elberfeld horses could figure out square roots and cube roots, even fourth power roots of numbers of six or seven figures. Moreover, using their hooves to tap out letters of the alphabet, they could communicate in their native tongue, German, and even in French. Professor Edoward Claparède of the University of Geneva, one of many scientists who studied the horses, called the phenomenon "the most sensational event that has happened in the psychological world."

As the well-documented story goes, in 1900, Wilhelm von Osten of Elberfeld, Germany (then Central Prussia) taught his horse, Hans, a Russian stallion (later called Kluger Hans, or Clever Hans), mathematics, including addition, subtraction, multiplication, and division. Von Osten first made Hans familiar with directions, such as right, left, top, and bottom. Then he would place skittles, or bowling pins, in front of Hans and count. He would then ask Hans to strike as many blows with his hoof as there were skittles in front of him. After a short time, the skittles were replaced by figures on a blackboard.

"The results were astonishing," Dr. Claparède reported. "The horse was capable not only of counting, but also of himself making real calculations, of solving little problems....But Hans could do more than mere sums: he knew how to read; he was a musician, distinguishing between harmonious and dissonant chords. He also had an extraordinary memory; he could tell the date of each day of the current week. In short, he got through all the tasks that an intelligent schoolboy of fourteen is able to perform."

After word spread of Claparède's independent investigation, a scientific committee was appointed in 1904. The committee found nothing suspicious but offered no explanation. A second committee was then appointed, including Oskar Pfungst of the Berlin psychological laboratory. Pfungst reported that the horse merely obeyed visual clues, whether conscious or unconscious, given by von Osten. This became known as the "Clever Hans effect," a term still used by animal trainers today. It was later revealed that of the 24 professors on the committee, only two of them actually observed Hans. The committee also stated that to accept such intelligence in horses would be subversive of the theory of evolution.

As a result of the committee's report, von Osten became something of a laughing-stock in the community. When he died in 1909, he left Hans to Karl Krall, a friend who had taken much interest in the horse in spite of the committee's report. Krall, a wealthy merchant, also bought two Arabian stallions, Muhamed and Zarif, and began to train them in the same manner von Osten had taught Hans. Within two weeks, Muhamed was doing addition and subtraction. He would distinguish tens from units by striking the latter with his right foot and the former with his left foot. By the end of the third week, he was doing multiplication and division; and by the time four months had passed, he knew how to extract square and cubic roots. Krall then devised a table with letters and numbers and Muhamed was soon spelling and reading.

Zarif was a little slower in learning, but was eventually able to do almost everything Muhamed was capable of. They could spell the names of their visitors, reply to questions put to them, and make little observations. Karl also trained Hänschen, a small Shetland pony, and Berto, a blind stallion with no sense of smell, how to count and communicate. He was unsuccessful with two other horses and an elephant. Meanwhile the aging Hans pretty much went to the back of the class, usually remaining in the barn, spending much of his time swatting flies with his tail.

Clever Hans at a demonstration of his abilities

Maurice Maeterlinck, a world-famous Belgian author, playwright, and Nobel prizewinner for literature, heard about the horses and decided to visit Elberfeld and observe them for himself. He was astounded. "I assure you that the first shock is rather disturbing, however much one expected it," he wrote. "I am quite aware that, when one describes these things, one is taken for a dupe too readily dazzled by the doubtless childish illusion of an ingeniously-contrived scene. But what contrivances, what illusions have we here?"

After Maeterlinck was introduced to Muhamed, Krall asked the horse to spell his name. Muhamed began by rapping out an "H." Krall then reprimanded the horse, but Muhamed continued with an "E" and an "R" before the two men realized that he was spelling Herr, the German equivalent of Mister. But Muhamed then struggled with the surname, first spelling M-A-Z-R-L-K. When told by Krall that it was incorrect, Muhamed groped a little before rapping M-A-R-Z-L-E-G-K. Krall then repeated

Maeterlinck's last name, and after two more attempts the horse spelled the name with one small error. The two men concluded that it was close enough.

Claparède had reported much the same experience with his name. After it was pronounced to him, Muhamed spelled it "Klapard." When a newspaper editor brought a friend and introduced him as Tauski, Muhamed spelled out "Tausj." When Zarif was asked to spell the name, he gave it as "Teauski" Maeterlinck was left alone with the horse as Krall tended to chores. Since the horses performed in the absence of Krall and gave some answers to questions that Maeterlinck himself did not know the answers to, he discounted the Clever Hans effect.

Maurice Maeterlinck

Another theory advanced was that of telepathy, as fantastic as the idea of a mind-reading horse seems. To test this theory, Maeterlinck took some large cards with Arabic numerals on them, shuffled them and placed them in front of the horse without looking at them himself. "Without hesitation and unasked, Muhamed rapped out correctly the number formed by the cards," Maeterlinck wrote. "The experiment succeeded, as often as I cared to try it, with Hänschen, Muhamed, and Zarif alike." Since Maeterlinck was the only person present and did not know the numbers, there was no mind to be read for the answers.

In one test, Maeterlinck wrote a surd—a number that had no square root—on the blackboard, not realizing that it was a surd. Maeterlinck looked to Muhamed for a square root. The horse lifted his hoof, paused, looked back at Maeterlinck and shook his head. This little test also opposed both the Clever Hans effect and the telepathy theory.

One day, Zarif stopped in the middle of a lesson by Krall. The horse was asked why and replied, "Because I am tired." On another occasion he stopped again and explained, "Pain in my leg."

Maeterlinck reported on tests run by a Dr. H. Hamel while Krall was on a trip. Hamel began by giving Muhamed simple math problems and ended with asking Muhamed for the fourth power root of 7,890,481, which Hamel himself did not know until after checking Muhamed's correct answer of 53, which took about six seconds before he began striking out the answer.

Claparède asked Muhamed to give him the fourth power root of 614,656, to which the horse correctly replied 28 after a few seconds. However, when asked to give the fourth power root of 4,879,681, the horse incorrectly replied 117. When told it was wrong, he corrected to 144, also wrong. The horse then gave up.

On another day, Krall and a Dr. Scholler decided to make an attempt to teach Muhamed to express himself in speech. The horse made several feeble efforts before stopping and striking out the message, translated from the German to read, "I have not a good voice." They then asked Muhamed what was necessary for him to speak. He replied, again in German, "Open mouth." They asked him why he didn't attempt to open his mouth, and the reply came, "Because I can't."

On another occasion Zarif was asked how he talks to Muhamed. "Mit Munt" (with mouth), he replied. Krall asked Zarif why he didn't tell him that with his mouth, to which Zarif replied, "Because I have no voice."

A *New York Times* article dated March 3, 1912, related how Zarif was asked for the date and correctly tapped out 25 for February 25. When asked how many days left in the month, he tapped out four, as it was a leap year. When asked how often leap years occur, he tapped out "every four years."

Maeterlinck was clearly flabbergasted: "You rub your eyes, question yourself, ask yourself in the presence of what humanized phenomenon, of what unknown force, of what new creature you stand," Maeterlinck reacted. "...You look around you for some sort of trace, obvious or subtle, of the mystery. You feel yourself attacked in your innermost citadel, where you held yourself most certain and most impregnable. You have felt a breath from the abyss upon your face. You would not be more astonished if you suddenly heard the voice of the dead."

As might be expected in a world where academia is locked into scientific fundamentalism, most modern references to the Elberfeld horses write it all off as the Clever Hans effect, completely ignoring the tests that clearly fell outside the scope of the Clever Hans effect, such as asking for a fourth root when the experimenter himself does not know the answer and when the horse trainer is not present to quickly figure out an answer and somehow signal it to the horse. It should be kept in mind that Claparède, Maeterlinck, and Hamel were not the only scientists or scholars who studied the horses. Dr. H. Kraemer and Dr. H. E. Zeigler, of Stuttgart, Dr. Paul Sarasin, of Bale, Professor A. Beredka, of the Pasteur Institute, Dr. William Mackenzie, of Geneva, Dr. R. Assagioli, of Florence, and at least a half dozen other respected academicians observed them and apparently ruled out fraud, including the Clever Hans effect.

Unfortunately, there is no indication that their reports have survived. They are simply referred to in the few surviving stories of the Elberfeld horses as being in agreement that there was no fraud and that the Clever Hans effect was not a satisfactory explanation. Moreover, it also must be remembered that Pfungst's findings applied only to Hans and von Osten, not to Krall and the horses he acquired.

But fraud, whether conscious or unconscious, is the only explanation acceptable to mainstream science. Telepathy defies the mechanistic laws of orthodox science, while the possibility that horses and other higher animals actually do have an intelligence that approaches or even exceeds humans cannot, as suggested by the committee investigating Clever Hans, be reconciled with evolutionary ideas.

If not the Clever Hans effect, if not some other type of fraud, if not telepathy, if not true intelligence on the part of the horses, then what other explanation is there?

Maeterlinck suggested that the horses were mediums, much like human mediums, through which some higher power was working. As to why it was necessary to teach the horses in the first place, he opined that it would be like asking an automatic writing medium to do her thing without knowing how to write. Whatever it is that is influencing her needs the organism to be accommodating. "Unconscious cerebration, however wonderful, can only take effect upon elements already acquired in some way or another," he explained. "The subconscious cerebration of a man blind from birth will not make him see colors."

However, Maeterlinck was clearly not a spiritualist as he rejected the idea that discarnate humans were overshadowing or in some way controlling the horses. He had studied the reports of psychical researchers like Frederic W. H. Myers, Richard Hodgson, Sir Oliver Lodge, and others, and accepted the reality of mediumship. But he could not bring himself to believe in spirits, primarily because all the spirits he had read about in the research material seemed to be still groping and groveling, not existing in a much more enlightened state. The spirit hypothesis seemed too much like religious superstition for the "intellectuals" of the day; therefore, those, like Maeterlinck, who accepted the reality of mediumship preferred to believe that the so-called "spirit control" of the medium was a secondary personality buried away in the subconscious, and this secondary personality was capable of subliminally tapping into some kind of cosmic consciousness or cosmic reservoir for information. In some respects, it was more fantastic than the spirit hypothesis, but still more appealing to the "intellectual" mind.

While not suggesting there is any precedent for animal overshadowing or control by spirits, Archibald Campbell Holmes, a spiritualistic phenomena historian and author of the day, believed that spirit influence was the most logical explanation for the Elberfeld horses. He reasoned that if spirits can take control of tables by tilting them and levitating them, and, at the other extreme, take control of human mediums, there was no reason to believe that they couldn't influence or control a horse. As to why they would do that is an unanswered question, although spiritualism teaches that there are many low-level and mischievous spirits hanging around the earth plane. Then again, it could have been a mathematically adept spirit who was experimenting or just having some fun.

There have been many anecdotal stories of birds and butterflies appearing regularly on window sills or otherwise acting strangely after the death of a loved one, as if to give a sign that the deceased person is still around. These stories also suggest some kind or control or influence by discarnates.

What can we believe about the Elberfeld horses? An open-minded, discerning person might easily conclude that the Clever Hans effect or conscious fraud of some other kind is the least likely explanations in spite of the fact that science has accepted it as the only explanation. To accept the position of mainstream science is to assume that distinguished men like , Claparède, Hamel, and all the others who shared their observations were complete incompetents or were involved in some kind of devious conspiracy with the two horse owners.

But back to the race horses. It occurred to me that if a horse were really smart, he or she might find some folly in silly running games and refuse to compete.

~ ~

The Unexplained Powers of Animals

Rupert Sheldrake

Horses capable of figuring out fourth power roots must exceed everyone's boggle threshold, even that of Dr. Rupert Sheldrake, the renowned British biochemist who authored the 1999 book, *Dogs That Know When Their Owners Are Coming Home*. Clearly, Sheldrake does not subscribe to the mechanistic theories of life dominant in orthodox science. "Dogs that know when their owners are coming home, cats that answer the telephone when a person they are attached to is calling, horses that can find their way home over unfamiliar terrain, cats that anticipate earthquakes—these aspects of animal behavior suggest the existence of forms of perceptiveness that lie beyond present-day scientific understanding," Sheldrake writes, adding that five years of extensive research on the unexplained powers of animals have convinced him that many of the stories told by pet owners are well founded.

As Sheldrake sees it, the study of dogs that know when their owners are coming home offers the most convincing evidence for telepathy between people and animals. While skeptics will claim that the phenomenon can be explained as a matter of routine, Sheldrake's research demonstrates that this ability exists outside of the routine as well as outside of smell and hearing. Sheldrake also considered the possibility that dogs have some kind of precognitive ability. While not completely ruling that theory out, he still sees telepathy as the most likely explanation. That is, the dogs are reacting to the thoughts, feelings, emotions, or intentions of a distant person. He quotes James Serpell, who studied human-dog relationships at Cambridge University, as saying that "the average dog behaves as if literally 'attached' to its owner by an invisible cord."

This cord, Sheldrake surmises, is elastic in that it can stretch and contract. "It connects dog and owner together when they are physically close to each other, and it continues to attach dog to owner even when they are hundreds of miles apart," he opines. "Through this elastic connection, telepathic communication takes place."

Much the same ability has been observed in horses. "Sometimes horses show anticipatory behavior hours in advance, especially when their person has been away for a long time," Sheldrake further writes, citing several cases, including one in which Fiona Fowler, an English nursing student, left her horse to be cared for by her mother. Even when Fowler would return to her mother's home at unexpected times, the mother noted that the horse would make his way from a lower paddock to the front gate well in advance of her arrival.

Sheldrake refers to the Clever Hans effect in the Introduction of the book, commenting that it is usually used to justify the dismissal of seemingly unexplained animal powers, attributing them to subtle cues rather than to any mysterious powers of the animal. However, he does not address the studies of Maurice Maeterlinck and other researchers who seemingly ruled out the Clever Hans effect as well as telepathy with Hans, but more so with the other Elberfeld horses. Contacted by e-mail for this article, Sheldrake said that his busy schedule has prevented him from looking at all the data from Maeterlinck's studies. "Personally I think it's very unlikely that the horse could give answers that he nor anyone else knew, which is why I'd have to look at the details of the tests to be able to form an opinion," he replied.

The Elberfeld horses seem destined to remain an enigma that clearly exceeds everyone's boggle threshold. —*Editor* ❧

A typical nineteenth century seance complete with table levitation

Science vs. Levitation

There Was a Time When More than Tables Were Up in the Air

Michael E. Tymn

The most celebrated levitation in recorded history took place on the Sea of Galilee some two thousand years ago and was witnessed by only a few humble fishermen. Science discreetly smiles at such fables.

Legend has it that on October 4, 1630, Joseph of Cupertino, an Italian monk, was assisting in a procession honoring St. Francis of Assisi when he suddenly was lifted into the sky and hovered there for some time before a crowd. Upon descending, he was so embarrassed that he ran to his mother's house and hid. It was the first of many "flights" that Joseph would experience while apparently in a trance state, or in a state of religious ecstasy or rapture. Joseph (1603–1663) was later canonized as a saint.

Levitations were reported with other saints, including St. Dunstan (918–988), St. Francis of Assisi (1186–1226), St. Thomas Aquinas (1226–1274), St. Ignatius Loyola (1491–1556), and St. Peter of Alcantara (1499–1562). The latter allegedly soared over the trees with his hands crossed over his chest as hundreds of birds gathered around him. The phenomenon has also been reported with a number of Eastern mystics.

Science superciliously smirks at such religious superstition.

During the 1850s, there were numerous stories about heavy tables being levitated by spirits working through mediums, and spelling out messages. The tables would hover off the floor and tilt one time for each letter of the alphabet, or the sitters would recite the alphabet and the table would tilt or turn at a certain letter. Judge John W. Edmonds, a justice of the New York Supreme Court, and Dr. Robert Hare, a professor of Chemistry at the University of Pennsylvania, were among a number of distinguished men and women who studied and attested to the phenomenon.

Science condescendingly snickered at such spiritualistic nonsense.

During the 1860s, stories circulated about levitations, spirit communication, and other strange phenomena surrounding Daniel Dunglas Home (pronounced "Hoom"), an American who had been born in Scotland in 1833, and had become a celebrated medium.

The most spectacular levitation purportedly took place on December 16, 1868 at the London mansion of Lord Lindsay and was witnessed by Lord Lindsay, Lord Adare, and Captain Charles Wynne. They reported seeing Home walk out a window on the third floor, float to the window of an adjoining room and re-enter there.

On March 4, 1869, Adare, Wynne, and Adare's father, the Earl of Dunraven, accompanied Home on a tour of the ruins of Adare Abbey. There they observed Home leave the ground and float horizontally for, according to Adare, "at least ten or twelve yards."

Science arrogantly sneered at the preposterous stories.

One of those sneering scientists was Professor William Crookes, a distinguished physicist and chemist, later knighted for his contributions to science, including the discovery of the element thallium and the invention of the Crookes tube, a high-vacuum tube that contributed to the discovery of the x-ray and television. Early in 1870, Crookes set out to prove that Home was a fraud. He opined that the increased employment of scientific methods would drive the "worthless residuum of spiritualism" into the unknown limbo of magic and necromancy.

But after 28 sittings with Home over nearly a three-year period, Crookes announced that he observed Home being levitated on three occasions—once while Home was sitting in an easy chair, once while kneeling on a chair, and once while standing up. "On each occasion, I had full opportunity of watching the occurrence as it was taking place," Crookes detailed, pointing out that he ran his hands under Home's feet to be sure there were no invisible supports of any kind.

Sir William Crookes

Crookes also reported hearing spirit voices and witnessing floating tables, luminous "spirit hands," and a floating accordion with beautiful music coming from it. In one sitting, Ellen Crookes, his wife, was levitated while sitting in a chair.

Crookes referred to Home and his wife "being levitated" rather than levitating themselves, as he came to understand that spirits were doing the lifting. In fact, when being levitated in the upright position, Home's arms were usually rigid and drawn above his head, as if he were grasping invisible hands. When he went horizontal, it was as if invisible hands were supporting his body.

It was further explained that Home could not be levitated at will. There had to be harmonious conditions. There were many sittings in which no phenomenon took place, apparently because of negative conditions. And it is why Home was levitated on only three of the 28 observations by Crookes.

Science now diplomatically scoffed at one of their own. It was assumed that Crookes had been the victim of a clever hoax.

"It is idle to attribute these results to trickery, for I would [point out] that what I relate has not been accomplished at the house of a medium, but in my own house, where preparations have been quite impossible," Crookes defended himself. "A medium, walking into my dining room, cannot, while seated in one part of my room with a number of persons keenly watching him, by trickery make an accordion play in my own hand when I hold it keys downward, or cause the same accordion to float about the room playing all the time. He cannot introduce machinery that will wave window curtains or pull up Venetian blinds eight feet off, tie a knot in a handkerchief and place it in a far corner of the room, sound notes on a distant piano, cause a card-plate to float about the room, raise a water bottle and tumbler from the table, make a coral necklace rise on end, cause a fan to move about and fan the company, or set in motion a pendulum when enclosed in a glass case firmly cemented to the wall."

But why such odd phenomena? The spirits explained to Crookes that they were experimenting with manipulating matter from their side, just as Crookes was experimenting on his side. In one sitting, Crookes overheard one spirit communicator giving instructions to another spirit communicator on how to effect a particular phenomenon.

Crookes was defended by Dr. Alfred Russel Wallace, co-originator with Charles Darwin of the natural selection theory of evolution. Wallace had been present at the Crookes' home for one of the sittings in which a table was levitated. The two famous scientists got on their hands and knees under the hovering table, but were unable to find any natural explanation.

A.R. Wallace

Now, science scoffed at science.

"I never said it was possible, I only said it was true." Crookes retaliated before retreating back to orthodox science.

Around the same time that Crookes first heard the stories about

Home, William Stainton Moses, an Anglican minister and English master in University College, London, was also reading about them in a book written by Lord Adare. Moses called it the "dreariest twaddle" he had ever come across. However, in 1872, Moses reluctantly began developing transcendental powers similar to Home. Serjeant Cox, a lawyer, described the swaying and rocking of a heavy mahogany table in the presence or Moses and seeing Moses lifted from the floor and onto the table, then lifted from the table to a sofa.

Initially, Moses thought it was the work of the devil and wanted nothing to do with it, but communicating spirits informed him that the levitations and other physical phenomena were simply a way of making themselves known so that they could impart some higher teachings through him. Moses developed into an automatic writer and over the next 20 years penned several books of profound wisdom from his spirit guides, much of it in conflict with his beliefs.

Frederic W. H. Myers, a Cambridge scholar who co-founded the Society for Psychical Research (SPR) in London in 1882, attended one of Moses' séances and reported that a table, untouched by any hands, rose from the floor and touched his throat and chest three times, and then, "I was three times raised on to the table, and twice levitated in the corner of the room."

Even though the SPR was formed for the purpose of thoroughly investigating paranormal phenomena, mainstream science wanted nothing to do with findings that seemed contrary to natural law and continued to frown on reports of levitations and spirit communication.

Perhaps the spirits decided there was no point in further levitating humans, or possibly there were too few who possess whatever it takes to be levitated, as there is not much in the way of human levitation reported by credible observers after Home and Moses. However, the levitation of tables and other objects continued through the first three decades of the 1900s. Dr. William J. Crawford, a lecturer in mechanical engineering at Ireland's Belfast University, began investigating the mediumship of 16-year-old Kathleen Goligher in 1914. The phenomena surrounding the young girl included communicating raps and table levitations.

In his 1918 book, *On the Threshold of the Unseen*, Sir William Barrett, professor of physics at Royal College in Dublin, tells of joining Crawford in one of Crawford's many sittings with the Goligher circle. At first, they heard knocks and messages were spelled out as one of the sitters recited the alphabet. Barrett then observed a floating trumpet, which he tried unsuccessfully to catch. "Then the table began to rise from the floor some 18 inches and remained suspended and quite level," Barrett wrote. "I was allowed to go up to the table and saw clearly no one was touching it, a clear space separating the sitters from the table."

Barrett put pressure on the table to try to force it back to the floor. He exerted all his strength but was unable to budge it. "Then I climbed on the table and sat on it, my feet off the floor, when I was swayed to and fro and finally tipped off," Barrett continued the story. "The table of its own accord now turned upside down, no one touching it, and I tried to lift it off the ground, but it could not be stirred; it appeared screwed down to the floor."

When Barrett stopped trying to right the table, it righted itself on its own accord. Apparently, the spirits were having a bit of fun with Barrett as he then heard "numerous sounds displaying an amused intelligence."

Somewhat similar folly had been observed by Crookes on April 12, 1871, during a sitting with Home, when sitter Frank Herne was carried out of his chair, floated across the room, and then dropped at the other end of the room.

Barrett described the medium and the small family group as "uncritical, simple, honest, kind-hearted people," and he was certain that what he had experienced was beyond any conjuring. "That there is an unseen intelligence behind these manifestations is all we can say, but that is a tremendous assertion, and if admitted destroys the whole basis of materialism," he concluded his discussion of the case.

Crookes, Myers, Wallace, and numerous other researchers had recognized that mediums were exuding a strange foamy substance from various orifices of the body that seemed to be responsible for producing various physical phenomena. With some mediums, it was very apparent and could even be photographed. With others, however, it was more of a vapory aura around the medium's body. This substance came to be called ectoplasm. Through much experi-mentation Crawford discovered that "psychic rods" emanating from mediums and made up of this ectoplasm were responsible for the levitations.

During his experiments with the Goligher circle, Crawford began communicating with spirit entities, one of whom said he was a medical man when on earth and that his primary function was to look after the health of the young medium. This spirit explained to Crawford that two types of substances were used in the production of the phenomena. One was taken in large quantities from both the medium and the sitters, then returned to them at the close of the séance. The other substance, apparently the ectoplasm (although never given a name by Crawford) was taken exclusively from the medium in minute quantities and could not be returned to her as its structure was broken up. It was pointed out that it came from the interior of the medium's nerve cells and if too much were taken she could suffer serious injury.

Some of the communication took place through Goligher's voice mechanism while she was in trance while much of it came through raps and table tilting. Crawford came to see the experimentation as a joint venture with the spirit "operators." He soon realized that these "operators" didn't understand much about the scientific aspects of the phenomena. "I am convinced that the operators know next to nothing of force magnitudes and reactions," Crawford wrote in his 1918 book, *The Reality of Psychic Phenomena*. "Their idea as to the prime cause of the phenomena is 'power.'"

On one occasion, a clairvoyant joined in the circle and told Crawford that she could see "a whitish vapory substance, somewhat like smoke," forming under the surface of the table and increasing in density as it was levitated. She could see it flowing from the medium in sort of a rotary motion. From other sitters, she could see thin bands joining into the much larger amount coming from the medium. She also saw various spirit forms and spirit hands manipulating the "psychic stuff."

Crawford brought in a scale large enough to hold the medium while she was sitting in her chair. He discovered that when a table was being levitated, the weight of the table was transferred to the medium through the psychic rods. Most of the time, the transfer of weight would be a few ounces short of the weight of the table. Further experimentation revealed that the extra weight was being transferred to the sitters in the room, who might have furnished small amounts of the "psychic force."

"I have come to the general conclusion from the results of my experimental work, and from observations of the circle extending over two and a half years, that all the phenomena produced are caused by flexible rod-like projections from the body of the medium; that these rods are the prime cause of the phenomena, whether they consist of levitations, movements of the table about the floor, rappings, touchings, or other variations," Crawford stated.

Some of Crawford's findings, such as the weighing of the medium, were objective and scientific. However, other aspects of it were based on things that were purportedly communicated by spirits or seen by a clairvoyant.

Thus, science sneered again.

In 1922, Dr. E. E. Fournier d'Albe had 20 sittings with the Goligher circle and observed no phenomena similar to what Crawford had reported. Crookes and other researchers had come to realize that too much skepticism causes a negative environment that defeats the production of phenomena, or to look at it another way, if the spirits didn't like a particular person they simply refused to perform. That may very well have been the case with Fournier d'Albe, as other researchers later reported phenomena similar to what both Crawford and Barrett had witnessed.

But science wanted nothing more to do with such unreliable and unrepeatable phenomena. Apparently, the spirits went away frustrated and decided there was no point in further demonstrating their existence to a doubting world.

And so, science still smiles, smirks, snickers, scoffs, and sneers. ❧

The Possession Factor

New Research Backs an Ancient Insight into Disturbing Human Behavior

Stephen Hawley Martin

I s demonic possession possible? The question crossed my mind as I was researching and writing my latest book, *A Witch in the Family*, about the Salem witch hysteria and my seven-times-great grandmother, who was hanged as one. How else, I wondered, could the extraordinary symptoms of those who were supposedly witchcraft victims be explained? One had vomited blood in the courtroom in front of the judges and other witnesses. Several had nasty skin lesions and deep impressions that appeared to have been made by human teeth. Others coughed up pins. All suffered fits and wailed or spoke in strange and exotic voices. Could those people have been possessed?

Professional historians have never considered the possibility. After all, the idea of demonic possession was thought to have been pure superstition for most of the nineteenth and twentieth centuries. But research into it today indicates a great many people, including many medical doctors, believe possession can and does happen. The Roman Catholic Church, which now recognizes the big bang theory, still trains a number of priests each year to conduct exorcisms. According to the memoirs of a former prefect of the pontifical household, Pope John Paul II successfully exorcised a woman in 1982. She was brought to him writhing on the ground. Father Gabriele Amorth told La Stampa, an Italian newspaper, that John Paul II successfully conducted three exorcisms during his pontificate.

John Paul II

Amorth said, "He carried out these exorcisms because he wanted to give a powerful example. He wanted to give the message that we must once again start exorcising those who are possessed by demons . . . I have seen many strange things [during exorcisms] . . . objects such as nails spat out. The devil told a woman that he would make her spit out a transistor radio and lo and behold she started spitting out bits and pieces of a radio transistor. I have seen levitations, and a force that needed six or eight men to hold the person still. Such things are rare, but they happen."

In recent years, a number of psychiatrists, psychologists, and other mental health practitioners have gotten into the business of what they call "depossession." They'd rather call it depossession than exorcism, apparently, because they don't approach it from a religious perspective. They say they rarely encounter Satan and his demons although they tend to agree Satan and his minions exist, and that obsession or possession by them can happen. According to Dr. Louise Ireland-Frey, a psychiatrist, "[Satan and demons] do not belong to the human kingdom, being the nega-tive aspect, composed of the 'fallen angels' and their slaves. This is not drawn from a religious source . . . I have been told these things by the dark entities [I have] encountered. A number of them have told us that they are delighted to get us to believe that they exist only when we think of them, speak of them, and 'believe in' them—it makes their work of invading easier! On the other hand, thinking fearfully of them, brooding compulsively, talking often of them certainly does predispose a person to attracting their focused attention."

Certainly, the people of 1692 Salem did a lot of thinking and compulsive brooding over them, and it appears they may have attracted their focused attention as a result. Nevertheless, lay practitioners indicate that in their practices obsession or possession by demons—entities that have never had a human body—is rare. More common are problems stemming from interference by the earthbound spirits of individuals who have died, but are still present among the living. The approach used to depossess a patient who is afflicted in this way is less confrontational than that of an exorcism by a Catholic priest. In addition, the therapist routinely tries to help the invading spirit find its way into the light.

I am not making this up. Much has been written about it. In the process of doing research for my book, I conducted a Google search and turned up a web site that offered a dozen titles on the subject. I'm going to relate some of what Dr. Louise Ireland-Frey has to say in her book, *Freeing the Captives: The Emerging Therapy of Spirit Attachment* (Hampton Roads Publishing, 1999) because her credentials are strong. She's a Phi Beta Kappa graduate of Colorado University, has a master of arts degree from Mount Holyoke College in Massachusetts, and a medical degree from Tulane University.

Dr. Louise Ireland-Frey

Dr. Ireland-Frey is a psychiatrist who uses hypnotism to help those who suffer past-life trauma. She also uses it to detach earthbound spirits who may be causing trouble for her patients. She says that when her clients are regressed to a previous life and come to the death experience terminating that lifetime, it's possible to continue the regression past the physical death into the after-death state. Similarly, when she contacts earth-bound entities—those who may or may not have attached themselves to a living person—she can also ask them to recall the circumstances of their physical death. Dr. Ireland-Frey uses an intermediary to make this contact. Essentially, she hypnotizes someone, either the patient she is trying to help or a willing assistant, and has the hypnotized individual channel the earthbound entity.

The doctor goes on to say that under normal circumstances after death the psycho spiritual part of a person—the mind, the psyche, or soul—finds itself floating above the body, still conscious of itself and aware of the people and activities around the dead body. This stage can be brief. The now disembodied consciousness usually feels free and light and relieved, and senses it can go wherever it seems to be drawn. For instance, it might be drawn through what some have called a dark tunnel and into the light that almost everyone in today's culture has heard about.

A life review may follow in which the activities, actions, thoughts, and words of the entire life are reviewed and evaluated as to their value and impact on others. The individual sees both his or her successes, weaknesses, and failures, and in this way judges for herself the worth and value of the life just past. Another stage sometimes called the "cleansing" is often described as the feeling of being embraced or surrounded by light. But apparently not all souls go through these stages.

An individual who is heavy with negative emotions and undesirable habits such as rage, cruelty, greed and so forth may be too negative to be attracted to the light, and will turn away, perhaps not even perceiving it, and go to a "place"—a vibrational frequency, or dimension—that is appropriate to its present nature, i.e., dark and heavy. You might say souls are a little like substances suspended in water, the "heaviest" after death sink to the lowest astral levels, the "lightest" float to the upper levels, and the rest find the appropriate levels in between. But not all follow a normal sequence.

Many die not having a clear idea of what to expect after death and become bewildered. It is as though they are alive, but their body is dead and they cannot reenter it. Rather than going to the light or finding an appropriate vibrational level, they remain on the earth plane where they are able to see and hear living persons but are invisible to and can't be heard by the living. Not knowing what to do or where to go, many such disembodied spirits begin to wander, either aimlessly, or perhaps to some chosen place or person.

Some wanderers remain near the body they inhabited in life—which may now be buried. I have a friend who is sensitive to the presence of the disembodied and will not go near a graveyard for this reason. Other wanderers may find a home in a house or other building and become the "ghosts" who haunt these places.

My first wife and I had friends, a couple, who owned a castle in Lorraine. Henri, the male half of this ménage, had inherited it and the land and village around it along with the title of count. The castle had fallen into disrepair when it came into his hands. Having done well in business, Henri decided to restore the place. He and his wife spend quite a bit of time there as it was undergoing renovation and were often disturbed by what seemed to be someone down in the basement banging and screaming in the middle of the night. Finally, they became so annoyed, Henri had the workmen tear out a wall he calculated might be the location of these night noises.

A Skeleton Was Found

Henri and his wife had no idea who the skeleton belonged to, but they gave it a proper Christian burial. Afterward, the couple was never again bothered by the nocturnal uproar.

Here's what Henri thought. Apparently, a man had been bricked up behind the wall while still alive—someone didn't like the guy—and he had died there, but had not realized he had died. The spirit of this dead man could easily have passed through the bricks, but he didn't know this, and had been screaming for help ever since. Of course, these were psychic screams, since the ghost had no vocal cords. The middle of the night was the only time the screams for help penetrated the minds of Henri and his wife because that was when all else was quiet, and they were sleeping or near sleep and sensitive to such things.

Let's hope the ghost of Henri's castle headed for the light once it got out from behind that wall. According to Dr. Ireland-Frey, many wanderers find a place that seems lighter or warmer than the chilly darkness of the earth-bound state in which they have been, and this turns out to be the body or aura of a living person—often without either the living host or the invading spirit being aware of the relationship.

What sort of person is a likely host for an invading spirit?

A person whose aura is weak or "open" is most susceptible. This may be because the individual has been in an accident, or suffered an illness, been under an anesthetic for an operation, or recently suffered an emotional shock such as grief or fear. Children whose auras are not yet fully protective are also vulnerable. Most of the accusers in Salem happen to have been children or young teens.

Several degrees of closeness of such attachments have been identified by therapists who work in depossession:

The first level is that of temptation of the living person by an aspect of the wanderer—not really an overwhelming compulsion but the thought or idea of doing or saying something that is contrary to the basic personality of the living individual, something out of character. The second level is called "influencing" or "shadowing" when the disembodied entity is affecting the host person mildly or intermittently, as with mood swings, irrational moments, sudden inexplicable fears or depressions. Third, when the entity is affecting the host's personal feelings and habits more noticeably and frequently, the words "oppression" and "harassing" are used. Someone who is clairvoyant may be able to see the entity attached to the host's aura or within it.

Obsession is next, and here Dr. Ireland-Frey's definition differs slightly from that of the Roman Catholic Church. She says it's a remarkably common condition in which the entity may invade not only the psyche but also the physical body of the host and meld its own personality traits and former bodily feelings with those of the host, often to the confusion and bewilderment of that person. The affected person may become aware of persistent pains, sudden changes in emotions unlike his or her normal feelings, unfamiliar attitudes, or even unnatural traits and talents.

And finally, "possession" is the condition wherein the invading entity takes over the body of the host completely, pushing out the host's own personality, or soul, and expressing its own words, feelings, and behaviors through the host's body. Dr. Ireland-Frey says complete possession is rare, but it happens, and can be spectacular when it does. Sometimes possession may alternate with obsession. A case when a person suddenly goes berserk, for example, may be the result of sudden, complete possession. The doctor writes that she has personally seen only one case of complete possession.

Based on the historical record, it seems to me the Salem afflicted may have experienced some or all of these states at different times throughout the Salem witch hunt of 1692. So maybe, just maybe, they were possessed.
ᚱ

8.

The Project Serpo Saga

*Did the Director of "Close Encounters of
the Third Kind" Know Something We Don't?*

Len Kasten

" I really found my faith when I learned that the government was opposed to the film. If NASA took the time to write me a twenty-page letter, then I knew there must be something happening."

—Steven Spielberg

In the movie, *Close Encounters of the Third Kind*, written and directed by Steven Spielberg and released in 1977, an alien spaceship lands, by pre-arrangement with the U.S. Government, on a high mesa called "The Devil's Tower" in a remote corner of Wyoming and an ambassadorial exchange takes place. A single alien disembarks and is escorted away, presumably to a secret site. Then, twelve American astronauts in orange jumpsuits and industrial-strength sunglasses, with duffel bags slung over their shoulders, ten men and two women, march into the spacecraft to be whisked away to the alien home planet.

In the previous scene, they are blessed by a clergyman, who refers to them as "pilgrims." Was this just some inventive touch conceived by Spielberg, or did he base it on something real? Since it is now widely believed in UFO circles that a pre-arranged alien landing did take place at or near Holloman Air Force Base in New Mexico in April of 1964, it seems not unreasonable, to true believers, to suspect that Spielberg may have had an inside track on classified information, and that the ambassadorial exchange with an alien race may also have been a real event.

Now, in what could be an unprecedented break with government secrecy policy, a few former military insiders have come forward to say that the exchange was indeed real, and actually took place almost exactly as depicted in the movie. Under the auspices of a Defense Intelligence Agency program referred to as "Operation Crystal Knight," or what is now being called "Project Serpo," it has been claimed that twelve astronauts left the earth in July of 1965, and were taken to the planet Serpo in the constellation Zeta Reticuli aboard an alien spaceship, as part of an exchange program. The bulk of the information about this program is said to have been dribbled out to the world via 21 e-mails from an individual referred to only as "Anonymous" to a closed circle of high-level UFO insiders beginning on November 2, 2005. Anonymous says that he was formerly a senior officer of the Defense Intelligence Agency, and is now the official spokesman for a group of six DIA personnel, three retired and three still currently employed there. It was decided by the group, and agreed to by Anonymous, that a web site should be created to publish all the e-mails on the Internet. One of the researchers in the group, Bill Ryan from England, volunteered for the job, and so began www.serpo.org, what has now developed into the official source for all Serpo-related information, including updates from Ryan, a link to a public forum, and supporting e-mails from other insiders who had knowledge of the Serpo project.

For the UFO community at least, the site has become something of a sensation. For what it's worth this is the story offered on the site.

A Presidential Decree

The tale told by Anonymous is indeed amazing. If it is true, then, at a minimum, the entire history of the government pretense of ignorance about UFOs and extraterrestrials is completely blown away. Not surprisingly, it all begins with Roswell.

Anonymous says that the Roswell crash did occur, but that it involved two alien craft. The first was found relatively intact, embedded into a hillside southwest of Corona, New Mexico on July 5, 1947 by a university archaeology team. This site is about 75 miles northwest of Roswell, and is famously referred to as the "Roswell crash" because all the remnants of the crash were brought to the Roswell Army Air Force base, where the military took control of the information. The second crash site wasn't discovered until August, 1949. Another downed craft, it is said, was found almost completely intact at a remote place outside of Datil, New Mexico by two ranchers. Evidently, the two spacecraft had collided somewhere near the Brazel ranch, thus accounting for the debris field, but the second craft, before hitting the ground itself, had limped on to the vicinity of Datil, about 80 miles west of Corona.

Betty and Barney Hill

Four dead aliens, the account goes on, were found at the Corona site, and six at the Datil site. However, one alien survived the Corona crash and was found hiding behind a rock. He was taken to Los Alamos, and became known as EBE #1 (Extraterrestrial Biological Entity #1). Although he "spoke" in tonal variations, just as in *Close Encounters*, the scientists at Los Alamos found a way to communicate with him, and he informed them that he was from a planet in the constellation Zeta Reticuli, about 40 light years from Earth. The constellation was also referenced in the famous 1966 UFO abduction account of Betty and Barney Hill.

EBE #1 also provided researchers with a complete explanation of all the devices found in the crashed spacecraft, one of which was a piece of equipment for communicating with his home planet that survived the impact. However, the Los Alamos scientists could not get it to work until they discovered how to hook it up to the energy source on the crashed Corona disc. That was in the early summer of 1952. However, EBE#1 died later that summer after sending six unanswered messages to his planet.

After the death of EBE#1, says Anonymous, the Los Alamos scientists figured out how to use the device correctly to communicate with the extraterrestrial race they had now named the "Ebens," and they received the first reply around December, 1952. Eventually, they were able to converse in rough English. Over the next nine years, the communications wrinkles were slowly ironed out, mostly by trial and error. Finally, in 1962, it was arranged that the Ebens would send another mission to earth in April of 1964 and that we would meet the craft at Holloman Air Force Base near Alamogordo, New Mexico. By this time President Kennedy was in office. Then, according to Anonymous, "Several months into the planning process, President Kennedy decided to approve a plan to exchange a special military team. The USAF was tasked as the lead agency. The USAF officials

President Kennedy

picked special civilian scientists to assist in planning and crew selection." It was arranged that we would send 12 astronauts to Serpo, and they would leave one Eben here in the custody of the U.S. Government.

As might be imagined, the selection and training of the 12 astronaut-ambassadors was an extraordinary undertaking. After months of discussion it was ultimately decided that they be career military, single with no children and preferably orphans themselves, and with multiple special skills. Originally, about 56,000 files were screened of which 158 were picked by the selection committee. The final 12, ten men and two women, plus four alternates, were chosen based on complex psychological, medical, and other tests. All the team members were "sheep-dipped," i.e., all identification records were purged, including social security, IRS, medical, military, et al, and they were all listed as "missing" and discharged, so that no connection with their former identities remained. They were then assigned three-digit numbers as new identities. They went through very difficult training for six months, mostly at Camp Perry in Virginia. Anonymous says, "Each team member had to endure extreme psychological and physical training. In one training test, each team member was locked inside a 5' x 7' box buried seven feet underground for five days, with just food and water, no contact with anyone else and in total darkness." Four of the team members who were pilots were taught to fly an Eben craft back to Earth, using for training the spaceship recovered in 1949, in case it was necessary to escape from Serpo. In addition to the four pilots, the team consisted of two linguists, one biologist, two scientists, two doctors, and one security man. They were all given suicide pills, and the team was assigned four 45 Colt revolvers and eight M2 carbine rifles.

The 1964 rendezvous occurred almost exactly as planned. Two Eben craft entered our atmosphere during the afternoon of April 24, 1964. After an initial mix-up, one landed just west of Holloman Air Force Base near the southern entrance to the White Sands Army Base, precisely at the designated location. The alien visitors were greeted by 16 senior U.S. Government officials. It is not known whether or not President Johnson was among them. The Ebens brought electronic translating devices with them to facilitate communications. The remains of the 11 dead aliens were taken on board.

Anonymous does not give the agenda of the meeting, but it is believed they presented us with the "Yellow Book," a complete history of planet Earth. The 12 astronauts were ready to board at that meeting and waited on a bus, but the aliens decided then that the exchange should wait until 1965. Then, in July, 1965, an alien craft returned, this time to the Nevada Atomic Test Site. Very much like the scene in *Close Encounters*, this was a simple, unceremonious, working meeting. The 12 courageous astronauts boarded the Eben craft along with 40 tons of supplies, for an intended stay of 10 years. Four of them would never see Mother Earth again. Two would die, and two would choose to remain on Serpo. The others would not return until 13 years later.

"We See Two Suns"

The trip to Serpo took 10 months, during which the astronauts experienced considerable discomfort. They were offered Eben food, but all agreed that it tasted like paper, and they stuck with the C-Rations they had brought along. The diary of the team commander recounts the second day on board: "We sat in the chairs and a clear container was placed over us and the chair. We were isolated in this bubble or sphere. We could breath (sic) OK and could see out, but we really felt dizzy and confused. I think I fell asleep or fainted. I think this is another day, but my watch says one hour since we sat." They used small metal containers for elimination, which the Ebens emptied for them. Eventually, they were able and allowed to wander freely around the enormous ship. The team was able to communicate with Earth HQ at Kirtland AFB, using the alien device, for the entire trip. Prior to reaching Serpo, the team member known as 308 had some sort of accident and died of a pulmonary embolism. The Ebens were respectful of the funerary rites of the astronauts, but they took possession of the body.

The team commander's account of the landing is vivid. "We see the planet for the first time. We walk down the ramp. Large number of Ebens waiting for us. We see a large Eben, largest one we have seen yet...I guess this guy is the leader. About one foot taller than the others. The leader tells us we are welcome to planet...we are lead (sic) to an open arena. Looks like a parade field. The ground is dirt. Looking up, I see blue skies. The sky is very clear. We see two suns. One brighter than the other. The landscape looks like a desert, Arizona or New Mexico. No vegetation that we can see. There are rolling hills but nothing but dirt...The brightness is almost too much for our eyes without sunglasses. What a planet." They were quartered in four huts that appeared to be adobe-like, and all their gear was stored in an underground facility. The temperature was 107. The buildings all had lights and electricity generated by a small box. They were able to plug their electrical devices into the box, and they all worked.

The one they called Ebe2 was a female and spoke English well. The team commander asked her for the body of 308. They were taken to a large building where they met an Eben doctor who spoke English. The commander's diary describes the confrontation: "This doctor told us that 308's body was not inside the container. The Ebens have done experiments with 308's body because they considered it an honor to have such a specimen to work with. The doctor told us they have used 308's body to create a type of cloned human being. I stopped the doctor at this point.

I told the doctor that the body of my teammate was the property of the United States of America, planet Earth. The body did not belong to the Ebens. I did not authorized (sic) any experiments on the body of 308." It was a tense situation. The Ebens were upset with the team's reaction, and

Climactic scene from *Close Encounters*

Ebe2 told them that "everyone should be nice," and repeated it several times. The astronauts had to back off to prevent a major escalation of the incident.

The commander and the scientists (700 and 754) were given permission to view what was left of the body of 308. This brought them into a building where biological experiments were being carried out. They were shocked by what they saw. The commander says they viewed "Strange looking bodies. Not human bodies, at least not all of them" from other planets being grown and maintained in tubs. The Eben doctor tried to explain the science behind their work, but the earthlings didn't comprehend because they didn't really understand DNA biotechnology in 1965. The team commander concluded that it was all evil stuff. He says, "I saw the dark side of this civilization."

The population of Serpo is about 650,000. Anonymous says that the Eben civilization is about 10,000 years old, originating on another planet that they were forced to leave 5,000 years ago due to volcanic destruction. The Ebens fought a devastating interplanetary war about 3,000 years ago and wiped out their enemies using particle beam weapons. The war lasted about 100 years. The Ebens have a "Council of Governors," which is in complete control of the population, with membership for life.

The astronauts observed no crime, but there is an army, which also acts as a police force. But no guns or weapons of any type were seen by the team. There is one large community, which is the center of the civilization. All the industry is concentrated there. The Ebens do not use any type of currency—they are all issued whatever they need from central distribution centers. All adult Ebens do some type of work.

A 3,000-Page Book

Timekeeping was a problem for the astronauts, since the batteries controlling the timepieces brought by the team eventually ran out. This meant they could not keep track of the calendar, so they eventually relied on Serpo time, which was governed by the movement of their suns. So they lost track of Earth time and ended up staying 13 years instead of 10. It was determined by Earth scientists that Kepler's Law of planetary motion did not apply to Serpo. Carl Sagan was consulted on this, and wrote about 60 pages of opinion on the subject, but ultimately had to ac-knowl-edge that earthly laws of physics do not necessarily apply out of this solar system.

The eight astronauts returned in 1978 and were debriefed for a solid year by the Air Force Office of Special Investigations, which resulted in a 3,000-page book. Anonymous claims to have a copy of this book. They were then released into civilian life. The last survivor of this brave and historic band of pioneers passed away in 2002. They had all absorbed large doses of radiation while on Serpo, and it is believed that this short-ened their lives.

In retrospect, it seems a shame that President Kennedy didn't live to see his initiative become a reality. He was assassinated only five months before the first landing. Would he have used the occasion to reveal the extraterrestrial connection, perhaps with worldwide TV coverage? Could that have been his plan from the beginning? Perhaps some powerful insiders didn't want that to happen. In any case, thanks to Steven Spielberg, maybe we got to see it after all. ☜

For complete information on Project Serpo with many related links, visit www.serpo.org.

Passion in Coral

*The Strange and Miraculous Obsession
of Edward Leedskalnin*

Frank Joseph

When what was, at the time, the worst storm in North American history struck Florida during 1991, only one structure in the city of Homestead, where Hurricane "Andrew" concentrated its fury, escaped damage. The surviving building was not a modern bank or skyscraper, but a "coral castle" completed by one lonely man in 1940. How could his private mansion have defied a cataclysm that devastated everything around it for thousands of square miles? This is only one of the numerous questions people have been asking about Coral Castle for more than 65 years.

The fortress-like complex was constructed of massive blocks of cut coral, many of which exceed five tons. These are imaginatively arranged and fitted together to form a central courtyard encircled by high, dominating walls. Entrance through them is made via a gate fashioned from a single block of coral weighing nine tons. This massive monolith is 80 inches wide, 92 inches tall, and 21 inches thick. It fit within a quarter of an inch of the walls surrounding it, and pivoted on an iron rod resting on an automobile gear. The enormous block balanced so perfectly on its center of gravity that a visitor could easily push it open with one finger.

Another gate, this one shaped into a large triangular configuration at the opposite wall, weighs three tons. Inside the courtyard, to the visitor's immediate right, rears a broad, square tower with a flight of stone steps ascending to a single doorway near the top. They lead to the highest point on the property and a small room. This chamber is occupied by only a leather hammock and a crude, wooden table piled with primitive tools—chains, saws, drills, wedges, hammers, chisels, and crowbars.

Tools also festoon the walls. This imposing tower was raised with approximately 243 tons of coral cut into cyclopean blocks weighing from four to nine tons each. The roof alone comprises 30 one-ton blocks neatly fitted together. Although electricity and plumbing are absent, oil lamps and a well of fresh water serve the living quarters—a sleeping chamber with twin beds, an outdoor cookery, and bathroom. A low but massive altar rests against the south wall. But to what god or gods it was dedicated, no one knows.

Through a single window looking out over the courtyard below, the extent of this peculiar place can be perceived in a glance. Among its oddities is a scattering of oversize chairs made of coral, each one weighing a half-ton. Although they

Coral Castle's entrance

look extremely uncomfortable, the chairs are, in fact, exceptionally restful and balanced into perfect rockers. Remarkably, not a single tool mark has been found on any of them. A smaller number of chairs resemble contour lounges oriented to the sun after dawn or at noon. But they are not the only Coral Castle features with celestial orientations. There are numerous stone representations of planets, moons and suns, many (perhaps all) of them deliberately aligned with various sky phenomena, as were the 25 larger chairs carefully positioned throughout the estate.

The site appears to be some kind of celestial observatory dating back to a time before the invention of the telescope. Twenty feet outside the walls stands a lensless, telescopic structure, 25 feet tall and weighing 20 tons. Crosshairs inside its aperture resemble those of a bombsight, but they are aligned with Polaris, the North Star. Nearby is a massive sundial calibrated to noon of the winter solstice, December 21, and the summer solstice, June 21. The sundial is adjacent to a fountain adorned with the representations of the moon in its first and last quarters, and when full. On Coral Castle's north wall are sculpted images of Saturn and Mars. The latter is shown next to a palmetto plant, signifying the artist's belief that life exists on the Red Planet. Other astronomical depictions and alignments abound throughout the mansion. Its astronomical identity is subtly reinforced here.

For example, a feature referred to by guides as the "bird bath" comprises three concentric circles: 124 inches, 62 inches, and 18 inches in diameter, respectively. These measurements represent the solar system. The concentric rings correspond to the three major division of planets. The innermost group includes Mercury, Venus, Earth, and Mars. Jupiter, Saturn, and Uranus make up the middle group, with Neptune and Pluto represented by the outermost ring.

An appreciation of the extraordinary labor that went into building this place may be gained by inspecting the north wall. Its center section, surmounted by the representation of a crown, contains the site's heaviest single block at 30 tons. Almost as massive is a 40-foot obelisk set in a pit six feet deep. There is also a two-and-a-half-ton banquet table surrounded by half-ton rocking chairs. These chairs are so perfectly balanced that they continue rocking long after a light touch has set them in motion.

The building, its furnishings and art objects were carved from 1,100 tons of coral. The average weight of cut rock used in its construction exceeds that of the stone blocks used to erect Egypt's Great Pyramid.

To visitors ignorant of its origins, Coral Castle might impress them as the ruin of some ancient, unknown civilization. But it was not built by astronomer-priests directing stone-dragging slaves of some prehistoric kingdom. No less incredible than its own stupendous construction is the fact that the entire complex was built between 1920 and 1940 by and for one, frail man working alone and in secret. His name was Edward Leedskalnin. He was born in 1887 into a farming family at Stramereens Pogosta, a small village near Riga, Latvia. Apprenticed to his grandfather,

Edward Leedskalnin

the young Edward became a stone cutter. Sometime before World War One, he left his homeland under mysterious circumstances. Agnes Scuffs, a young woman some years his junior, promised to marry him, but she left him waiting in vain at the church. Broken-hearted, he left to seek his fortune in America, where he hoped to amass enough wealth to lure his "sweet sixteen" to his side in the New World.

This is what he repeatedly told visitors to his Florida castle, but this version of events is transparently false. Interviewed during the 1970s, Agnes Scuffs said she never promised to wed Leedskalnin, with whom she was only remotely acquainted. She never left Latvia, and married in the early 1920s, shortly after Ed arrived in North America. In truth, he fled his homeland under threat of a warrant issued by the Czarist police for his arrest on subversive activities. Latvia was then, circa 1913, under the dubious "protection" of Imperial Russia. While the precise nature of Leedskalnin's "subversion" is not known, it would appear he made his way across Northern Europe, where he contracted a serious respiratory disorder. He claimed later to have gone to Canada, where he worked at a logging camp, but his debilitating illness and slight stature would have prevented him from becoming a lumberjack.

Between his departure from Latvia prior to the First World War and his arrival in Florida during 1920 nothing is known, save that he contracted a serious, lingering sickness and somehow learned the building secret of Coral Castle. With his puny savings, he purchased an acre of virtually worthless land near Florida City for twelve dollars. Here he began building his strange monument. At five feet tall, weighing 100 pounds and in delicate health, Leedskalnin seemed unable to quarry and move the more than a thousand tons of coral that even the most robust man would have found impossible to budge. And his fourth-grade education hardly qualified him as a construction engineer. His tools were handmade saws, chisels, chains, hoists, and hammers of the most primitive kind, and his only mode of transportation was a dilapidated bicycle without tires.

Ed was a fanatic for secrecy and worked only after sundown, when he was certain no one was watching him. If anyone did stop by to inquire how he was getting along, he would immediately put aside his labors and chat pleasantly with visitors until they left. Only then would he resume construction. When we consider that he cut, moved, and positioned every block in the megalithic structure during the dead of night, the man's achievement assumes a truly incredible scale. Some children spying on him one evening claimed they saw him "float coral blocks through the air like balloons," but no one took them seriously. If their testimony can be believed, they were the only eyewitnesses to the building of Coral Castle.

In 1936, when developers threatened to set up a subdivision near Florida City, Leedskalnin bought 10 acres in nearby Homestead with money saved through years of performing odd jobs for neighboring farmers. He dismantled the largely finished Castle and transferred it piece by piece to its new location. Each enormous block was placed on a pair of iron girders mounted on a makeshift truck chassis, then transported over 10 miles to Homestead. For this major operation, he relied on outside help for the first and last time. He hired a flatbed but insisted that its driver not be present whenever the blocks were placed on the truck. The driver showed up every morning, returning in late afternoon to find the chassis loaded with immense coral monoliths.

The real function of the coral monoliths is still unknown.

Once, the driver absentmindedly returned after less than half an hour for a lunch he had forgotten on the seat of the cab. He was astounded to see several multi-ton stones already laid neatly on the girders. "It was impossible to have stacked those gigantic blocks in under thirty minutes," he recalled, "even with a steam-powered derrick. And Ed had no equipment, just a simple tackle and chain hoist. Yet, there they were, piled like cord wood." Their mysterious mover was nowhere in sight, and the driver, somewhat apprehensive, left before Leedskalnin returned.

Relocating Coral Castle progressed with easy pace. Leedskalnin accomplished this amazing engineering feat in less than a month and re-erected his stone complex, working always under cover of darkness, from dusk until dawn. It took him four years of unrelieved labor, during which time he added a wall eight feet high and four feet wide at the base, with an average thickness of three feet. After his work was completed, he opened Coral Castle to restricted tours, charging twenty-five cents per visitor, but he preferred to live behind the great walls in otherwise perfect seclusion.

He never shared the secret of its construction with anyone, saying only that he understood the same laws of magnetism used by the Ancients, and that these same principles somehow involved a relationship of the earth to certain positions of the heavenly bodies. Leedskalnin was quoted as saying, "I have discovered the secrets of the pyramids. I have found out how the Egyptians and the ancient builders in Peru, Yucatan and Asia, with only primitive tools, raised and set in place blocks of stone weighing many tons."

Ed's work was his life. Material pleasures meant nothing to him, and he merrily subsisted in his solitary existence on a diet of sardines, crackers, eggs and milk. His meager garden yielded green vegetables and some fruits. He worked tirelessly throughout each night and spent much of his day reading, mostly about magnetic current and cosmic forces, resting only a few hours in late afternoon. Leedskalnin passed away in his sleep in 1953 of malnutrition and kidney failure. Today, Coral Castle is open to the public as the self-made monument of a reclusive man's strange genius. But how he built it is no more mysterious than why he did so. He had no interest in money, consistently resisting efforts by entrepreneurs to advertise his place and turn it into a tourist attraction. Indeed, outsiders could only gain entrance after pulling a bell cord, to which he may or may not have been in a mood to respond. He rarely left the site, and what he mostly did behind its sheltering walls, no one ever knew.

Like the enigmas of its construction, its real function is still unknown. Why did he make so many sculpted references and astronomical orientations to the heavens? For whom were the 25 half-ton rocking chairs designed? To what or whom was his barbaric altar dedicated? What need could have demanded so massive a complex as Coral Castle? And why did Edward Leedskalnin devote his whole life to it?

Perhaps an answer lies in an e-mail I received three years ago from a reader in the Cayman Islands. She told me of a German physician, Dr. Albert Bender, who arrived in the Caymans 50 years ago to build a natural healing clinic based on his experiments with coral. Apparently, he discovered that patients in physical contact with the hard, stony skeletons secreted by many millions of certain marine polyps to form reefs in tropical seas experienced remarkable tissue regeneration. Sufferers, who ingested finely pulverized coral in a protective solution while laying on a coral bed in a small room with coral-lined walls Dr. Bender had specially constructed at his Munich office, reportedly enjoyed a spectacular recovery rate from infectious diseases caused by the tubercle bacillus.

Consumption, pulmonary phthisis and various serious lung ailments, Dr. Bender supposedly demonstrated, could be regressed, even cured in some cases, by the proper application of coral. He had come to the Cayman Islands for their abundant reefs, from which he intended to build a medical facility entirely out of coral. For reasons I could not discover, nothing came of his project, and I learned little concerning Albert Bender, other than confirming his established medical reputation and death in the early 1960s.

But what most struck me about his healing work with coral was its parallel with Ed Leedskalnin: the reclusive builder of Coral Castle fought a life-long battle with TB. Did he know something about the curative powers of coral, with which he built south Florida's strange structure to heal himself of the disease? If so, how could he have found out about coral's supposedly therapeutic properties? After more than six decades, his unique castle still keeps its secrets. ❧

10.

The Peca-Gasha, also known as
the Monument to Humanity

The Legend of Markawasi

*The Geologist Who Redated the Sphinx Explores
Monumental Stone Sculptures on an Andes Plateau*

Robert M. Schoch, Ph.D.

"Natural adapted features in a sanctified landscape."

These words (from John Michell, *Confessions of a Radical Tradition-
alist*, 2005, p. 127) resonated in my mind as I explored the
Markawasi Plateau. I had come to this small plateau (about 2 miles
long by a little over half a mile wide) in the Andes, towering above the
town of San Pedro de Casta (50 miles northeast of Lima), at an elevation
of 12,000 feet above sea level, to view for myself the reputed ancient mon-

A gigantic ancient turtle; the head is to the right of the photograph.

umental stone sculptures. Here, some claimed, were to be found the remains of a lost culture that dates back thousands of years, if not tens of
thousands of years or more. Supposedly they created monumental carvings from the granodiorite cliffs, boulders, and outcroppings on the top
of the plateau—carvings of an anthropomorphic and zoomorphic nature,
including peoples of many different races and animals found not just in
the immediate vicinity, but from other continents as well. There was even
an alleged sculpture of the Egyptian divinity Ta-urt (Thoueris), goddess
of childbirth and maternity, in her typical form as an upright female hippopotamus.

If these reports were true, this would indicate a pre-Columbian culture that had transoceanic ties, and just perhaps it represented a branch
of the primordial global lost civilization of which many writers and
philosophers have speculated over the centuries. Certainly such reports
piqued my interest, especially since I have championed both the concept
of a very ancient high civilization and the idea of significant global contact
among cultures long ago.

Before leaving the U.S., I was warned that Markawasi is a landscape
of strange, anomalous phenomena, be they encounters with extraterrestrials (many UFOs, which the Peruvians refer to as ovni/ovnis, have been
sighted from the plateau) or inhabitants of the reputed tunnels that lie
beneath the Andes. Visitors to the plateau have experienced altered states
of inner consciousness, accompanied by telepathic and clairvoyant abil-

ities, whether in the dream or waking state. What might await me in this preternatural setting?

Markawasi has attracted the attention of some obscure, but nonetheless influential, figures in the arcane and occult sciences over the past fifty-some years. Foremost among these are Daniel Ruzo (1900–1993) and George Hunt Williamson (1926–1986).

Born in Lima, Daniel Ruzo was trained in law, but is best known for his studies of the esoteric, occult, and protohistory as exemplified by his interpretation of the monuments of Markawasi. Ruzo amassed a large collection of works by and about Nostradamus and wrote a book, El Testamento Auténtico de Nostradamus, on the seer that went through a number of editions. He was also a 33rd degree Mason.

Most importantly relative to Markawasi, however, Ruzo became convinced as early as 1924–1925 that an incredibly ancient culture once existed in Central and South America, almost entirely destroyed by a cataclysm many thousands of years ago—a belief he based on traditions and legends passed down from pre-Spanish times. Perhaps the ancient culture was the American remnants or branch of a worldwide primordial culture, the lost civilization of primal times. It was from this long-forgotten culture, Ruzo suggested, that our present humanity inherited the roots of our own civilized ways.

The few survivors of the cataclysm, which Ruzo thought might have been the same as the Biblical Noachian Flood, may have hidden in underground chambers, caves, and tunnels. Ruzo searched for physical evidence of this very ancient culture, from the time immemorial that he referred to as protohistory. He thought he found such evidence in gigantic stone figures found along the Peruvian coast, but they were not clear enough to be convincing—most people dismissed Ruzo's "sculptures" as simply natural erosional features. It was all rather like seeing faces and animals among the clouds.

Ruzo called the protohistorical culture and people (or beings) he sought the Masma. The name was not original to Ruzo, but came to the Peruvian esoterist Pedro Astete (1871–1940) in a dream while he resided in Andahuaylas, Peru. In 1905 Astete dreamt of a huge, ancient subterranean hall, filled with scrolls containing the knowledge of the most ancient ones. And Astete heard a voice repeating the name "Masma." Astete studied extensively myths, legends, and esoteric symbolism, and believed that sacred and mysterious treasures were buried in some cavern or tunnel system in the Huanca region of Peru. Astete lived in Buenos Aires, Argentina, from 1911–1923, and in 1913, a Buenos Aires periodical recounted another dream by a second person that matched in many features Astete's dream of 1905. Furthermore, in 1915, Astete discovered that the name Masma has Biblical connections. Genesis 25:12-16 names Masma (Mishma in some translations, and one of his brothers is Massa) as one of the twelve sons of Ishmael (the son of Abraham, by the Egyptian Hagar [also known as Agar]). Each of these twelve brothers was a ruler of his own tribe. Could the tribe of Masma have reached the Pacific coast of South America? Could the mysterious land of Ophir, to which Solomon's fleet traveled to return with gold (1 Kings 9:26-28), be located in modern Peru?

Ruzo came to know Astete in the 1920s, and was convinced that the Masma of the dream were real, and this was the protohistorical culture that he devoted most of his life to uncovering. Despite his penetrating analyses of myth, legend, and tradition, Ruzo made little headway uncovering physical evidence for the Masma until 1952 when he was shown a photograph of what appeared to be an enormous sculpted head. This was the Peca-Gasha, or "head of the narrow pass" (Williamson, 1959, p. 34), of Markawasi, also sometimes referred to as "The Head of the Inca," that Ruzo and others would later refer to as the "Monument to Humanity."

Ruzo quickly mounted a small expedition to Markawasi that year, and was stunned to find not just the 80-foot-tall Peca-Gasha, but also numerous other gigantic sculptures in the rocks and cliffs of the plateau. Ruzo intensively studied the Markawasi monuments from about 1953 to 1960, living on the plateau for extended periods of time. He lectured about his findings at scientific confer-ences in Mexico, Lima, and Paris, published scientific papers on the sculptures and wrote a book about Markawasi. Not everyone was convinced, however, and many archaeologists continued to regard the supposed sculptures as natural landforms sculpted by erosion. In some circles the subject became known as "Ruzo's Folly."

The Peca-Gasha is actually not just one head, but two major faces melded Janus-like, with one facing each way. These faces are evidently of different races, and according to Ruzo and others, a dozen smaller faces of various races, nationalities, genders, and ages can be found on the structure, hence the name Monument to Humanity.

George Hunt Williamson first popularized Markawasi among the English-speaking world in a chapter of his 1959 book, *Road in the Sky.*

A profile in one of the cliff faces known as the Inca Head,
with local guide Don Manuel in the foreground.

Williamson based his account on a visit to the plateau in 1957, and he also had a chance to interview Dr. Ruzo (who then lived near Lima). Williamson, an advocate of UFO contact in ancient and modern times, associated the Markawasi structures with extraterrestrials and giants of past aeons. Indeed, *Road in the Sky* is a book about extraterrestrial contact with humans on earth, from ancient to modern times, with speculations on the future of such communion. For Williamson, Markawasi is a "Sacred Forest" in stone where the "gods" (extraterrestrials, or crosses between extraterrestrials and earthlings?) met to plan the future.

So what are the structures, the monuments, the gigantic megalithic sculptures, found at Markawasi?

I interpret the monuments of Markawasi as incredible simulacra— that is, in this case, natural objects that in the mind's eye take the shape of forms of other entities, such as human faces and animals. I believe they were recognized as such even in very remote ancient times. The weathering and erosion of the granodiorite of which the plateau is composed gives rise to rounded anthropomorphic and zoomorphic features that, with a little imagination and insight, can be seen as very convincing sculptural forms. Indeed, the longer one stays on the plateau, and the harder one looks, the more sculptures appear.

Just possibly a little retouching on the part, a human hand has enhanced some of the natural monuments, but given their heavily eroded condition, I could not be certain. I found examples where the sculptures seem to have been created in stages, whether or not the creative forces were natural or man-induced. Furthermore, following a Rupert Sheldrake morphogenic (morphogenetic) field type of idea, continued viewing and interpretation of the structures may have reinforced later interpretations.

The Markawasi sculptures are point-of-view manifestations, not typical sculptures in the round. Most can only be seen from a particular angle, and in many cases under particular lighting conditions, be it in morning, evening, a solstice sunrise, by the light of a full moon, or under other special conditions. Believers in the sculptures feel there are special spots that have been designated as viewing locations, and to move even a few feet from some of the spots means that the sculpture is obscured or not visible at all. Certain sculptures appear to change forms as one moves or the light changes, perhaps from a face of one race to a face of another race. Such apparent subtlety and precision in sculpting and viewing has been used to argue for the reality of the artificiality of the monuments, but likewise has been advanced as strong evidence that they are simply natural structures to which humans bring their own meaning and interpretations. Essentially the stones and cliffs of Markawasi are like a huge Rorschach test. Among the forms that various people, including Ruzo and others, have identified at Markawasi are men and women of diverse races and nationalities, from native South American to Semitic to African, mostly these are facial profiles, but some of the figures consist of standing or reclining forms. Along with people are a diverse array of animals such

A reclining man; the head is to the left.

as horses, camels, elephants, lions, frogs, seals, turtles, sphinxes, a hippopotamus, sea lions or seals, a crocodile, lizards, and many other forms.

The indigenous Andean peoples had a traditional concept of wakas (guacas), which could in an abstract sense refer to laws (as laws of nature) or knowledge, or could at times be personified as heroes and deities (similar, perhaps, to the Egyptian concept of neterw, also spelled neters, or divine principles) or as cult ancestors. Wakas, it was believed, could sometimes take the physical form of uniquely shaped rocks or other natural structures. This is exactly what we may behold in the simulacra of Markawasi. The perfection and abundance of the manifestations of the wakas would make this an incredibly sacred place indeed.

Markawasi during the dry season (my visit was in August 2005) is a place virtually guaranteed to induce and enhance psychical, paranormal, mind-altering, preternatural, consciousness-bending experiences. It is a natural laboratory for heightened sensory perception. It is no wonder that this would be a perfect site for shamanistic gatherings and ritual invocations, whether in the guise of the traditional language of symbolism and hallucinations, or modern interpretations (such as a mecca for those bent on experiencing an unidentified flying object).

The plateau is shrouded in mystery at many levels. There is even disagreement as to the derivation of the name Markawasi (Marcahuasi). Daniel Ruzo stated that the name is relatively recent and means "two-storied house," referring to the stone buildings (which Ruzo regarded as Inca military garrisons) found, along with burial huts, on the plateau. In contrast, Lisa Rome states that marca in Quecha means the land belonging to a community, and huasi means town, so the name Marcahuasi refers to the land for the town or entire community, and from this etymology she suggests that the plateau was a communal religious center for the surrounding area.

Virtually no ancient inscriptions are known from the plateau. There is one major petroglyph remaining at Markawasi, although Ruzo suggested that once there must have been many. Occurring on the neck of the Peca-Gasha, it takes the form of sixteen squares arranged in a four-by-four checkerboard pattern. According to Williamson (1959, p. 41–42), citing Astete and Ruzo, this is a very ancient and primordial symbol, from which many later symbols were derived, and incorporates among other ideas, the ascent and harmonization of the individual, and hence humanity, with the forces of nature and the cosmos.

The cosmos are manifest at Markawasi. I went the skeptic, and came-back convinced that it is a very special, mystical, spiritual, mind-altering place. It is an incredible site that raises many issues concerning lost civilizations, the past history of humanity, varying states of consciousness, and the nature of reality. Markawasi is a location where, more than most sites, each person brings their own notions, molds the landscape to their own thoughts, is affected in unique ways, and brings back their own perceptions. This, in my opinion, is part of the mystery and draw of Markawasi. I am determined to return to this enchanted plateau. ◌

Part TWO
Lost History

The Georgia Guidestone Mystery

*Do the Monuments in a Georgia Cow Pasture
Bode Well or Ill for the Future of Earth?*

Robert M. Schoch, Ph.D.

Recently I had the opportunity to visit an enigmatic granite structure that superficially mimics various ancient megalithic constructions. Surrounded by mystery and intrigue, inspiring awe and animosity ever since it was unveiled on March 22, 1980 (two days after the Vernal Equinox), "The Georgia Guidestones" monument (alternatively called "The American Stonehenge") is located among the farms and cow pastures of Elbert County, Georgia. Some praise its beauty and the hope it bodes for the future of humankind. Others see it as a symbol of Satan and his cohorts, an attempt to usher in a vile New World Order. Reinforcing the latter theory, a coven of witches once used the monument as the setting for their rituals and, as I discuss further below, alleged paranormal phenomena have occurred at the site. The controversy is fueled by both the engraved message on the monument's surface and the secrecy of those responsible for its erection. It all began on a Friday afternoon in June 1979 when a well-dressed, apparently well-educated, middle-aged man visited the office of Joe H. Fendley, Sr., president of Elberton Granite Finishing Company.

Introducing himself as "Mr. Robert C. Christian," he explained that he represented a "small group of loyal Americans who believe in God" who wanted to build a monument so as to "leave a message for future generations." After speaking with Mr. Fendley and getting a very rough estimate of how much the monument might cost, the gentleman went (on the recommendation of Mr. Fendley) to the Granite City Bank in Elberton where he spoke to the president, Mr. Wyatt C. Martin.

In the course of conversation, it was revealed that "Robert C. Christian" was a pseudonym that the gentleman had chosen because he was of the Christian faith. Only after Mr. Martin was sworn to the utmost secrecy did "Christian" reveal his real name and other necessary information to the bank president. From then on, Mr. Martin acted as the intermediary to see the project carried through. Thus, ostensibly Mr. Martin is the only known person entrusted with the true identity of "Christian," knowledge he has never divulged.

In due course, the considerable funds necessary to underwrite not only the construction of the monument but the purchase of the two-hectare (five-acre) site on which to place it, were transferred to the bank and paid out to the landowner, to Elberton Granite Finishing Company, and to other construction workers, craftsmen, and consultants who participated in the project. "Mr. Christian" delivered plans and a wooden model for the monument to Mr. Fendley before he disappeared. By the following spring the monument was complete.

Composed of four solid granite monoliths each approximately five meters tall by two meters wide by half a meter thick positioned in a star pattern radiating out from a central monolith of the same height and thickness but half the width, and topped by a capstone three meters by two meters and half a meter thick, the entire monument is estimated to weigh 107,840 kilograms (237,746 pounds) and is oriented to the cardinal points.

A hole drilled through the center column locates the celestial North Pole, while a slot carved in the same column marks the annual path of the Sun throughout the year. A hole in the capstone allows a sunbeam to be used to mark noon each day. The eight sides of the four main monoliths are engraved with the same message in eight different languages— English, Spanish, Swahili, Hindi, Hebrew, Arabic, Chinese, and Russian. This message consists of ten "guides" or precepts, as follows:

MAINTAIN HUMANITY UNDER 500,000,000
IN PERPETUAL BALANCE WITH NATURE
GUIDE REPRODUCTION WISELY
IMPROVING FITNESS AND DIVERSITY
UNITE HUMANITY WITH A LIVING NEW LANGUAGE
RULE PASSION – FAITH – TRADITION
AND ALL THINGS WITH TEMPERED REASON
PROTECT PEOPLE AND NATIONS
WITH FAIR LAWS AND JUST COURTS
LET ALL NATIONS RULE INTERNALLY
RESOLVING EXTERNAL DISPUTES IN A WORLD COURT
AVOID PETTY LAWS AND USELESS OFFICIALS
BALANCE PERSONAL RIGHTS WITH SOCIAL DUTIES
PRIZE TRUTH – BEAUTY – LOVE
SEEKING HARMONY WITH THE INFINITE
BE NOT A CANCER ON THE EARTH
LEAVE ROOM FOR NATURE – LEAVE ROOM FOR NATURE

The four edges of the monument's capstone are inscribed with the following message translated into Babylonian Cuneiform, Classical Greek, Sanskrit, and Egyptian Hieroglyphics: "LET THESE BE GUIDE-STONES TO AN AGE OF REASON." This has been viewed as an obvious reference to Thomas Paine's *The Age of Reason* (1794 and later), which espouses a deistic interpretation of the universe (accepting a Creator or God who does not generally interfere with our worldly affairs) and heavily criticizes organized religion, including Christianity. Such an allusion to Thomas Paine and his radical ideas seems ironic for a man going by the pseudonym "Robert C. Christian" in reference to his faith.

The message engraved on the Guidestones is subject to multiple interpretations and thus has been alternatively praised and condemned. What does it mean to "maintain humanity under 500 million"? Is this focus on global population simply an outgrowth of ideas that were trendy at the time? In the 1970s many people contended humanity would be

Guidestone inscribed with the
precepts in English

doomed before the end of the twentieth century—subject to widespread famine, disease, and social unrest as limited supplies of natural resources were exhausted— if global population growth was not brought under control. Or is there something more sinister in the message?

The global population in 1980 was close to 4.5 billion and today it has passed the 7 billion mark. Are the creators suggesting that there should be massive genocide to decrease the world population? In terms of present numbers, should 13 out of every 14 people on Earth be exterminated? Or does the second precept, "guide reproduction wisely," imply that limiting reproduction should slowly lower the population? And if so, which persons or groups will be discouraged or banned from reproducing? Should a program of eugenics be established? Should certain people and races be forcibly restricted in their reproduction? Or should Darwinian-like natural selection be allowed to take place, such that the strongest and fittest will be those who reproduce in the greatest numbers while those who are weak die out?

Researcher Jay Weidner has proposed that a conspiratorial plan, which he calls "The Culling," has already been put in place by secretive wealthy ruling elites (including members of the Rockefeller family, the Bush family, the Trilateral Commission, the World Trade Commission, and the Club of Rome) to reduce the population of the world to around 500 million.

According to Weidner, The Georgia Guidestones are telling us what will (or must) happen, if only in a symbolic manner, once the elite have their way. An alternative, but related, theory is that the monument is intended to speak to survivors of a global catastrophe during which 95% or more of the human population is destroyed. The injunction is not to allow the population to increase over 500 million in the post-apocalyptic world. Either interpretation is rather unsettling. The global catastrophe scenario suggests that the designers perhaps had secret information. Using top-secret classified scientific data, had they determined that a comet or asteroid will hit Earth in the near future? Or had they calculated when the Sun will undergo a major solar outburst, causing devastation across the planet? Or could they predict future earthquake and volcanic activity and other Earth changes? Or were they concerned about nuclear holocaust?

Maybe their methods involve the paranormal ability to look into the future. The precepts "unite humanity with a living new language" and "resolving external disputes in a world court" strike many as advocating a New World Order and global government. Is the secret group responsible for The Georgia Guidestones the same group who will rule the world in the future? Is the message on the Guidestones related to the ostensible secret plans of the United States Government to continue even in case of total disaster and societal breakdown (sometimes referred to as "Continuity of Government," or COG), such as during a nuclear attack or a catastrophic natural disaster? (Note that if the U.S. is the dominant, or only, superpower, then the U.S. government can be seen as effectively the world government of the future).

Polaroid photograph of an "energy beam" at The Georgia Guidestones, 21 June 1985.

And what about the precepts that state "prize truth – beauty – love – seeking harmony with the infinite" and "be not a cancer on the Earth – leave room for nature"? Are these simply vague expressions of environmental-ism, as was so popular at the time of the monument's erection, or are they calling for a new religion to accompany the New World Order?

It is well demonstrated that religion can be one of the best ways to control the masses. Is this new religion intended to be a method to lull the general populace into complacency, even as they line up like docile sheep to be sterilized so that they cannot reproduce and thus be "a cancer on the Earth"? Will Earth and humanity be better off if the thoughts on the monument are followed, or are they the commandments of a dark force, a secret and nefarious group that plans to take over the world?

Conspiracy theories are only reinforced by the secrecy of those who arranged and funded the construction of the monument. It has been as-serted that it was a group of Masons, or Freemasons, who were behind the design of The Georgia Guidestones. While producing a documentary titled *2012: The Odyssey*, Jay Weidner interviewed Gary Jones, the editor of a local newspaper, the *Elberton Star*. According to Jones, the Guide-stones were erected by local Masons. Or, alternatively, was it another—even more secretive—group?

Remember that the man who arranged the monument's construction used the pseudonym "Robert C. Christian." Who was he in reality? One popular hypothesis asserts that his name is a not so subtle reference to the Rosicrucians, mem-bers of the Order of the Rosy Cross, a secret soci-ety ostensibly founded by Christian Rosenkreuz in the fourteenth century but possibly having its roots in ancient Egyptian hermeti-cism. According to re-searchers, such as Lynn Picknett and Clive Prince, it was Rosicrucians (and those I would label as Her-metic Illuminati) who were behind the Invisible College, which is gener-ally viewed as the immedi-ate precursor, in the 1640s

Another Polaroid photo taken the same day.

and 1650s, of the Royal Society (Royal Society of London for Improving Natural Knowledge) founded in 1660 (see the article by Picknett and Prince in *Darklore*, vol. 6, 2011).

Is the Invisible College much more extensive geographically and longer lived temporally than generally suspected? Is it a branch of the Rosicrucians that dates back to antiquity and exists secretly to this day? Have the Rosicrucians and/or members of the Invisible College inherited or discovered knowledge from the ancient world about the end times?

According to an extreme version of the theory, this ultra-secretive group is even now instigating global chaos (as evidenced by the current worldwide financial meltdown, with accompanying wars and riots), which will only be exacerbated by impending solar outbursts, devastating the surface of our planet and resulting in the death of the vast majority of humanity. The Rosicrucians, following this line of thinking, are the lineal descendants of sages who have been monitoring solar activity for thousands of years—sages who have figured out the cycles of the Sun on timescales of tens of thousands of years—and so they know the next catastrophe will soon arrive. When the Apocalypse comes, they will be ready to step in and take charge of the New World Order.

The enigmas of the message on the stones, and the secrecy of those responsible for the monument, are not the only mysteries surrounding this site. While he etched the lettering on the granite monoliths, sand-blaster Charlie Clamp reported hearing "strange music and disjointed voices" unlike anything he had ever experienced before. Supposedly the general location at which the monument is erected was traditionally considered "the center of the world" or the "belly button or navel of Earth" by the local Native Americans (Indians).

Some have suggested that the area might be a potential landing site for UFOs (unidentified flying objects); viewed from above, the monument looks like the letter X, as if to mark the spot for extraterrestrial contact. Could it be that "Robert C. Christian" was not actually a human at all, but an extraterrestrial alien in disguise? Or a human body, effectively a zombie-like being, taken over by alien forces?

No, I do not believe either to be the case, but such ideas are out there. They are indicative, perhaps, of just how enigmatic The Georgia Guide-stones are to some people. I visited the Guidestones on September 23, 2011, kindly guided by a woman from Georgia (she wishes to remain anonymous and does not live in the immediate region of the Guidestones) who was familiar with the area and happy to recount some of her personal experiences. She, as well as various family members and friends, had experienced strange energies in the presence of the Guidestones over a 22-year span, from 1985 through 2007, and although no one visually saw the energies, they could sense them.

On several occasions Polaroid cameras captured on film what were claimed to be "energy beams" that appear to be descending down from the sky in the

Another Polaroid shot one year later with different camera again shows "energy beam."

vicinity of the monument. I had the chance to inspect some of the original Polaroid photos as well as the cameras used to take the photographs, and although I cannot state for certain what exactly is captured on the film— be they simply overexposures from the bright Sun, reflections in the camera lens, defects due to the film or cameras, psychically imprinted images on the film, or genuine energy beams—I certainly find the evidence tantalizing that perhaps something strange was happening.

Interestingly, the best photos were taken on the Summer Solstice of June 21, 1985 and then exactly one year later on the Summer Solstice of June 21, 1986, and the photos from both years show similar phenomena although they were taken with different cameras (one camera in 1985, and a second camera in 1986) and using different batches of film.

Ultimately I am not sure what to make of The Georgia Guidestones. Do they represent a genuinely profound mystery? Did "Robert C. Christian" really appear in Elbert County? Or is the entire story a fabrication, a local hoax, and the monument nothing more than a simple tourist attraction concocted by local residents to bring in revenue? Is this why Elberton Granite published (in 1981) a 50-page "guide" to the monument, including a handy map locating the site?

Supposedly "Mr. Christian" hoped that other people or groups would come forth in the future to add to the monument; for instance, it is said he envisioned an outer circle of 12 more stones carrying the message in another 24 languages. Of course this would conveniently mean more business for the Elberton Granite Finishing Company! For over 30 years, however, no one has come forth to add to the monument.

The truth behind The Georgia Guidestones may never be known for certain. ◛

Robert M. Schoch, a full-time faculty member at Boston University, earned his Ph.D. in geology and geophysics at Yale University. He is best known for his redating of the Great Sphinx of Egypt. His latest book is The Parapsychology Revolution *(Tarcher/Penguin, 2008). Dr. Schoch currently has a new book in the works, tentatively scheduled for publication by Inner Traditions, Fall 2012. Website: www.robertschoch.com.*

Survival of a Different Kind

The True Story of Journalistic Pioneer
William Thomas Stead

Michael E. Tymn

S everal survivors of the *Titanic* disaster, 100 years ago April 15th, reported seeing William Thomas Stead at various places in the two hours, 40 minutes that elapsed between the time the floating palace on its maiden voyage hit an iceberg and then made its plunge to the bottom of the North Atlantic. All told of a very composed and calm man, one prepared to meet his death with courage and hope.

Frederick Seward, a 34-year-old New York lawyer, said that Stead was one of the few on deck when the iceberg was impacted. "I saw him soon after and was thoroughly scared, but he preserved the most beautiful composure," Seward, who boarded lifeboat Number 7, recalled.

Andrew Cunningham, a 35-year-old English cabin steward serving Stead and several other passengers, recalled that Stead had not been feeling well all day and had supper in his room. "I did not see him again until after the accident," Cunningham related. "Then I went to see all my passengers. He had gone on deck but soon came back. I said, 'Mr. Stead, you'll have to put on your life-belt.' He said, 'Cunningham, what is that for?' I said, 'You may need it.' I put the belt over his head. We bade each other good-bye, and that was the last I saw him."

Racing through the first-class smoking room on his way to lifeboat Number 9, George Kemish, a 24-year-old ship's fireman and stoker, observed Stead sitting alone there while reading, as if he had planned to stay there—whatever happened.

Juanita Parrish Shelley, a 25-year-old second-class passenger from Montana who was traveling with her mother, saw Stead assisting women and children into the lifeboats. "Your beloved Chief," Shelley later wrote to Edith Harper, Stead's secretary and biographer, "together with Mr. and Mrs. (Isidor) Straus, attracted attention even in that awful hour on account of their superhuman composure and divine work. When we, the last lifeboat, left, and they could do no more, he stood alone at the edge of the deck near the stern in silence and what seemed to me a prayerful attitude, or one of profound meditation. You ask if he wore a life belt. Alas! No, they were too scarce. My last glimpse of the *Titanic* showed him standing in the same attitude and place."

Stead, a 62-year-old English journalist, author, editor, and peace activist, was on his way to New York City to deliver a speech on the subject of world peace at Carnegie Hall on April 21. He had been invited by the Men and Religion Forward Movement, an organization dedicated to bringing business methods into religion. Among the other speakers on the program was President William Howard Taft.

Though Stead had psychic abilities, including the gift of automatic writing, he apparently did not foresee his death on the Titanic, at least on a conscious level. Subconsciously, on the soul level, however, he seemed to have known what was coming. In one of his many stories, *From the Old World to the New*, a novel published in 1892, Stead described the sinking of a ship after hitting an iceberg in the North Atlantic. A psychic on another ship, the *Majestic*, received a clairvoyant message of the sinking in time to warn the captain of the ship about the icebergs in the area. In Stead's story, the *Majestic*, like the *Titanic,* a White Star Line ship, was captained by Edward J. Smith, the captain of the *Titanic* on that fatal maiden voyage. However, Smith did not take over the *Majestic* until 1895, three years after Stead's article.

In an 1886 story for the *Pall Mall Gazette*, which he edited, Stead wrote about the sinking of an ocean liner and how lives were lost because there were too few lifeboats; and in a 1909 book, Stead, in explaining why he believes in life after death, wrote: "In order to form a definite idea of the problem which we are about to attack, let us imagine the grave as if it were the Atlantic Ocean…" In a speech delivered by Stead to members of the Cosmos Club that same year, he pictured himself as being shipwrecked and drowning in the sea, calling frantically for help.

While the *Titanic* was being built, the Rev. Venerable Archdeacon Colley printed a pamphlet entitled *The Fore-Ordained Wreck of the Titanic* and sent a copy to Stead, who replied: "Dear Sir, Thank you very much for your kind letter, which reaches me just as I am starting for America. I sincerely hope that none of the misfortunes, which you seem to think may

happen, will happen; but I will keep your letter and will write to you when I come back. Yours truly, W. T. Stead."

Titanic Sinking (Willy Stöwer)

Harper noted that before Stead departed Southampton, he appeared very somber, unlike his numerous previous trips abroad. He told her that he felt "something was going to happen, somewhere, or somehow. And that it will be for good." He also gave her directions as to arranging some of his business affairs.

Stead's career as a journalist and author began during the 1860's when he became a reporter for a newspaper called the *Northern Echo*, advancing to editor in 1871. In 1880, he accepted a position as assistant editor of the *Pall Mall Gazette*, then became its editor in 1883. In 1890, he founded the *Review of Reviews*. Stead is credited with introducing the interview technique to British journalism and inventing the "New Journalism," bringing important topics in bright, colorful prose to the man in the street.

In a story written by B. O. Flower, the editor of *Arena*, a popular American publication, Stead is referred to as a cosmopolitan journalist "with a rare blending of intellectual force with moral conviction, idealism with utilitarianism, a virile imagination, and a common sense practicality that strove to make the vision a useful reality."

Stead is not listed among the 334 victims, whose bodies were recovered as they floated in their lifejackets, having frozen to death. The only record of what happened to his body came 15 days later, on April 27, when Stead communicated with Dr. John S. King, a Toronto physician, through a medium King had been studying. Stead had indeed survived, but it was his consciousness, not his body, that survived the calamity. "Even my plight was preferable to some, for I was hurt by something like a blow, and so I quickly sank below the surface of the sea," Stead communicated to King. One might infer from that message that Stead was hit by one the ship's funnels that broke loose.

Stead was to have accompanied Etta Wriedt, a Detroit, Michigan, direct-voice medium, to England on his return trip so that she could be further studied and observed. Vice-Admiral William Usborne Moore, a retired British naval commander turned psychical researcher, had told Stead about Mrs. Wriedt two years earlier after visiting her in Detroit and being very much impressed by her mediumship. Mrs. Wriedt had visited England in 1911 and was being brought back for further study by Stead, Moore, and others.

In the "direct-voice," the spirits communicate independent of the medium's body, usually in the same voice associated with them when alive in the flesh. A floating trumpet is used to amplify the voices. While Mrs. Wriedt did not require darkness, Moore observed that the voices were stronger when it was dark. It was reported that as many as four spirit voices would be talking simultaneously to different sitters and, although Wriedt knew only English, spirits communicated in French, German, Italian, Spanish, Norwegian, Dutch, Arabic, and other languages. Occasionally, apparitions of the spirits could be seen by the sitters.

Mrs. Wriedt was in New York City at the time the news came of the disaster, and according to her host, Stead communicated three days after his passing. "He was weak in articulation, but we quite understood him; his stay was short," Moore quoted the host. "His stay was short. The next night, Thursday, Mr. Stead came again; his articulation and personality were much stronger, and he went into details of his passing. The following night, Friday, he came again very strong and clear, again giving us full details of his passing. He particularly desired that Mrs. Wriedt go over to London to fulfill her engagement, which she is now about doing."

Back in England, Major-General Sir Alfred Turner, a retired British army officer, recorded his first experience in hearing from Stead, about 10 days after the disaster. "No professional medium was present, but Mr. Stead's private secretary and her mother (who lived at Cambridge House, Wimbledon) were among the sitters. We had hardly commenced when a voice, which came apparently from behind my right shoulder, exclaimed, 'I am so happy to be with you again!' The voice was unmistakably that of Stead, who immediately (though not visible to anyone) commenced to tell us of the events of the dire moments when the huge leviathan settled down to her doom and slowly sank to her grave two miles below the surface of the sea.

For himself, he felt no fear whatever. He had a premonition of his physical ending, as we know, from the last letter written by him from Cherbourg a few days before the disaster, that he felt that the greatest event of his life was impending, but he knew not what it was. When the *Titanic* sank there was, as regards himself, a short, sharp struggle to gain his breath, and immediately afterwards he came to his senses in another state of existence. He was surrounded by hundreds of beings, who, like himself, had passed over the bourne but who were utterly dazed, and being totally ignorant of the next stage of life to come, were groping about as in the dark, asking for light, and entirely unconscious that they were not still in the flesh. He set himself at once to do missionary work by enlightening these poor and unprepared creatures; and in such work, he told us, he was still employed, with the assistance of numerous spirit inhabitants of the next plane, whose task and bounden duty is to help and enlighten those who pass over."

Stead then had a long conversation with his secretary, Edith Harper, during which he gave some instructions to her. "Asked by me if he would show himself to us," Turner continued, "he replied: 'Not tonight, but if you go to Cambridge House on such and such a day, I will do so.' The voice then died away."

Mrs. Wriedt made the trip to England and gave her first sitting on May 5, 20 days after Stead's death. According to Moore, Stead manifested

Epitaph on W.T. Stead's memorial reads: "This tribute to the memory of a journalist of worldwide renown is erected by American friends and admirers. He met death aboard the *Titanic*, April 15, 1912, and is numbered amongst those who, dying nobly, enabled others to live." Followed by the Latin, *Finis Coronat Opus—* "The Ending Crowns the Work."

and "gave three admirable tests of his identity," including some details about a conversation Stead and Moore had had at a bank building the last time they met. The following night Estelle Stead, Stead's daughter, attended a sitting with Wriedt. "A fortnight after the disaster I saw my father's face and heard his voice just as distinctly as I heard it when he bade me good-bye before embarking on the *Titanic*," she recorded, estimating that her father talked for over 20 minutes. Moore, who heard the conversation, estimated that it was closer to 40 minutes and described it as the most painful but most realistic and convincing conversation he had heard during his investigations of mediumship.

Count Chedo Miyatovich, a diplomat from Serbia, sat with Mrs. Wriedt on May 16, 1912, accompanied by his friend, Dr. Hinkovitch. Wriedt began by telling Miyatovich that a young woman, a spirit friend of his, stood in front of them and wondered if he could see her. Miyatovich could not see her, but Hinkovitch said he saw some "illuminated mist." Wriedt then said that the woman whispered to her that her name was Adela or Ada Mayell. "I was astounded," Miyatovich declared. "Only three weeks before died Miss Ada Mayell, a very dear friend of mine, to whom I was deeply attached. The next moment a light appeared behind Mrs. Wriedt and moved from left to right. There in that slowly moving light was, not the spirit, but the very person of my friend William T. Stead, not wrapped in white, but in his usual walking costume. Both I and Mrs. Wriedt exclaimed loudly for joy. Hinkovitch, who knew Stead only from photos, said, 'Yes, that is Mr. Stead.' Mr. Stead nodded to me and disappeared. Half a minute later, he appeared again, looking at me and bowing; again he appeared and was seen by all three of us more clearly than before. Then we all three distinctly heard these words: 'Yes, I am Stead. William T. Stead. My dear friend, Miyatovich, I came here expressly to give you fresh proof that there is life after death. You always hesitated to accept that truth.' "

Miyatovich said that an old friend of Hinkovitch's, a physician when alive, then carried on a conversation with Hinkovitch in the Croatian language. He called it the "most wonderful experience of my life."

The Reverend Charles Tweedale recorded that Stead was seen and heard on July 17, 1912, at the home of Professor James Coates of Rothesay, a well-known author and investigator, who had Mrs. Wriedt give a sitting with a number of witnesses. "Mr. Stead showed himself twice within a short time, the last appearance being clearly defined, and none will readily forget the clear, ringing tones of his voice," Coates said, "There in our own home, and in the presence of 14 sane and thoughtful people, Mr. Stead has manifested and proved in his own person that the dead do return."

Stead later communicated with his daughter through another medium. He stressed that in transitioning to the spirit world one does not immediately become part of the "Godhead," nor does the "spirit" have full knowledge on all subjects. "I cannot tell you when your grandson will next require shoes...nor can I tell you the settlement of the Irish question. I can only see a little farther than you, and I do not by any means possess the key to the door of All Knowledge and All Truth. That, we have each to work for...and as we pass through one door we find another in front of us to be unlocked....and another, and another." He added that as progress is made and Earth's inclinations and habits put aside, other interests take their places and then comes the desire for true knowledge.

"Life here is a grander thing—a bolder thing, and a happier thing for all those who have led reasonable lives on Earth," Stead further communicated to his daughter, "but for the unreasonable there are many troubles and difficulties and sorrows to be encountered. There is a great truth in the saying that 'as ye sow, so shall ye reap.' " ❧

A more complete story of William Stead can be found in Transcending the Titanic, *authored by Michael E. Tymn, published by White Crow Books, and available at Amazon.com.*

13.

Whence Went Thomas Aquinas?

*Did the Medieval Theologian
Travel Out of His Body?*

John Chambers

Only the sacristan heard the words—the sacristan and the tall, stout, balding, red-faced priest kneeling before the crucifix from which these words were issuing:

> "You have written well of me, Thomas. What do you desire as a reward for your labors?"

The kneeling priest was Thomas Aquinas, the greatest Christian theologian of the Middle Ages. The date was December 6, 1273. Now Thomas murmured in reply:

> "Lord, only yourself."

The congregants of the modest chapel of St. Nicholas, in Naples, Italy, before whom Thomas had just celebrated the Mass of St. Nicholas, didn't hear these words. But they likely stared in bewilderment as the beloved and revered scholar and teacher, newly arrived from the University of Paris, remained stock-still on his knees for several minutes, not uttering a word. His head quivered slightly; he was lost in some form of rapt concentration they'd never seen before. Then he got to his feet and, walking slowly with eyes half-closed, like a man in a trance, crossed the floor and went out the chapel door without a word.

Thomas Aquinas had lately, here and in Paris, been seen in this trance state. Recently, he had revealed to his socius, or assistant, Reginald de Piperno, that he had been speaking personally with Christ and the Apostles. In 1319, at the process of Thomas's canonization as a saint, Bartholomew of Capua, quoting Bernard Gui (who heard it from Reginald), testified that, "Once, Thomas was puzzling for days over a passage from Isaiah, praying and fasting and asking God for understanding. Reginald then overhears his master speaking with someone at night. Soon afterward, he is called into Thomas's room to take dictation on the Isaiah passage for one hour and then sent back to bed. But before he goes, Reginald begs Thomas to tell him with whom he was speaking. Thomas at first refuses, but finally says, with tears running down his cheeks, that God had sent Peter and Paul, and these had told Thomas what he had desired to know. Reginald was told never to tell anyone this as long as Thomas lived."

When he arrived in Naples in the fall of 1273, Thomas, who would die the next year, aged 49, was exhausted in body and soul. Born in his father's castle in southern Italy, he had been engaged in furious theological study since the age of 14. He had to his credit roughly a hundred works:

commentaries on Scripture, collections of patristic commentaries, sermons, philosophical treatises, explorations of disputed subjects, commentaries on Aristotle and Proclus and Boethius, and a couple of Summas.

When Thomas entered Naples in 1273, he had written one million words of his final work, the immense *Summa Theologica (A Summation of Theological Knowledge)*, which would offer a comprehensive synthesis of Christian doctrine and the philosophy of Aristotle and serves to this day as the definitive Catholic manual for preachers. Thomas would leave the Summa unfinished, Reginald later adding sections from previous treatises to round off the enormous fragment.

The *Summa Theologica*, illuminated manuscript

Certainly the 35 years of continuous, hard-driving, impassioned work had sapped every last drop of creative energy from Thomas. That might explain why, after the brief exchange with Jesus via the crucifix in the chapel, Thomas virtually never wrote another word. Bewildered and frightened at his master's refusal to lift a pen, Reginald drew from him the begrudging admission that, during the few minutes Thomas had knelt in stunned silence following Christ's words, he had been taken up by God on a wondrous journey. He had seen and heard such prodigious things that he could not continue his own writing because, compared to that, "everything I have written seems to me like straw." Thomas swore Reginald to silence, saying: "I adjure you by the living almighty God, and by the faith you have in our order, and by charity that you strictly promise me you will never reveal in my lifetime what I tell you. Everything that I have written seems like straw to me compared to those things that I have seen and have been revealed to me."

Many commentators believe that at that time Thomas had had a stroke or some form of physical or nervous breakdown. (One contemporary Catholic scholar, Father James A. Weisheipl, suggests he had both at once, along with a mystical vision.) Whatever the case may be, Aquinas remained in a semi-trance for several days. Additional documents from the Canonization Enquiry attest that, soon after the St. Nicholas chapel visitation, "Thomas went to visit a sister (the Countess of San Severino) to whom he was very close, and who was disturbed on seeing her brother in such a 'dazed' state." Apparently, there was a reoccurrence of the "straw" statement: Reginald, still worried by his master's behavior—thinking that his hard work "might have effected his master's brain"—followed him to the Countess's estate and, questioning him about why he was no longer writing, received the same answer about "so much straw."

Bernard Gui remarks that, "Thomas not infrequently during this period fell into a 'trance,' and that the trance at the Countess's home lasted longer than any prior incident, such that Reginald had to question him multiple times and 'tug violently at his cloak' before he could get any reply from Thomas." Gui also notes that "Thomas was 'insensitive to pain' during this period. He did not, for example, seem to feel a leg cautery, and one night, while dictating comment on Boethius' De Trinitate to Reginald, the candle burned down to Thomas' fingers without him noticing."

Thomas died in Fossanova on March 7, 1274, on his way to the Council of Lyons.

Born in Roccasecca in southern Italy on January 28, 1225, the man who would be the supreme theologian of the Middle Ages was of noble lineage; his mother Theodora was related to the Hohenstaufen line of Holy Roman emperors. His brothers would eventually enter the military; Thomas himself was intended by the family to follow in his uncle's footsteps as abbot of the original Benedictine Abbey at Monte Cassino. The boy advanced in leaps and bounds at the Monte Cassino school and at the new university founded in Naples by Emperor Frederick II, astounding his teachers with his powerful intellect. Thomas was deeply impressed by his teachers from the Dominican Order, John of St. Julian and Petrus de Ibernia, and resolved at the age of 19 to become, not a Benedictine, but a Dominican priest.

This thoroughly frustrated his parents, who had set their hearts on their brilliant son's becoming the Abbot of Monte Cassino. They had Thomas kidnapped by his brothers while he was on his way to Paris to join the Dominicans and kept their son a prisoner on the family estates for 15 months. The ruddy-complexioned scholar did not budge in his determination to become a Dominican. His brothers thought the pleasures of the flesh might weaken his resolve (the Dominican Order demanded celibacy) and introduced a prostitute into Thomas's bedroom to seduce him. He sent her flying with blows of a burning cudgel. That night, according to legend, two angels appeared in his dreams to reinforce him in his desire to remain a virgin. By 1244 his parents had given up; Thomas's mother, Theodora, maneuvered to save face by arranging for her son to escape at night through his window. She hoped the world would never know she had totally capitulated to the Dominicans.

Albertus Magnus

Thomas went up to the University of Paris's Faculty of Arts in 1245, very quickly becoming the pupil of Albertus Magnus, or Albert the Great, the Dominican scholar who, before he was eclipsed by his own beloved pupil, Thomas, was the leading theologian of the time. Thomas followed Albert to Cologne, Germany, then back to Paris. When Thomas failed his first disputation, Albert declared: "We call him the dumb ox [the nickname given to Thomas by his fellow students because he studied silently and relentlessly], but in his teaching he will one day produce such a bellowing that it will be heard throughout the world."

Albert the Great's inquiring mind roamed over the whole universe. It did not exclude the study of alchemy, though Albert's approach was more circumspect and critical than most. Serge Lequeuvre writes, in *Thomas d'Aquin: Le Saint Alchimiste (Thomas Aquinas, Holy Alchemist)* in Historia that Albert "notably doubted the possibility of the transmutation of metals into gold. Did he drag his young and brilliant collaborator into the 'Great Work?'" Lequeuvre says, yes. "Every subject mobilized his [Thomas's] energies: from the most arduous of philosophical questions to [the mundane practical matter of] how to transport water…. There was no way then that he could not have been interested in alchemy, the new science that had aroused the enthusiasm of Europe's elite and was playing a part in the revival of learning. Was he an alchemist?

Lively polemics have surrounded the part of his work—it was minimal—dedicated to alchemy. Only a tiny treatise on the subject has been attributed with certainty to him, the Treatise on the Art of Alchemy. Lequeuvre observes that Thomas's references to alchemy were not typical. "Far from the impenetrable hermeticism of numerous alchemical texts, they are remarkably easy to read. They unveil without esoteric flourishes the details of the operations necessary to purify a substance and, were it not for the mysterious character of certain matters obscured beneath medieval designations [whose meanings were known to Albert the Great and Thomas, but are not known to the twenty-first century], modern readers, in reading Thomas, would find themselves on the threshold of undertaking the 'Great Work.'"

Thomas's final words on alchemy, as preserved by Reginald: "Do not pay much attention to the words of modern and ancient philosophers who have worked with that science, because alchemy is purely a matter of the depth of our understanding [i.e., of how intelligent we are] and demonstrations by experimentation. Philosophers, wanting to hide the truth of some sciences, have almost always spoken figuratively." Lequeuvre adds: "As for the quest after gold or material riches, that didn't concern brother Thomas, since he refused prelacies of the highest order."

Thomas's overriding concern, however, was to synthesize the thought of the ancient Greek philosopher Aristotle with the doctrines of the Church. Only over the preceding century had Aristotle's works become known again to the western world. The pagan philosopher's naturalist and empirical approach to the understanding of the universe, with its assertion that all knowledge can be acquired solely through reflection on sense data (even to understanding the nature of God), ran counter to the passionate conviction of medieval Christianity that only revelation through faith can unveil the secrets of God.

Thomas achieved his synthesis, insisting that while someone looking at nature could tell that an intelligent creator exists and therefore it is necessary to follow the Aristotelean path, only someone who has imbibed the doctrines of the Church can tell whether that creator is good or if he might work in history.

Thomas's *Summa*, and all his works, stands today as a single solid monument to learning. But, in Thomas's time, many viewed Aristotle's writings suspiciously, since they came from the pen of a pagan. Many considered that Thomas's synthesis was close to being heretical and that it might even have crossed the line. The great author of the *Summas* had to fight for his views in a way we cannot imagine today; and dark rumors persisted in the corridors of the Sorbonne that he was a practitioner of the black arts. These gossips considered, though, that Thomas was less given to heretical practices than some others: Lequeuvre writes, "A legend circulated according to which Albert the Great was supposed to have breathed life into an automaton, after which Thomas destroyed the automaton with blows from a stick."

From the beginning, Thomas's prodigious intelligence was aided and abetted by his prodigious memory. Sheila Ostrander and Lynn Schroeder tell us in Supermemory that, "Aquinas's memory was literally encyclopedic. As a boy he could remember verbatim what his teachers said. As a young man he impressed Pope Urban by putting together a compendium of writing by Church fathers. He didn't copy it; he remembered it." Thomas told his pupils he had never read a book he hadn't thoroughly understood; Gui testified at the Canonization Enquiry that, "his memory was such that he never forgot what he had once read. According to Reginald, he used to dictate to three and occasionally four secretaries on different subjects at the same time, speaking fluently, 'never seeming to search.'"

It was not until the sixteenth century that Thomas's teachings were hailed as preeminent and a chief bulwark against Protestantism. In 1879, the Papal Bull *Aeternis Patris* endorsed Thomism as an authentic expression of doctrine and said it should be studied by all students of theology. Pope Benedict XV recently declared that, "This (Dominican) Order ... acquired new luster when the Church declared the teaching of Thomas to be her own and that Doctor honored with the special praises of the Pontiffs, the master and patron of Catholic schools."

Thomas's achievement is a prodigious and abiding one. But the question remains: Where did Thomas go and what did he see and hear on December 6, 1273, to make him believe that all that prodigious achievement was less than a bit of straw? ଔ

Mary Magdalene, in her ubiquitous orange robes, lands in Septimania.

Mary Magdalene and the House of Orange

European History Would Not Be the Same Without Her

Ralph Ellis

Mary Magdalene founded the royal Dutch house of Orange? Is this an all-fools'-day joke? Actually, no. And one of the primary reasons for thinking that this may be so is that the House of Orange is not Dutch, nor was it French. In fact, the House of Orange was originally from Septimania—the small province in the south of France in which the fabled City of Orange is situated, the province where Mary Magdalene is supposed to have been exiled in the first century AD.

In my previous works, *Cleopatra to Christ* and *King Jesus*, I followed the new historical evidence for the biblical family, provided in the works of first century historian, Josephus Flavius. It is commonly said that there is no historical evidence whatsoever for the biblical Jesus, but this is not true; if readers only understand that the biblical Jesus was called Jesus of Gamala, then we suddenly find that there is a whole host of contemporary historical information about the biblical Jesus. And, not surprisingly, this new evidence concurs very well with the biblical accounts.

Thus we find that Jesus (of Gamala) was the leader of a new and radical sect of Judaism, called the Fourth Sect, or the Galileans; and he was said to be the leader of 600 rebel fishermen. This is why the New Testament calls its hero "Jesus of Galilee" and the "Fisher of Men." It is also said that Jesus (of Gamala) became high priest of Jerusalem, just as Hebrews Chapter 7 affirms. In addition, if you follow the threads given to us by the Talmud and the research of Professor Robert Eisenman, we find that Jesus (of Gamala) was also married to Mary of Bethany, a lady who turns out to be one and the same as Mary Magdalene.

So far, so interesting. But here is where we begin to diverge from biblical history.

Royal Prince

If we continue to follow these records of real first century history, we eventually find a family history for Jesus (of Gamala) that is rather different from the one we have been taught by the religious authorities. We begin to discover that Jesus was actually rather wealthy: he owned a castle near Tiberias, and he controlled a 600-strong army (of so-called fishermen). In addition, Mary Magdalene was called Mary Boethus, in the historical record, and she was said to have been the richest woman in Judaea. And it was Mary Magdalene who supported Jesus and the disciples financially, out of her great wealth, just as it says in Luke 8:2-3. This might seem like a radical departure from biblical history, but it actually makes sense. King Herod would never have been afraid of a pauper carpenter, but he might well have been afraid of the strategic ambitions of a popular aristocrat and royal prince.

And there is more. If you begin to link the various threads of this new history together, we begin to discover that Jesus (of Gamala) was actually a royal prince called Izates, the son of Queen Helena of Adiabene (Queen Thea Muse Ourania). And we know that these two characters are closely linked, because Josephus Flavius specifically blames the leaders of the Fourth Sect (including Jesus of Gamala) for the Jewish Revolt. But later on, Josephus says that the leaders of the Revolt surrendered to the Roman army commander, Titus, and the foremost leader was called King Izates, the King of the Jews. But Josephus also mentions the fact that Izates had a nickname, and that was Izas. If you have an open mind to these matters, it is quite clear that King Izas was the biblical Jesus, who was also called the King of the Jews.

Enscription above Jesus cross: INRI, which stands for "Jesus the Nazarene, King of the Jews."

Remember that Jesus was only being hailed as a king in the New Testament because Mary Magdalene had enthroned him as the King of the Jews when she anointed him with the sacred oil of spikenard at the house of Simon in Bethany. This anointing was, after all, the traditional ceremony for the coronation of a monarch—the same ceremony and anointing that was applied to Queen Elizabeth II of Great Britain—and Mary Magdalene's central role in this enthronement ceremony clearly demonstrates her power and authority within the Nazarene Fourth Sect.

So here we have the royal couple of Judaea—King Jesus, the King of the Jews, for that is how he was known in this era, and his wife Queen Mary Magdalene. And, as the first century Talmud and the Medieval Golden Legend both indicate, they were not only royal but the richest couple in Judaea.

Perhaps the biggest deviation from biblical history here is the late date for these events, for King Izas (King Jesus) only became embroiled in a war with the Romans in the late AD 60s—the Jewish Revolt that was quelled by Vespasian and Titus, the two Roman army commanders who eventually became emperors of Rome. The reasoning for this late era is not going to be explained, at this moment in time, as the reasoning is quite complex; and besides, in some respects the date of these events is largely immaterial. But nevertheless there is copious evidence in my books to demonstrate a later date for the crucifixion; an event that Josephus describes as happening in the Kidron valley after the siege of Jerusalem in AD 70.

King Izas (King Jesus) lost the war against Rome, and was exiled to England, but that is yet another story. Instead, what we want to look at in this article is the fate of Queen Mary Magdalene. From here on the evidence and history is mostly based upon mythology, but there is a strong body of rumor and myth that indicates that Queen Mary Magdalene was exiled to the south of France. She is said to have landed at St Maries de la Mer in Provence (Septimania), and this would have been in the early AD 70s, according to this new chronology. And from there the trail of mythology grows thin and weak until it tails off into rich speculation and bizarre theories.

Orange

So did Mary Magdalene sail to France? And if so, how is this connected to the Dutch House of Orange?

I am not sure how well this Medieval history is known in Holland— not very well, I think—but the House of Orange is not Dutch. The House of Orange was originally founded in the independent City of Orange in southern France, in the region then known as Septimania.

The first Prince of Orange that we know about was the eighth century Guillaume de Orange (Guillaume de Gellone), a well connected prince who had Judaic origins and a Judaic aristocracy. In fact, the influential book Holy Blood, Holy Grail tried to link Guillaume directly to the bloodline of Jesus, through the line of the Merovingian kings of France. That link is not entirely certain, but what is known is that Guillaume was so powerful and well connected that his sister became Queen of the Franks, and he was able to openly threaten King Louis of France at a court banquet. Here was a powerful baron or prince, if ever there was one. Indeed, it was Guillaume and his influential Jewish banking family who financed the Septimanian-Frankish army that defeated the Muslim invaders of France and reclaimed Western Europe in the name of Christianity.

Of course in later centuries, as this family gained ever greater links and ties to the Germanic House of Nassau, the family name "Guillaume," meaning "guide and navigator," changed to Guillhalme, then Wilhelm, and eventually to the English William. This is, of course, where the current holder of the royal title, Prince Willem-Alexander of Orange, got his name and why the Dutch Orange celebrations are … well … so orange.

The St. Bartholomew's Day Massacre of the Huguenots in France. Many Orange citizens were not simply Protestants, but Huguenots, too, as were the later Princes of Orange.

So how did this royal title get transferred from Septimania, in southern France, to Holland? This answer lies in the Wars of Religion, the great century-long war that prosecuted the Orange Reformation and the Enlightenment Era. The Dutch princes had inherited the independent City of Orange, the city that had become one of the primary supporters of the Protestant Reformation. So King Williams I, II, and III, from the sixteenth and seventeenth centuries, were not only involved in a desperate struggle to save northern Europe from Catholic hegemony and oppression, they were also desperately trying to keep the little principality of Orange in the south of France safe, too. This was no easy matter, for the War of Religion was a bitter and divisive, century-long civil war that set Protestants against Catholics across all of Europe—a bitter struggle that saw all of the French Huguenots killed or forced into exile, while the population of Germany fell by more than a third.

Victory in the Wars of Religion was at last achieved in 1690, when William III of Orange became King of England, and thus had sufficient power to threaten the Catholic Louis XIV of France. The City of Orange was safe at last, and the Orange Reformation and the Age of Reason were allowed to blossom and the Industrial Revolution could begin. Everything we see in the modern world around us, all of our technology, all of our modernity, all of our freedoms of speech and freedom of thought, came from the great victory by William III, King of England and Prince of Orange, over James II of England and King Louis of France. Catholic oppression and terror had been put back into its Medieval box, and freedom of speech and freedom of research could flourish for the first time since the Roman-Greek era. Science was no longer a heresy to be persecuted and exterminated; it had become an essential tool to improve the human condition.

Unfortunately, while the Orange Reformation left a lasting legacy in northern Europe and the modern world was able to take shape, the rather lonely City of Orange in Septimania was not so lucky. King William died without issue in 1702, and the English throne was filled by Queen Anne, whose father was the despised and exiled Catholic King James II. Thus King Louis XIV of France, emboldened and vengeful, wasted no time in taking revenge upon the lonely, unprotected Protestant City of Orange. In a deliberate genocide, each and every citizen of Orange was killed or forced out of the town and into permanent exile. Here was a brave city that had withstood 100 years of civil war—a golden beacon for the Orange Enlightenment in the midst of a sea of Catholic darkness—and yet its defiant golden light was extinguished at the very last minute and the city was left as an empty shell, a mere husk of its former self. Liberal and free-thinking Orangeism had been irrevocably displaced from southern France and relocated in the progressive, tolerant and prosperous lands of Holland.

Magdalene

But what, readers may ask, does all this have to do with Mary Magdalene? The answer lies in the fact that Mary and Martha are said to have lived in Tarascon, just south of the City of Orange. But did they move further north by a few kilometers? It so happens that Orange was known in antiquity as the Latin Aurania, a name that is very similar to the Dutch pronunciation for Orange. But the family of Jesus, that I have been tracing for the last ten years, was also called Aurania–for they were descendants of the Egypto-Persian Queen Thea Muse Ourania (nee Helena of Adiabene). In the original Greek, the name Aurania (or Ourania) referred to the Heavens above—ouranos ouranos. But in the Latin, that same name has been transferred on to all things golden—'aur' in the Latin or 'or' in the French, meaning "gold."

The link between these two strands of etymology (between 'heaven' and 'gold') is the Sun itself. Like King Louis XIV of France, the Ouranian royal family were known as Sun Kings and so the symbology they adopted was of all things golden and circular, just like the Sun. That is, of course, where the orange symbology for the royal House of Orange came from— for the humble orange fruit was an obvious similitude for the sacred Sun. This is why the coat of arms for the City of Orange is graced by three oranges. Since Mary Magdalene was linked to this royal family, she, too, was linked to all things golden. Thus she invariably wears golden or orange clothes, and she is always depicted with ginger or golden hair— just like William Alexander, the current Orange prince. This was the Midas family—the royal House of Orange and House of Gold.

There is more evidence than this, of course, but the evidence to be found in France will never proceed beyond the circumstantial. This was a family in exile, so it would be foolish to believe that there would be some great monolithic tomb waiting to be discovered. No, the evidence is circumstantial, yet strangely compelling, for the Mary Magdalene we know from the Nag Hammadi Gospels was clearly a Gnostic; yet it was similar independent gnostic thought (independent scientific thought) that powered the Reformation. The Orange Reformation, that great Europe-wide revolution in thought and freedom, was for some reason centered upon the small and isolated City of Orange in the south of France, and promoted by its fearless and tenacious Princes of Orange.

New Vindication
for James Churchward?

*Or Maybe Not... Are New Reports Confirming
a Secret Library to Be Credited?*

Philip Coppens

New evidence suggests that James Churchward, who claimed to have seen evidence of the lost civilization of Mu, was indeed shown a secret library. German tour operator Thomas Ritter says he has been able to enter it, but are his claims too good to be true?

Churchward was a patented inventor, engineer—and a man who claimed that he had found evidence of a lost civilization: Mu. Said to have been the Pacific equivalent of Atlantis, Mu was, Churchward believed, the original colonizer of the later Atlantic empire.

The first modern researcher to write about Mu was Augustus LePlongeon, best known in archaeological circles as the first to make a photographic record of the ruins of Chichen Itza. In his books, *Sacred Mysteries Among the Mayans and Quiches* (1886) and *Queen Moo and the Egyptian*

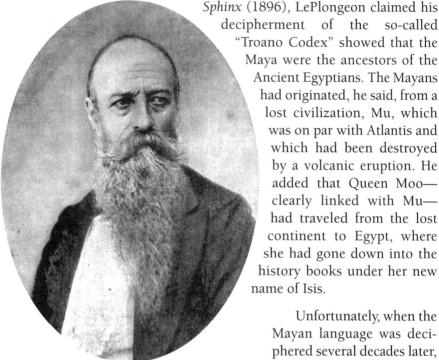

Augustus LePlongeon

Sphinx (1896), LePlongeon claimed his decipherment of the so-called "Troano Codex" showed that the Maya were the ancestors of the Ancient Egyptians. The Mayans had originated, he said, from a lost civilization, Mu, which was on par with Atlantis and which had been destroyed by a volcanic eruption. He added that Queen Moo—clearly linked with Mu—had traveled from the lost continent to Egypt, where she had gone down into the history books under her new name of Isis.

Unfortunately, when the Mayan language was deciphered several decades later, it turned out that LePlongeon's interpretation was completely erroneous, sometimes even using letters that were, in fact, no such thing. Jack Churchward, a descendent of James Churchward, states that LePlongeon relied on the translation of Brasseur de Bourbourg. Jack Churchward received an email from one of de Bourbourg's descendants who stated that the translation was done by channeling a spirit. That may explain why LePlongeon erred so much in his interpretation.

LePlongeon, however, did put the lost civilization of Mu on the map, but it was left to Theosophist Helena Blavatsky to popularize it, claiming it was the mystical birthplace of occult traditions. The man, though, who may fairly claim to have brought Mu from theory and speculation to purported history was James Churchward, a friend of LePlongeon's, who said he had been shown physical evidence for Mu's existence in a secret library in India.

Born in Britain, Churchward eventually settled in the United States. But it was during earlier years, while living in Sri Lanka where he owned a tea plantation with his wife, that he traveled to India. During this journey, he later claimed, he discovered a lost epoch of mankind's history. In India, he had befriended a priest who taught him to read an ancient dead language. Allegedly, only the priest and two others in the entire world were able to read it. The language was written down on numerous tablets, which the priest allowed Churchward to see and read.

Churchward intimates in his books that he tricked the priest into showing him the tablets as well as teaching him the meaning of the language. As he did so, Churchward claimed, he realized that the tablets he saw were not the complete library. Nevertheless, by consulting other sources and people, he was able to piece together a coherent picture of the lost civilization of Mu. Years later he would claim that he received further corroborating material in the form of tablets found by archaeologist William Niven in Mexico.

The earlier events happened in the late nineteenth century, even though Churchward did not go public with his Mu material until 1924. That he had remained silent for such a long time about such a momentous discovery was seen by many skeptics as just too good to be true. It is known, however, that Churchward's interest in ancient civilizations was of very long standing. In the 1890s, he had personally discussed the subject of Mu with LePlongeon and his wife Alice. Moreover, Jack Churchward points out that a previously unseen publication from his ancestor is "Copies of Stone Tablets Found By William Niven at Santiago Ahuizoctla Near Mexico City." It is established that the two exchanged letters in 1927.

Churchward's discovery became famous when a major news story appeared on November 10, 1924, in the *New York American* newspaper. In it, the central framework of Churchward's claims about Mu was put forward. The civilization was labeled "Empire of the Sun." Mu, claimed Churchward, was once a civilization of 64 million inhabitants known as the Naacals, the priestly brotherhood, keepers of the sacred wisdom, who lived 50,000 years ago. All known ancient civilizations—India, Egypt and the Mayas —were but the decayed remnants of its many colonies.

In 1926, at the age of 75, Churchward published *The Lost Continent of Mu: Motherland of Man*. Mu, he said, extended from north of Hawaii to the Fijis and Easter Island. Most geologists, however, find it difficult to imagine dry land in that locale, as the area is intersected by the so-called Andesite Line, making it geologically unlikely there could have been a landmass here. Since Churchward never produced any concrete evidence for his visit to the Naacal Library, many treat his claims with considerable suspicion.

So was Churchward a liar, or someone with genuine experiences? To understand the man better, it is important to note that some aspects of the Mu legend are original to Churchward. Some aren't. It was LePlongeon who had first written about the "Nacaal," in 1896, where he identifies them as Maya adepts and missionaries, with the word Naacal meaning "the exalted." But LePlongeon identified their homeland as Central America, not Mu in the Pacific Ocean, a notion that was specific to Churchward.

What about connections with Madame Blavatsky's account? Both Churchward and she claimed that, in India, they had been exposed to "lost knowledge." In the case of Blavatsky, the source was said to be the "Book of Dzyan," said to be written in Atlantis and presented to her by the Indian Mahatmas.

Madame Helena Blavatsky

Indeed, though it could be argued that Churchward merely copied from the likes of Blavatsky and LePlongeon to create his own stories of Mu, it could also be said that his story is totally new and that it confirms Blavatsky's assertions. It can also be argued that Churchward spent several decades cementing his case before going public and writing his series of books on the subject. Churchward lived in India in the 1880s, before moving to the United States in 1889. It was during this period that he allegedly made contact with the Indian adepts—allowing for a period of roughly a decade, more than sufficient time—where he could have learned and studied the language. Churchward said he studied for more than two years the "Naga-Maya" language, purported to be mankind's original tongue.

After having read the Naacal documents, he continued his quest for further information. In Burma, he visited an ancient Buddhist temple in search of the missing records, carrying letters of introduction from the Indian high priests with whom he had studied.

But what is lacking from his account is any verifiable information. His story truly hinges on whether or not he met and befriended the Indian priest who, in turn, introduced him to the numerous rare tablets. As a consequence, the story of Churchward has remained for years strictly a legend, even as his books were widely published. Nothing new emerged that might change the status quo. Recently, though, the German independent researcher, author and travel agency manager Thomas Ritter has made quite a stir by claiming to have personally entered a "secret library" underneath Sri Ekambaranatha Temple in Kanchipuram, India, in which he has found corroborating evidence of the lost civilization of Mu.

Ritter claims that on July 23, 2010, he was contacted by one Pachayappa who invited him to enter the underground complex—and even allowed him to photograph some of its contents! Ritter relates, "at chamber no. 4 the priest only allowed me to take pictures from two tablets, not from all the books there. The two tablets he showed me are a little bit damaged. But you can see clearly the inscriptions."

The two tablets, ostensibly, were from the so-called Naacal tablets, which James Churchward claimed to have seen many decades before. When Ritter published the material, there was immediately a torrent of disbelief, not helped by the realization that what Ritter apparently showed was a tablet unearthed in Byblos (Lebanon), discovered by French archaeologist Maurice Dunand. Despite the small amount of writing on the tablets, they have, so far, not been deciphered, though the script has been identified as Proto-Byblian and therefore not related to India. Indeed, the tablet presented by Ritter can be found in the Beirut Museum (Cat. 16598) and not a secret library in India.

Ritter claims, though, that in July 2010, he was not welcomed by the usual young priest Narjan, whom he knew well, but, instead, an elder man, Pachayappa, who, unlike Narjan, did not speak English. Pachayappa took him down into the underground structures of the temple complex. Ritter relates: "Before an iron-bound door he stopped and pointed with some gesture to the bottom: 'Rishi place!'" Then he opened the door, behind which the Nacaal library was located.

Whether Ritter is lying or not, he has, at least, specifically identified a specific spot as the location of the library: the Sri Ekambaranatha Temple in Kanchipuramin the state of Tamil (India). The gate of the temple complex measures more than 60 meters tall, making it the largest temple tower in Southern India, and is made from granite, decorated with the images of gods, goddesses, and heroes. The complex is a Hindu temple dedicated to Lord Shiva and is one of the five major Shiva temples, each representing a natural element. The Sri Ekambaranatha Temple represents the element earth. It's history dates back to at least AD 600, though it could be older and is notorious for its "hallway with a thousand pillars," as the temple's inner walls are decorated with an array of 1,008 Shiva lingams, a symbol of the male energy.

Ritter has drawn attention to the subterranean system of this complex, where he claims there are 10 chambers. In nine of these chambers are stored the tablets. Each room measured 25 meters long and 15 meters wide, with the ceiling so low he could touch it. Pachayappa claimed that the inscriptions detailed the Rishi Puranas, the lives of the culture bringers of Ancient India. Inside were black granite tables, and there were tens of thousands of stone tablets. Ritter notes that "both sides of such postcard-sized stone tablets engraved with tiny lines were narrow characters covered in an unfamiliar script. Other plates showed fine geometric patterns on running, technical drawings, maps and astronomical images." When he asked what they contained, he was told it was the legacy of the Seven Sages.

In the first three chambers, the tablets are made from black granite; in the next three, from gold. Each golden tablet was 14 by 10 centimeters, about two to three milimeters thick, and were bound like a book. In the final three rooms, he found silver and bronze tablets that were hard to read, so Ritter used a handkerchief to polish the tablet, restoring it to its original state. Ritter claims he was only allowed to photograph two tablets. All of these chambers have inscriptions, describing the lives and deeds of the rishis, and who has produced photographs of these inscriptions.

The tenth room was located at the end of the corridor. In the middle of the room rose a column of about 1.50 meters high from a solid black material; and according to Pachayappa, the material was not stone. Behind the lingam were statues of the Seven Rishis, placed in a semicircle, made from a shimmering metal, which Ritter thought could be gold or silver plate. One of them he was able to identify as Aghasthiya, who is always depicted as a dwarf.

Throughout the rooms, Ritter also saw rolls of metal foils, one of which Pachayappa opened. Ritter claimed they were easy to unroll and that the material was very thin, reminding him of titanium, as it did not tear or wrinkle. The characters inscribed on it were equally etched, rather than engraved, and Ritter says he realized that he had seen one of these rolls before—in Churchward's book.

At the back of this room was another door, but Pachayappa indicated that he would not open this for Ritter. He did learn that the door led to a large underground system of tunnels, some of which are said to connect to towns several tens of miles away. Ritter states that non-Hindus and foreigners normally find the library closed to them and that even access to the central part of the temple is forbidden. But it is Ritter's conviction that it was here that Churchward was shown the Naacal tablets and that he, more than a century later, stepped into Churchward's footsteps.

Jack Churchward has studied the material of his ancestor in detail and remains skeptical of Ritter's claims. Ritter claims that some of the scrolls he found were the same Churchward found. Jack Churchward, however, adds: "If James was there, then the tablets would have been wrapped and put away in what James referred to as 'chatties' and therefore not visible. James said as much in his books. Ritter does not say anything other than he saw a symbol, he doesn't know that the tablets James saw were unfired clay or that the tablets would have been packed away. Just my two cents."

Ritter is definitely no stranger to the arena of sensational claims. He once asserted that in a crop circle in England he had been approached by a mysterious stranger who handed him a crystal. For some time Ritter argued that this was the long-lost and much sought after thirteenth crystal skull. Ritter presented it at lectures, wrote articles, and even offered paid sessions with the skull. Subsequently, he dropped his claim that it was the notorious thirteenth skull. The discovery had, apparently, been based on a prophecy of dubious origin.

Understandably, Jack Churchward has queried Ritter for more evidence for his "Naacal" discovery, including photographs, to back up his latest extraordinary claims. In March 2011 Churchward managed to speak to him by phone, following which Ritter sent him a small set of photographs. Unfortunately, the picture of the so-called Naacal Tablets were quickly identified as being artifacts from Byblos (Lebanon) currently held by the Beirut Museum (item 16598). A small brass plaque, allegedly presented to Ritter by the priests, was identified as a Tablet of Union used in sixteenth-century England and later by the Hermetic Order of the Golden Dawn. When Churchward pointed out that he had learned the true origins of the photos and that they were not from India, Ritter merely commented that there was "maybe a coincidence" between the civilizations. He told Churchward he would provide more evidence during the summer of 2011, but nothing was ever forthcoming. My own two attempts to contact Ritter likewise received no reply.

Gopuram (Gate Tower) of the Sri Ekambaranatha Temple in Kanchipuram

Swiss researcher Armin Risi appoached frequent temple visitor Annett Friedrich to see if her contacts could corroborate any details of Ritter's story. Risi was told that Ritter has several elements plainly wrong and that his story is clearly fiction. Risi adds that in a 2006 book Ritter had published another hoax story about the Sri Ekambaranatha Temple. He described how a priest led him into a secret part of the temple "which has never been shown to another white man before."

In this "secret part" of the Sri Ekambaranatha Temple, Ritter tells of having seen a gallery of more than 70 statues of former high priests: "Their slender but strong physical structure appeared to be almost reptilian, and I got the impression that these were amphibic beings who could live in the sea and on land at the same time." Risi believes that Ritter is trying to exploit the gullibility of people in the West, as the notion of reptilian overlords has become quite the popular theme for many so-called alternative researchers. ✧

For more information on Jack Churchward, visit jack.churchward.com and www.my-mu.com.

16.

The Rushton Rebus

When Three Is a Charm

The Very Strange Legacy of Sir Thomas Tresham

Philip Coppens

Rushton Lodge—better known as the Triangular Lodge—is considered by many to be only a folly—a building without a real purpose, other than decoration. But the history of the structure is more than interesting, inviting the question whether it might not actually contain a veritable secret message, so far not uncovered. Such questions arise from the strange Elizabethan saga of Sir Thomas Tresham. What happens when you release a Catholic from jail? The answer in the case of Tresham is: the Triangular Lodge. The small building near Rushton, in England's Northamptonshire, at the edge of Tresham's estate was, ostensibly, built to serve as a very enigmatic home for the rabbit warden. It is referred to in the Rushton estate documents as "The Warryners Lodge."

Tresham was released from prison in 1593. He had been held because he was a Catholic and was considered a threat to the ruling Protestant order. It is said that his prison cell contained drawings and material that would ultimately find their way into the design of the Triangular Lodge. As the story goes, while in prison at Ely in 1590, he was reading a treatise on proofs of the existence of God. Suddenly three loud knocks startled him and inspired upon him the overwhelming theme for his lodge-to-be: the number three.

Sir Thomas Tresham

The political history of the Tresham family is interesting. In 1559, Thomas became one of the largest estate owners in the country. The family were supporters of Mary Tudor (later Mary I); and while Henry VIII suppressed the Order of St. John of Jerusalem, when it was reinstated in 1557–1558, Thomas Tresham the elder—the grandfather of the lodge builder—became Grand Prior. Thomas "the builder" was knighted by Elizabeth I at Kenilworth Castle in 1575. About 1566, he had married into another Catholic family, to Meriel, the daughter of Sir Robert Throckmorton, of Coughton Court in Warwickshire. Together, they would create one of the most impressive libraries in Elizabethan England.

However, in 1570, Pope Pius V launched a bull declaring Elizabeth deposed and released her Catholic subjects from their allegiance. When Spain launched the Armada against England in 1588, English Catholics were expected to assist, but few felt "called upon." Penal laws against Catholics were passed in 1581, 1585, and 1593. As a consequence,

Thomas was continuously in prison, subject to house arrest, or under surveillance between August 1581 and April 1593. He would find himself in prison again for a few months in 1594 and again in the winter of 1597–1598.

Work on the lodge stared on July 28, 1594 and it was completed by 1597. It is not the only enigmatic building Tresham created. He also built New Bield at Lyveden, which he started in 1594, and which was left unfinished at the time of his death in 1605. Here, he commemorated the Crucifixion rather than the Holy Trinity, with a cross-shaped plan and a frieze of carvings of the Instruments of the Passion.

But what is remarkable about the lodge is that it is all about the number three. Seeing that Tresham was a Catholic, Triangular Lodge is seen as a symbolic hymn to the Trinity. However, a few have noted that the Trinity is not exclusively Catholic, and hence, the question arises: was Tresham's devotion to the number three "merely" Catholic, or something more?

At a basic mathematical and visual level, the entire structure represents three. Each of the three exterior walls is 33.3 feet long, each has three triangular windows and is surmounted by three gargoyles. The inside has three floors. Decoration-wise, there are three Latin texts, each 33 letters long, which run around the building. They read: Aperiatur terra and germinet salvatorem (Let the earth open and… bring forth salvation, Isaiah 45:8); Quis seperabit nos a charitate Christi (Who shall separate us from the love of Christ?, Romans 8:35); Consideravi opera tua domine et expavi (I have contemplated thy works, O Lord, and was afraid, a paraphrase of Habakkuk 3:2).

Though three is the common denominator, there is great variation within the details. The windows all have different designs. The largest is a trefoil, the family emblem; the basement windows are small trefoils with triangular lights. Around the windows on the first floor are plaques for the family emblems, some of them left empty, no doubt to be filled in by future generations—that never accomplished their assigned task.

Above the entrance door is the Tresham coat of arms and the Latin inscription: "Tres testimonium dant," meaning "The number three bears witness" or "Tresham bears witness." Such a pun was precisely what most such "Elizabethan follies" attempted to incorporate: several layers of meaning.

So far, so good, but above the door is also the number 5555. Some experts have speculated that this originally might have been 3333, which would indeed fit nicely with the three-theme, but where to go from there? Hence, others argue that 5555 could be the year 1593, for according to the Reverend Bede, it was in 3958 BC that the biblical flood occurred. Others, however, see 55 as a reference to "Jesus Maria" (each containing 5 letters), though others see it as "Salus Mundi," "Saviour of the World".

The beauty of such follies is that one might not necessarily have to choose which one is correct; all solutions could be correct. The important question however is: Is it all quite benign or is there far more to this, and might the monument contain a secret code, a layer that so far no one has cracked? Is this building a rebus? (According to Wikipedia, a rebus is an allusional device that uses pictures to represent words or parts of words. It was a favorite form of heraldic expression used in the Middle Ages to denote surnames.)

Continuing our exploration of the building, the principal room on each floor is hexagonal, thus leaving the three corner spaces triangular; one of these spaces contains a spiral staircase—the remaining two are small rooms. The building is crowned by three steep gables each surmounted by a three-sided obelisk at the apex. But as soon as the devotion to the number three is once again apparent, the emblems on the gables begin to pose deep and interesting questions. There is a seven-branched candelabrum; another depicts the seven eyes of God; a Pelican picking her own chest; a hen and chickens; a dove and serpent; and the hand of God touching a globe. Finally, the triangular chimney is adorned with the holy monogram "IHS," a lamb and cross, and a chalice. Confused? Or, indeed, nothing more than a folly and not to be taken seriously?

Carved in the gables are the numbers 3509 and 3898, which some have argued should be taken as dates: that of Creation and the calling of Abraham. But there are also other dates, like 1580, which is thought to have been the date of Tresham's conversion to the Catholic faith—by Edmund Campion, a missionary priest, though no one can be sure of the date.

Others have continued the numerical path, arguing that all of them are divisible by three; and that, when one subtracts 1593 from them, they end up giving 33 and 48 as dates, which is the alleged date of Jesus Christ and the Virgin Mary. Numerical coincidence, or evidence that there is, indeed, a clever rebus encoded into this building? Again the question whether it is merely a puzzle or whether there is an even deeper layer, one that might lead to some important message that Tresham could only encode within the fabric of a building. The Lodge is indeed an Elizabethan device, and Tresham himself said that the harder a device was to interpret, the more commendable it was "so long as it be perspicuously to the purpose." The question is therefore: what is the purpose?

Alan Moore has featured the lodge in his novel, *Voice of the Fire*, which tackles Tresham's son Francis, who was one of the Gunpowder Plot conspirators. Moore takes the story into magic, but historians believe that the Lodge was indeed a sacred building. Treshem leased a deer park at Brigstock, which contained a small lodge, where it is believed Mass was said. Historians believe that the Triangular Lodge was equally used as a "chapel" and an inscription in the upper room, SSSDDS, "Sanctus Sanctus Sanctus Dominus Deus Sabaoth," hints that this was indeed "hallowed ground."

That the Triangular Lodge is a celebration of the number three is obvious. Furthermore, Tresam means "I am three." And seeing that the Treshams were Catholic, the conclusion many jump to is that it is all about the Trinity. But is it? Again, the Trinity is not specifically Catholic. Furthermore, the family's involvement with the Gunpowder Plot is highly in-

Closer view of the Rushton Rebus

triguing for we know that several of the plotters had a rather "magical mission" in mind, which is why the entire episode is so captivating to the likes of the magically minded Alan Moore.

The Treshams were one of England's most important families and they had fought for the Catholic cause. It is known that the Catholic cause had several "magical" dimensions at that moment in time, including the presence of Giordano Bruno on English soil. Bruno spent two years living with Sir Philip Sydney, a man instrumental not only in the creation of the Shakespearean literature but who also operated on many other levels.

Specifically, Bruno was a student of the Corpus Hermeticum, the secret tradition, which had been popularized during the Renaissance and which, in the sixteenth century, remained more popular than ever. Bruno had studied from the best: the writings of Ficino, who had helped the de Medici family of Florence shape the Renaissance with artists like Donatello and Botticelli. And within this wider context, we need to ask whether the reference to "three" is not to a magical person who was specifically identified with the number three: Hermes Trismegistus, Hermes Thrice Great, the "father" of the Corpus Hermeticum, a religious book that has as many levels as an Elizabethan device.

Though there are numerous references to three, there are also numerous references to three times three, which is underlined by the fact that there are a total of nine angels holding water spouts under the gables for draining water off the roof, each inscribed with two letters, or with one letter and a triangle. These give: SSSDDS and QEEQEEQVE, or "Sanctus Sanctus Sanctus Dominus Deus Sabaoth, Qui Era et Qui Est et Qui Venturus Est", or "Holy Holy Holy Lord of God of Hosts, Who was, and who is, and who will be." It could be a reference to the Trinity, but if we read this on the magical layer, then nine is an important number, as are the nine principles that surround the creator father—a Hermetic concept, if only because the Florentine Academy founded by the de Medici contained nine—and only nine—members. Coincidence, or design? Though historians are quite open to the possibility that Mass was said in the lodge… could it have been a slightly different type of Mass than the traditional?

Thomas was succeeded by his son Francis, who died imprisoned as a traitor in the Tower of London for involvement in the Gunpowder Plot. The main instigator of the plot was his first cousin, Robert Catesby, though it is Guy Fawkes who is popularly associated with the failed blowing up of Parliament.

On October 26, 1605, Tresham's brother-in-law, Lord Monteagle, received an anonymous letter warning him not to attend meetings at the Houses of Parliament. The letter almost certainly came from Francis Tresham. Monteagle communicated his concerns to the government, which uncovered the plot in time. Though Francis died in prison of natural causes, his corpse was decapitated, and his head was set up over the town gate of Northampton. Opinion now has it that he had known of the plot but was not directly involved.

And with that, the Treshams have gone down into history as good Catholics; the Lodge itself has gone down as an Elizabethan folly. But perhaps the decoration of some of the more bizarre numbers on the walls might lead us into an even more esoteric dimension, one given to the Lodge by the likes of Alan Moore but, so far, not converted into hard historical facts—that what the Treshams were up to could have been far deeper than a puzzle to occupy one's mind. A man who had worked on this building in prison, did he do so merely to entertain his mind? Or did he instead use it as a means to encode certain knowledge, which he would set out to realize, as soon as he was set free? ෬

17.

Nicholas Roerich, wearing his Dalai Lama robe.

Roerich and Tibet

*The Road to Shambhala Can Take
Some Very Surprising Turns*

Andrei Znamenski

In the fall of 1923, a peculiar sage-looking European appeared in Darjeeling in the northernmost part of India near the Tibetan border. A plump man with a round face and a small Mongol-styled beard, he moved and talked like a high dignitary. He announced that he was a painter, and, indeed, from time to time people could see him here and there with a sketchbook, drawing local landscapes.

Yet, even for an eccentric painter, he acted strangely. To begin with, he argued that he was an American, although he spoke English with a heavy Slavic accent. He also demonstrated a deep interest in Tibetan Buddhism, particularly in the Maitreya and Shambhala legends, which was not unusual—except that the painter had a ceremonial Dalai Lama robe made for himself and donned it occasionally, hinting he was the reincarnated fifth Dalai Lama, the famous reformer in early modern Tibet. His behavior raised the eyebrows of local authorities who passed this information along to the British intelligence service.

As strange as it might sound, the "sage" did strike a chord with some local Tibetan Buddhists, for several visiting lamas did in fact recognize him as the reincarnated Dalai Lama by the moles on his cheeks. At that time, no one except a few close relatives and disciples of the painter knew that he had formed a grand plan, which included dislodging the sitting Dalai Lama and installing instead the Panchen Lama, second in the Tibetan hierarchy after the Lhasa ruler, reforming Tibetan Buddhism, and establishing in the vast spaces of Inner Asia a new theocracy, which he planned to call the Sacred Union of the East. On his occult map, which was tied to Tibetan-Mongol prophecy of Shambhala, the timing was right, he declared, to launch this exciting new project. The name of this ambitious dreamer was Nicholas Roerich.

What was so special about the Shambhala prophecy that made it so attractive for various spiritual and political seekers in the first three decades of the twentieth century—a time of great turmoil on the vast spaces of Eurasia? Shambhala was a prophecy that emerged in the world of Tibetan Buddhism between the tenth and twelfth centuries CE, centered on a legend about a pure and happy kingdom located somewhere in the north; the Tibetan word Shambhala means "source of happiness."

The legend said that the people of this mystical land enjoyed spiritual bliss, security, and prosperity. Having

The sixth Panchen Lama, spiritual leader of Tibet, 1920s.

mastered special techniques, they turned themselves into godlike beings and exercised full control over the forces of nature. They were blessed, it was said, with long lives, never argued, and lived in harmony as brothers and sisters. At one point, as the story went, alien intruders would corrupt and undermine the faith of Buddha. That was the time when Rudra Chakrin (Rudra with a Wheel), the last king of Shambhala, would step in and, in a great battle, would crush the forces of evil called mlecca (or people of Mecca).

After this, the true faith, Tibetan Buddhism, would prevail and spread all over the world. The image of Shambhala as the Buddhist paradise and the motif of the final battle between good and evil (elements missing in original Buddhism), which may have been borrowed from neighboring religious traditions, particularly from Islam, which had violently dislodged Buddhists from northern India in the early Middle Ages.

Rudra Chakrin (Rigden Djapo), the King of Shambhala. From Nicholas Roerich's painting, *Command of the Teacher*.

In most recent times, indigenous lamas and Western spiritual seekers muted those "crusade" notions of the prophecy, and Shambhala became the peaceable kingdom that could be reached through spiritual enlightenment and perfection. Yet from olden times to the early decades of the twentieth century, the Shambhala prophecy was frequently revived whenever the Mongols and Tibetans had to face foreign invaders. In order to fully comprehend the geopolitical significance of this legend, it is important to remember that although old Tibet was ruled by the Dalai Lama ("Ocean of Wisdom" in Tibetan), the chief religious leader and administrator, he did not enjoy total power. The Panchen Lama (Great Scholar), abbot of the Tashilumpho monastery, traditionally exercised control over the eastern part of the country. Most important, people believed that one of the Panchens would be reborn as the king of glorious Shambhala.

Theologically speaking, the Great Scholar stood even higher than Dalai Lamas. Tashilumpho abbots were considered the reincarnation of

Buddha Amitabha (one of the five top Buddhas, in addition to Gautama), whereas Dalais were only reincarnations of Avalokitesvara, who was only a bodhisattva and the manifestation of Buddha Amitabha. Panchen Lamas, whom many viewed as the spiritual leaders of Tibet, did not pay taxes and even had small armies. In modern times, this privileged status of the Panchen Lamas became a liability, undermining and chipping away at Tibetan unity and sovereignty, to the joy of its close neighbors, some of whom did not miss any chance to pit the Ocean of Wisdom against the Great Scholar. In 1923, when the thirteenth Dalai Lama attempted to curtail the autonomy and tax-exempt status of Tashilumpho, the conflict between the two powerful Tibetan leaders reached its peak; and the Panchen Lama, in fear for his safety, had to escape to Mongolia.

The flight of the Panchen Lama stirred diplomatic and spy games that involved England, Japan, China, and Red Russia. Surprisingly, each, for its own reasons, wanted the Panchen Lama back in Tibet. Driven by spiritual and geopolitical dreams of his own, painter Roerich joined this game. He is mostly known as a talented Russian émigré painter and a spiritual seeker. (Roerich's paintings were exhibited throughout Europe and America; his designs for the original production of Stravinsky's *Rite of Spring* won much acclaim; and his many ardent supporters included Albert Einstein, H.G. Welles, and George Bernard Shaw. In 1929 he was nominated for the Nobel Peace Prize. —*Editor*)

Yet few know that Roerich's spiritual quest led him to form a geopolitical plan that would have drastically changed the entire map of Inner Asia. By the early 1920s, he and his wife Helena had delved deeply into Theosophy, reading Helena Blavatsky's works, frequenting occult and spiritualist salons, and eventually pioneering Agni Yoga, a school that was an offshoot of Theosophy. They also came to believe that the Great White Brotherhood, the hidden masters of Shambhala, acting through their otherworldly teacher Master Morya, chose them to speed up human spiritual evolution by establishing a great Buddhist theocracy in the heart of Asia.

For the couple, the flight of the Panchen Lama from Tibet in December 1923 was an important and occult sign of the coming new age. The painter was convinced that he needed to act assertively by bringing the Panchen Lama to Lhasa, repairing the situation, and making sure that the thirteenth Dalai Lama would be the last. Roerich was convinced that all Tibetans were awaiting "the prophecy that a new ruler from Shambhala, with numberless warriors, shall come to vanquish and to establish righteousness in the citadel of Lhasa." An expedition to Inner Asia, headed by the painter and disguised as a scientific archeological enterprise, was to accomplish this task. (The expedition was carried out under the auspices of the United States Department of Agriculture headed by Henry Wallace, later to serve as vice president under Franklin Roosevelt; and Wallace was one Roerich's closest disciples.—editor)

The final goal was to bring all Tibetan Buddhist people of Asia, from Siberia to the Himalayas, together into the Sacred Union of the East with the Panchen Lama and Roerich presiding over this future theocracy. The spiritual tool to rally Buddhists around this plan would be the power of the Shambhala prophecy boosted by the Maitreya legend, another potent Mongol-Tibetan prophecy that announced the Buddha of the new coming world.

This theocracy was to be guided by reformed Buddhism, cleansed from what the painter and his wife considered "shamanic superstitions," adjusted to the original teachings of Buddha, and injected with the Roeriches' Agni Yoga. The couple envisioned this utopia as a common-wealth of people who would live a highly spiritual life and work in cooperatives—the economic foundation of this new state.

To accomplish such an ambitious project as the unification of all Tibetan Buddhists into a grand theocracy required a powerful sponsor. Yet, far from being helpful, English colonial officials of India were very suspicious of the adventurous painter and attempted to disrupt his plans that came to light after he turned up wandering along the Indian-Tibetan border. So, Roerich, who liked to call himself a practical idealist, decided to seek the help of Red Russia, which was obsessed with spreading its own gospel, Communism, to Mongolia, Tibet, and further to India, and which was fiercely competitive with England for influence in the region.

In the spring of 1924, the Reds, whom the Roeriches had previously viewed as the servants of Satan, suddenly became allies. Their other-worldly teacher Morya had blessed this political turnaround Roerich announced: "Now business needs to be done with the Bolsheviks." Soon, after receiving these revelations, Helena noted in her diary, "Now everything has changed. Lenin is with us."

Roerich openly approached Bolshevik diplomats in Paris and offered to gather intelligence on England in India and Tibet in exchange for logistical assistance. Red Russia became interested and eventually invited the painter to visit Moscow. On June 10, 1926, the Roeriches were in Moscow, where they met Chicherin, Soviet secretary for foreign affairs,

Nicholas Roerich with visiting Buddhist monks, who recognized
him as a reincarnation of the fifth Dalai Lama, Darjeeling, India, 1924.
Standing, right to left : George Roerich, Lama Lobzang Mingyur
Dorje, and Nicholas and Helena Roerich.

and Meer Trilisser, head of the foreign espionage branch of the Bolshevik
secret police. Without beating around the bush, Roerich laid out for the
Bolshevik leaders his program to secure the alliance between Communism
and Tibetan Buddhism:

1. Buddha's teaching is revolutionary.
2. Maitreya represents the symbol of Communism.
3. The millions of Buddhists of Asia can be drawn into the movement to support the idea of the commune.
4. The basic law of Gautama Buddha easily penetrates the minds of
   the masses.
5. Europe will be shattered by the alliance between Buddhism and
   Communism.
6. The Mongols, Tibetans, and Kalmyk now expect the fulfillment
   of Maitreya prophecies, and they are ready to apply them to the
   current evolution.
7. The escape of the Panchen Lama from Tibet provides an incredible opportunity to stage a revolt in the East.
8. Buddhism explains the reason for the negation of God.
9. The Soviet government needs to act quickly, taking into consideration cultural conditions and prophecies of Asia.

Although they swallowed some of the Roeriches' bluff, the Bolshevik leaders were not so naïve as to immerse themselves completely in such a reckless plan. Although they did provide logistical help for the painter's expedition to Inner

Tibetan Stronghold, from Nicholas Roerich's painting.

Asia, Chicherin and Trilisser made it clear that the direct involvement of Red Russia in their Tibetan venture was out of the question.

In 1927, the Soviet embassy in Mongolia provided automobiles, which allowed the Roeriches to quickly reach the southernmost border of Mongolia. There they switched to camels and entered western China, an area populated by warlike tribes, infested with bandits, and contested by several Chinese warlords. From Moscow the Bolshevik secret police sent a radiogram to a warlord friendly to the Bolsheviks, asking him "to provide all possible help to Roerich's expedition."

The traveling party, which, in addition to the Roerich couple, included their son George, three occultist friends, and twenty Buryat and Mongol armed guards, took the form of a spiritual march. Proceeding as an American expedition under the Stars and Stripes, the party also carried the Shambhala banner (tanka) attached to a flagpole. En route, the Roeriches spread word about the coming new age of spiritual bliss and prosperity. Special efforts were made to promote rumors among local nomads about the party as messengers of Shambhala and the new age of Maitreya. The painter constantly reminded his travel companions to remember that now they were all walking heroes: "All our steps are destined to become legends, which people will compose about our journey. And who knows, they might be great legends. On the threshold of the coming of the sixth race, all events are destined to become special."

Otherworldly teacher Morya was pleased with how the legend-making was developing and encouraged his earthly students: "The legend is growing. You need to proceed to Tibet without hurry, sending around rumors about your Buddhist embassy. The appearance of the embassy under the banner of Buddha is something that has never been seen before in the history of humankind. In the name of Maitreya Commune, you need to topple false teachings. . . . Each evening talk about Shambhala! Shambhala prepares the coming of Maitreya. . . . Plan your movement to make sure that each phrase you utter turns into a legend. Remember, you already stand above regular human beings."

Yet, despite an official permission to enter the snow kingdom, when they reached the Tibetan border, Dalai Lama's border guards suddenly detained them and marooned them on a high plateau in the freezing weather for five months without any explanation. Little did the travelers know that the formidable wall on their way to Tibet was erected by Lt. Colonel Bailey, the English spy stationed in Sikkim entrusted with monitoring all Bolshevik activities in Inner Asia. The English spymaster recommended that Tibetan authorities immediately block the movement of the "American" expedition, and Lhasa followed this advice.

On February 17, 1928, after prolonged deliberations, Lhasa officials finally worked out a solution, forcing the party to quickly proceed straight to Sikkim and letting Bailey deal with them. Lt. Colonel Bailey welcomed the exhausted travelers into his residence, acting as if nothing had happened. It took the experienced operative only a brief chat with the painter to figure out that Roerich was not a Bolshevik but simply someone Bailey took to be a dangerous eccentric.

After parting with the hospitable Bailey, the painter suddenly announced to his friends that he, along with Helena and George, would leave the rest and proceed straight to the forbidden Shambhala kingdom—the Great White Brotherhood was calling them. Exclaiming "It is nice to believe in the fairy tale of life," the Roeriches parted with their comrades. Although the Shambhala war that was to bring all Tibetan Buddhists into the Sacred Union of the East had apparently fallen through, it was not the end of the Roeriches' ventures. The second part of this geopolitical drama, which unfolded in northeastern China and which involved FDR and his Vice-President Henry Wallace, was no less exciting and intriguing. But that is another story. ❧

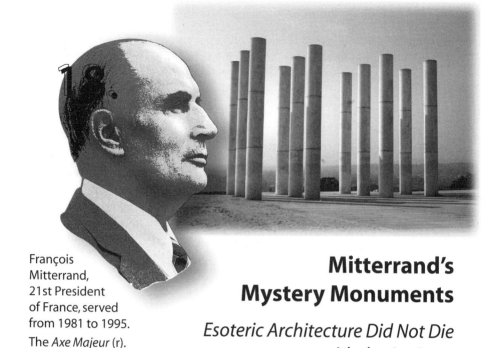

François Mitterrand, 21st President of France, served from 1981 to 1995. The *Axe Majeur* (r).

Mitterrand's Mystery Monuments

Esoteric Architecture Did Not Die with the Ancients

Philip Coppens

The *Glass Pyramid of the Louvre, La Défense*, and even the quaint *Monument to the Rights of Man* are known to be part of the French President François Mitterrand's enigmatic building obsession. But Cergy-Pointoise's *Axe Majeur*, the largest, is seldom cited as work developed under Mitterrand's reign. Why is it so unknown?

When the pharaoh Khufu (or whoever) built the Great Pyramid, it probably would not have occurred to him that millennia later, his masterpiece would be remembered as the greatest monument ever erected by a head of state. Still, it is easy to believe that even in those days, the pyramid was seen as a major accomplishment.

In modern France, President François Mitterrand, who, indeed, was nicknamed "the Sphinx," may also be remembered as a man who tried to accomplish similar ends. His modifications of Paris, especially the pyramid of the Louvre and the extension of the main Parisian axis towards *La Défense*, have captured the imagination of many, including Dan Brown and Robert Bauval. The latter wrote that this "Great Work" was a series of subtle modifications with a hidden, esoteric meaning in line with sacred Egyptian town planning and stellar alignments.

Some authors have also drawn attention to the "Monument to the Rights of Man and the Citizen," a small building in the shadow of the Eiffel tower, modeled after an Egyptian funerary temple. It is aligned to the summer solstice when the sun at noon penetrates a shaft between its two columns. It is said that Mitterrand came here during the night, apparently to think, meditate, or reflect.

Few, however, have noticed one of the grandest, most enigmatic and impressive creations of Mitterrand's regime: the *Axe Majeur* in Cergy-Pontoise, where one of the most infamous alchemists of all times, Nicolas Flamel, was born.

Unlike other new towns that derive their names from existing villages or geographical features, there was no previous place named Cergy. The story goes that someone noticed that paths in the upper part of the *Axe Majeur* (major axis), which was already integrated into the general layout of the project, looked like the letter Y and proposed naming the new town Cergy, the inversion of "Y Grec"—the Greek Y—in French. The letter Y was one of the favorite symbols of the Pythagoreans, indicating that the course of anyone's life divided into the two paths—vice and virtue.

The axis is the primary feature of Cergy-Pontoise, a suburb of Paris, roughly between the city center and Charles de Gaulle airport. It is the creation of artist Dani Karavan and is the "soul" of this new town. It stretches for three kilometers; if future archaeologists ever stumble upon its remains, they may call it a ley line. Though many doubt that ley lines have earth energy attached to them, the "axe majeur" actually might. But, primarily, the axis was intended to inspire creative energy from the local community and offer the town's inhabitants a place to walk, relax, and attend

Axe Majeur in Cergy-Pontoise

festivals.

Karavan, an artist born in Tel Aviv in 1930, devoted his life—from 1963 on—to monumental art. He started with the *Negev Monument* in the desert around Beersheba, and created similar works in Spain, Italy, Korea, and Germany, where, in Nuremberg, he created a sculpture in homage to human rights.

The idea for a feature at Cergy-Pontoise existed as early as 1975 and, in 1978, became more than just talk when Karavan's works in Florence were noted by officials of the Cergy project. A long exchange of letters began, and in 1980, Karavan visited the town and accepted the project, making a wooden model over the next month, which he submitted for approval.

The idea of the *Axe Majeur* thus predates Mitterrand's regime, which began in May 1981. This may explain why it does not feature on his list of Great Works. But, as was so often the case with this enigmatic French leader, things are not so simple. Even though Karavan's project predates his Great Works, it still is—remarkably—the last to be completed. Hence, it is the concluding statement providing the closing period for everything that went before.

Mitterrand's Great Works were constructed not only in a precise location, but also in a precise time frame. The greatest, size-wise, was *La Défense*, or the *Grand Arche de la Défense*, commissioned in 1982 and completed in 1989. A gigantic inverted U-shape, the structure was meant to express Masonic and Pythagorean symbolism. The design was by Johan-Otto von Spreckelsen, who called it a "porte cosmique"—a cosmic door, or star gate. It sits at one end of the major axis that runs from the Louvre through the Champs Elysées. Bauval has noted that on specific days of the year, the sun can be seen to set along this axis, its disc framed by the Arch.

In front of the Arch, there is the commercial center of the "Four Times" (a reference to the four ages of the esoteric tradition, the Age of Gold, Silver, Bronze and Iron). Here, time and space have become entwined.

But it was no coincidence that the Arch itself was inaugurated on July 14, 1989, the 200th anniversary of the French Revolution, while the G7 Summit was hosted in Paris. As Jules Boucher observed: "It were, of course, seven masters that participated in the search." Seven is, indeed,

Le Grand Arche de la Défense

one of the most holy numbers. And, of course, the letter G is an important Masonic letter, referring to God. Masons normally depict the letter G in the center of the Blazing Star. All of these "coincidences" make it clear that Mitterrand was working to a preconceived timeline, with subtle clues containing major significance.

Before focusing our attention on the "Major Axis," indeed, its name suggests that there is a smaller axis. This "Minor Axis" runs from the local train station with the *Place de l'Horloge*, a giant watch, which is visible from one end of the Major Axis. Hence, both Minor and Major Axes are linked, especially in time, as indicated by the giant watch. Time is also a primary component of this Great Work.

Furthermore, just as the Minor and Major Axes interrelate, some have argued that the "axis" of the Champs Elysées is also integrated with the *Axe Majeur*. A plotting of the two axes shows that they cross—or link— on an island in the river Seine, in the town of Carrières-sur-Seine. Coincidence, or design?

The *Axe Majeur* has gone through several phases, and it remains a work in progress. As a whole, it has twelve stations, some of which are more recognizable than others. They are: the observation tower, the "place des colonnes Hubert Renaud," the Impressionists' Park, the Esplanade de Paris, the terrace, the garden of Human Rights Pierre Mendes France, the amphitheatre, the scene, the bridge, the astronomical island, the pyramid, and the "Carrefour du ham."

The axis is thus a complex artistic realization, involving several components. Its point of origin is a tower, known as the *Tour Belvédère*, a phenomenal structure, rising to a height of 36 meters. Originally, the now square tower—with sides of 3.6 meters each—was intended to be circular. It sits in the center of a semi-circle of buildings and at the center of a ring of 360 paving stones, each 36 centimeters on a side. The axis commences, cutting its way through the 3.6 meter opening between the two semi-circular buildings. The number 36, incidentally, is clearly a key in the overall design.

The tower thus acts as a solar gnomon casting its shadow on the surrounding pavement, while the axis throws itself in between buildings created by Ricardo Bofill but which were not originally part of the design. The two are oriented exactly East-West. One is a semicircle symbolizing the sky, oriented westward, while the other, half a square, symbolises the earth, oriented eastward, the inversion of the traditional orientation. Bofill incorporates the same orientation in two other buildings located on top of the highest hills around Paris.

On the other side of the building are well-maintained gardens in which apple trees grow. It is said to be an homage to the impressionists that loved to paint the countryside and especially fruit trees that were covered by flowers in springtime. Of course, the apple is a very symbolic fruit, which might make us wonder about the fact that Mitterrand labeled one of the skyscrapers to be designed around La Défense "Eve." Unfortunately, the first series of planted trees did not produce any apples. In 2007, new trees were planted—which hopefully will bear fruit.

Much has been made about the *Glass Pyramid of the Louvre*, if only because of its prominent inclusion in Dan Brown's *The Da Vinci Code*. Brown adjusted the number of glass panels to 666, to imbed even more symbolism. But what is often overlooked is that to make room for this structure, some of the old—and beautiful—paving stones of the "Court Napoleon" had to be removed. The stones were carefully dug up and transferred to Cergy-Pontoise, where they are now positioned in a semicircle, an official part of the *Axe Majeur*. Coincidence? Or design?

It is not the only Louvre connection that raises eyebrows. Perhaps the signature feature of the Axis is the enigmatic group of twelve columns with the same dimensions as those of the arch of the *Carrousel* at the Louvre. These twelve columns, as well as the twelve components that make up the axis, underline that apart from the number 36, the number 12 is equally important. Twelve and 36, of course, are no strangers to each other. Twelve is a primary number in the zodiac and timekeeping, whereas 36 and 360 were key features of the Egyptian calendar—a time, and a place, of which Mitterrand was enamored.

In fact, some argue that Mitterrand believed he was the incarnation of an Egyptian pharaoh. Some believe these twelve columns also refer to the twelve gates of the New Jerusalem, and some claim that the *Arche de la Défense* is also built on twelve columns. Its outer shape is that of a cube, as the New Jerusalem is described in the Revelation of St. John, though it is empty (even as in the *Axe Majeur* where the twelve columns support nothing), while the New Jerusalem, although containing no temple, is filled with God's Glory.

The site's "ley line" connection is concretized between the slabs that were formerly in the Louvre and the twelve columns: the "Fountain of Vapors," which was designed to evoke the geothermic qualities of the site where underneath resides a hot water reservoir. One might even wonder whether this feature—less impressive than most others on this line—may nevertheless have been one of the primary reasons the axis was located as it was. The vapors emanate from the Dogger Phreatic layer, found at a depth of 1000 to 1500 metres beneath the Ile de France. Its temperature varies from 56 to 85 Celsius degrees and is used to provide heating to 34 locations, Cergy being one of them. Some observers have thought the vapors rising from below symbolized the Underworld.

From the twelve columns, a series of steps descends to the river Oise below. It is in this garden that the personal involvement of François Mitterrand can be proven: on October 18, 1990, he planted an olive tree, which had been specially imported from Vinci in Italy. Some may wonder whether that was a coincidence, or a symbol, and whether this is yet another, if not the actual, Da Vinci Code—or Vinci Code.

The project was conceived as one whole, yet certain sections were constructed only at precisely set times. Though this would often be given ordinary practical explanation (funding, a special occasion, etc.), sometimes, its phased realization resulted in higher costs. Hence, some have suggested that the project had a prescribed or secret timeline that was not necessarily communicated to all. So, because of a timeline that both preceded and post-dated the French President, the idea that the project was

Pyramid in the Lake

Mitterrand's Great Work has ofter been rejected, but such purely three-dimensional considerations might be totally misleading.

Though conceived in the 1970s, it was only in 1986—well into Mitterrand's regime—that the first three sections were completed: the "Place de la Tour", the "Tour Belvèdere" itself, and the "Vergers des Impressionistes"—the apple tree garden. Then, on August 26, 1989, the year France was celebrating its bicentenary and six weeks after the G7 summit in Paris, the twelve columns were inaugurated in the presence of 10,000 people. The following year, the laser light between the Tour and the Carrefour du Ham became operational, materializing the layout into an axis of light. The following year, Mitterrand personally visited the site— to plant a tree. Any Great Work has an idea, a realization, and a completion. And the realization clearly involved Mitterrand.

The third and lowest level of the Axis involves structures around the river and an artificial lake. No doubt the most ingenious of these is a pyramid that seems to be emerging from the lake's surface and which sits just off the axis itself. The pyramid was completed in 1992 and is meant to symbolize the harmony between Man and Nature. It was designed so that the wind, one of the Four Elements, would play with its layers causing a type of natural music to be created on this island reachable only by boat. Those who make the journey will find the pyramid is hollow and open on one side, revealing a blue azure-like interior. By coincidence or design, it has become a breeding site for migrating birds. Are they to represent the Egyptian Bennu bird—the phoenix—or are they instead references to those birds that carried the soul of the deceased? Or is it just coincidence?

For several years, little if anything happened. Then, in 2002, a red bridge was added to the complex, which crossed the river. In 2007, work began on the last stage of "the Path," which made it possible to walk from one end of the Axis to a circular island next to the submerged pyramid: the "Astronomical Island." This island is intriguing, both in visual appearance and in name, providing a stellar connotation to the project. The remnant of an old sandpit, the island is equally unfinished, as it is expected eventually to see the installation of a sundial, a meridian stele, an observational staircase, and various other instruments that will make it true to its name. Whatever the axis of the Champs Elysées might represent, it is clear what the *Axe Majeur* is meant to be.

As mentioned, in 2007 the bridge over the Oise was extended so that it would finally reach the island. Why someone would build a bridge in 2002 and then wait five more years to build a relatively small extension that would complete the design is a question that a few have posed. The reason cannot be funding and it is clear that the timing was intentional and that, indeed, the entire project has followed a specific timeline. As with any sacred building, the creation of sacred space requires a knowledge of sacred time. And only by mixing those ingredients, correctly, can one perhaps realize the Greatest of Works. ◌

This article appeared in Les Carnets Secrets *(2007)*.

Mary Magdalene in Penitence (El Greco)

Legend of the Three Marys

There's More to the Story than Reported in The Da Vinci Code

Steven Sora

The Acts of the Apostles describes the days and weeks after the Crucifixion. Jesus was dead and the Apostles and his closest companions were stunned. What was the next step? Where the Acts leaves off, legend takes over. According to *The Golden Legend*, the stoning of the first Christian martyr St. Stephen was the writing on the wall. The followers of Jesus were in danger. They had to leave Palestine.

According to the thirteenth century Italian chronicler Jacob Voragini, author of *The Golden Legend*, a handful took to the sea in a rudderless raft later translated as a "radeau." The passengers included Mary Magdalen, her servant Martilla, Mary Salome, Mary the mother of James, Lazarus (who Jesus had brought back from the dead), Martha (the sister of Lazarus) and Sara, described as a dark Egyptian servant. Without rudder or oars, they were guided by the hand of God through the perilous seas, if *The Golden Legend* is correct. They landed at a place named Ratis near Marseilles in France. They took refuge under a "porch" of a temple of the "people of that country." What Voragini does not say is that it was a temple to three goddesses. He was writing in an era where pagans and their goddesses were forced to assimilate into Christianity.

Ratis, later renamed Les Saintes-Marie-de-la-Mer, became the cradle of Christianity in France. The authors of *Holy Blood, Holy Grail* introduced the world to the importance of that seemingly unimportant town of Rennes-le-Chateau not far from Ratis. The town where a certain Father Berenger Sauniere would go from impoverished priest to millionaire in a few short years because of secrets he uncovered. The town was known alternately as Rhedae and Razes. It was in the center of a kingdom once known as Septimania where a king of the Jews was said to live. The conclusion of that book was that one of the three Marys, the Magdalen, had carried the child of Jesus. Heirs of that child then became a dynasty in hiding with a bloodline to David.

In modern times, it is hard to separate fact from legend. When religion is added, it becomes extremely difficult.

The Legend in the Medieval Period

Lazarus, it is said, moved to Marseilles where he preached to the pagans and converted many to Christianity. He survived the persecution of Nero and went on to become the first bishop of Marseilles. He didn't survive the persecution of Domitian. He was arrested and beheaded in a cave under what became the prison of Saint-Lazare.

Martha settled in the small town, which was later named Tarascon. Here she bested the Tarasque, a dragon, who lived in the Rhone and plagued the town. It is unknown where the mythical creature came from, but it had a turtle-like body, six short legs and a scaly scorpion tail. While the king's knights could not defeat it, Martha charmed the beast with hymns and prayers. The townspeople then killed it. Her feat is celebrated every year in a colorful annual pageant on the last Sunday in June. As penance for killing it even after it was tamed, the people changed the town's name to honor the dragon. While this legend seems to be more of a fable with an allegorical lesson, it has become more important over the years. A fifteen-foot model of the green dragon is paraded through the town and the parade is followed by concerts, fireworks, and a "historical" reenactment of the event.

Two of the three Marys faded into obscurity while the importance of the Magdalen grew.

Mary Magdalen preached the word of Jesus. When a local prince and his wife could not conceive, she told them if they would stop worshipping pagan idols and persecuting Christians she would intervene. The bargain was struck. It was her first miracle, and she continued to perform miracles until she was too old. Then she settled in a grotto at St. Baume, a name that might relate to her anointing Jesus with a holy balm. She was buried at St. Maximin where from the early fifth century a small group of monks became the guardians of her remains. Under her basilica was a much older Gallo-Roman sanctuary again putting a Christian figure over a former pagan Goddess. Such practice is most evident in Rome where one landmark, Santa Maria sopra Minerva, shows in its name it was literally built "sopra Minerva," or "over Minerva" the goddess of Rome.

While the mother of Jesus, the Blessed Virgin Mary, might be the most significant woman in Christianity, Mary Magdalen might have been the most significant woman among French Christians. Many believe the appellation Notre Dame, "Our Lady" refers to her and not the mother of Jesus. The Cistercian monks, allied closely with the Knights Templar, declared themselves to be the "Knights of Our Lady." Instead of the New Testament version that brands Mary a sinner from whom Jesus had to cast out demons, other traditions exist. Rabanus, the Archbishop of Mainz, wrote in the ninth century that she had been wealthy, highborn, and amassed further wealth beyond that of her family through buying properties. For her faith she had sacrificed all of this and became a refugee.

In Charlemagne's time, her remains were said to have been moved to Vezelay in Burgundy. Here the relics of Our Lady still performed miracles. It is said a man left his list of sins in her church. He prayed for forgiveness. The next day he went back to her church and the list was blank. His sins were gone. Vezelay became a rival site to Les Saintes-Mariede-la-Mer and Pope Eugenius III and St. Bernard preached the need for Crusade at her shrine.

This most remarkable era had seen the combined Cistercian and Templar orders fighting for the holy land while building cathedrals all over Europe. As East met West legends were filtered through an expanse of knowledge that had flowed back to Europe. Europe emerged from the Dark Ages, thanks to the import of books of the Greeks and Egyptians, which may have been forgotten or ignored for centuries.

The Legend in Ancient Times

When Jacob put his *Golden Legend* to paper, he may have been aware of a more ancient origin. In the *Egyptian Book of the Dead*, the dead enter a boat that is without sail with only an image of Ra to guide them. That boat is the Radeau or Ratis and Les Saintes-Marie-de-la-Mer may have actually already existed as the place of Ra or Ratis. The "porch" over the heads of the three Marys was a Gallo-Roman temple dedicated to three goddesses. In 4 BC, Isis Pelagia, Cybele and Artemis were those goddesses.

Cybele was regarded as a mother goddess and often depicted with her dying son, Attis. Those who view the sculptures of Cybele and Attis can not be faulted for believing they are seeing Mary and Jesus post-Crucifixion. Christianity did all it could to drive her out of the public consciousness. Her most famous temple was in the Vatican where it is now under

St. Peter's Basilica. Artemis was the moon-goddess whose most famous shrine was in the city of Ephesus. Once Christianity became dominant, this temple was destroyed; and it was claimed that Mary, Mother of Jesus, had moved to that city. Her "house" can be seen today. Isis Pelagia is the goddess of the Seas. She protects sailors and sea travelers from disaster. A coin of Cyme, an Asia Minor city, depicts her standing in a boat.

The Egyptians regarded Isis as the mother of all. Her Son was Ra. Her cult was popular in Rome circa 80 BC and spread through Europe. One of the numerous titles of Isis was Stella Maris, Star of the Sea. She traveled in her own rudderless boat, which actually was the crescent moon.

Did the Christian legends actually incorporate the pagan triple goddess into the legend of the three Marys?

The early Christian Church was not in favor of a feminine entity in any form being regarded as sacred. Church father Epiphanius said let the Father, Son, and Holy Spirit be worshipped, not Mary. She was not, he declared, the mother of God. Anastasius said she was just a woman. The Eastern Christian churches replaced a triple goddess, or a trinity of goddesses, with a Father-Mother-Son Trinity. Rome, however, made no allowance for the feminine; and Sophia, once the spirit of Sacred Wisdom, simply became the Holy Spirit, or more inexplicably, the Holy Ghost.

Eastern Influence Adds to the Legend

In more modern times, the most celebrated passenger to land at Saintes Marie de la Mar became Sara. Gypsies claim that Sara was not actually Egyptian but a Gypsy "Sarah la Kali" meaning Sara the Black. The shrine to her is a pilgrimage spot sacred to her. Under the choir of her shrine is a crypt where her relics are preserved. The crypt contains a statue of her garbed in seven robes implying that she is more important than simply a servant. The statue has been kissed so many times the black paint is coming off. In 1686 the servant Sara actually became a saint, and the cult objects were put in the crypt.

Every year Gypsies flock from around the world for a two-day celebration (May 23 and 25) that includes flamenco, bullfights, horse races and a more serious all-night candle procession.

The story of "saint" Sara might again have much older connotations. Sarah recalls the Hindu Goddess Kali. Sara-Kali became Queen Kali of the Gypsies. They may have actually originated in the Hindustan region. They appeared in tenth century Persia and were known as Kalenderees. As "Kali Ma" she was the triple goddess of creation, preservation and the destroyer. Later, Brahmins, like the Christian fathers in Rome, gave these aspects to Brahma the creator, Vishnu the preserver, Shiva the destroyer. The feminine goddess was, however, never erased by succeeding religion.

In the Sinai peninsula priestesses of the Moon Goddess called themselves Kalu. In Ireland, pagan priestesses were known as kelles. The goddess then is the source of the name Kelly and possibly the name behind the *Book of Kells*. The continent had a Saxon goddess Kale who was regarded as Mother Earth.

Isis Nurses Horus (Philae)

The Goddess (Hidden) in Christianity

The Church had always attempted to assimilate the gods of the past into Christianity. Pagan sites regularly became Christian sites. Pagan myths became Christian stories. Is it possible, that in preserving in secret the role of the goddess, some church leaders actually believed in the same gods and goddesses they attempted to eliminate?

St. Bernard had a fascination with the Black Virgin shrines that existed throughout Europe. Such sites originated in the twelfth century and could not be explained by the Church as to what they implied. Some believed they were originally shrines to Isis, often depicted with child, or Cybele or Artemis. Diana is another choice, as she is sometimes called the Queen

145

of the Witches. Ean Begg, author of *The Cult of the Black Virgin*, found fifty black virgin sites where the Magdalen was worshipped. His book discusses that such sites are often chosen for meetings of the Order of the Priory Notre-Dame of Sion. The group was forced to the spotlight when *Holy Blood, Holy Grail* was published.

While some of the source material for the Priory of Sion was discredited, much of it pointed to a reality that was hardly a secret within the Catholic Church. St. Bernard was devoted to Mary Magdalen and picked Vezelay to be the place to preach the Second Crusade. It was he who claimed that God's secrets existed in the science of Geometry. Bernard declared, "What is God? He is length, width, height and depth." The Feast of the Magdalen was July 22. Expressed as 22-7 or 22 over 7 it gives us that most important concept of pi.

The shrines built by the Templars and Cistercians from Mellifont to Tomar to the tiny Baltic island of Bornholm would often incorporate both the octagon and the circle. They were notably built after the famous Mosque in Damascus and the St. John Church in Rome, meaning such science was not truly forgotten.

The Gypsies claim that all the cathedrals of France were arranged to show an earthly reflection of the Constellation Virgo. While at one time that might have seemed farfetched, recently David Ovason's *The Secret Architecture of our Nation's Capitol* exposed the numerous zodiacs and hidden cosmological symbolism built into Washington DC. He also discussed the role of Virgo in determining not only the placement of major structures but also their dedication dates. "The importance of Virgo, and her connections with the Egyptian Goddess Isis, had been recognized in Masonic circles from the very early days of America."

The far-off, quaint myth-history of a tiny coastal village in the south of France may conceal much greater and more ancient secrets as well. ∞

Interior of
Rosslyn Chapel,
Louis Daguerre
(1824)

The Rosslyn Bones

*Is the Tale of the Murdered Apprentice
More than Just a Legend?*

Jeff Nisbet

P hotographic pioneer and artist Louis Daguerre's 1824 painting, *The Interior of Rosslyn Chapel*, shows two workmen crouching by the base of a pillar, with three Templar Knights nearby. One workman is staring intently at some bones they have found beneath the flagstones.

For a bizarre example of life imitating art, let's fast-forward 186 years... On March 1, 2010, Scottish Television reported that workmen at Rosslyn, the chapel made famous by *The Da Vinci Code*, had discovered remains in an area with no recorded burials. The remains, continued the STV report, had been "removed from the site to be examined by archaeologists to discover their age, type and if they are human or animal."

The local police confirmed the find but said "it was not being treated as a crime." Rosslyn Chapel declined comment.

Two things aroused my interest.

First, I was sure that even an untrained eye would be able to distinguish between animal and human remains and wondered why the archaeologists could not do the same. Second, I wondered exactly where the remains had been discovered. The idea they might have been found in the spot Daguerre showed in his painting made me chuckle.

It would take me a year to get some answers.

During that time, I searched for news updates. There were none. I also broached the subject with two St. Clair/ Sinclair clan online forums. Since a William St. Clair had built the chapel in the mid-fifteenth century, these groups share an abiding interest in its history. No one knew anything.

Finally, on Feb. 21, I wrote to a Rosslyn Chapel executive. There was no reply.

Someone knew more, but no one was talking.

Two weeks later, however, my inquiries finally bore some fruit—an Email containing four remarkable photos of the excavation, before the remains had been moved.

One showed leg bones that were undoubtedly human, confirming that one of the stated reasons for their removal was, as I suspected, clearly bogus.

Two showed the exact location of the remains, but it was not the area shown in Daguerre's painting. Instead, they had been found at the threshold of the west door.

The fourth showed a skull, face down, with a ragged-looking wound just a short distance above the foramen magnum, the natural aperture that allows the spinal cord to connect with the brain.

Taking just a small leap of the imagination, what might this tell us?

There's a long-lived legend that Rosslyn's master mason, returning

The leg bones

from Rome after studying the design of an exquisite pillar in person, found an apprentice had carved the pillar in his absence. Flying into a rage, he slew the apprentice with a blow to the head, a legend that resonates with the eponymous murder of Hiram Abiff, chief architect of Solomon's Temple, absolutely central to the Freemasonic ritual of the Third Degree.

Could the skull belong to the apprentice? The teeth were in remarkably youthful condition, and the shape of the head wound appeared consistent with the stone-trimming end of a mason's hammer.

Researchers skeptical of the chapel's claimed Masonic roots scoff at the legend, protesting that it's not exclusive to Rosslyn. While there are indeed similar tales told about other ecclesiastical buildings of the day, I'm not so quick to throw the baby out with the bathwater. As a speculative researcher, and in the absence of the forensic evidence already more than a year in coming, I'm happy to present some speculative thoughts about the Rosslyn bones.

Above the area of discovery are three carved heads. Rosslyn tradition describes the one in the southwest, gazing northeast, as the head of the apprentice; the one in the northwest, gazing southeast, as the head of the master mason; and, on an adjacent wall, the apprentice's mother, weeping for her son. The chapel's website describes the master's gaze as his punishment, forever condemned to look southeast towards the now-famous Apprentice Pillar. Not much of a punishment for murder, certainly.

I have since received, however, another dispatch that suggests a stiffer sentence: There were two skeletons found at Rosslyn, in a single grave. Could one be the master?

That they were found at the threshold of the chapel conjures up a plump scenario of darkly poetic justice.

History records many examples of human remains being buried in the foundations of buildings, and at their thresholds, but the reasons are varied. Legend has it that Saint Dunstan ordered his own burial to be under the threshold of Winchester Cathedral as a testament to his humility; Scotland's St. Columba, by contrast, is said to have buried a man alive at the foundations of a cathedral in order to ensure the building's structural stability with blood sacrifice; and I will give a third example, later on, where the practice was meant as an insult to the deceased.

Another robust legend that may connect Rosslyn with threshold sacrifice is the widespread belief that the chapel's ground plan is based on that of Solomon's Temple, although skeptics point out that Rosslyn's is identical to that of Glasgow Cathedral, which, except for the enormous difference in scale, is true.

But what if the similarities between Rosslyn and Solomon's Temple, at least for Freemasons, were meant to be more symbolic than actual and that both skeptics and true believers have been looking at things the wrong way?

In Albert Mackey's *Encyclopedia of Freemasonry* is the following entry: "Over the Sacred Lodge presided Solomon, the greatest of kings, and the wisest of men; Hiram, the great and learned King of Tyre; and Hiram Abiff,

The Murder of Rizzio (1787, John-Opie)

the widow's son, of the tribe of Naphtali. It was held in the bowels of the sacred Mount Moriah, under the part whereon was erected the Holy of Holies. On this mount was where Abraham confirmed his faith by his readiness to offer up his only son, Isaac. Here it was where David offered that acceptable sacrifice on the threshing-floor of Araunah by which the anger of the Lord was appeased, and the plague stayed from his people. Here it was where the Lord delivered to David, in a dream, the plan of the glorious Temple, afterward erected by our noble Grand Master, King Solomon.

And lastly, here it was where he declared he would establish his sacred name and word, which should never pass away—and for these reasons this was justly styled the Sacred Lodge."

Might not the floor of Rosslyn Chapel be symbolic, then, of a place that predates Solomon's Temple—the threshing floor of Araunah and a place of great Biblical sacrifice, which in many ways it still is? Claimed as a holy place by Christians, Jews, and Muslims, the rock over which now stands Jerusalem's Dome of the Rock has become, over millennia, a most costly piece of real estate.

Also revered as "The Foundation Stone," the rock from which the world was made, it was the place where Biblical patriarch Jacob is said to have dreamt of a ladder reaching to Heaven, with angels ascending and descending—which brings us to Scotland's unique connection with the place. Whether or not the block of stone now safely enshrined in Edinburgh Castle is Scotland's fabled Stone of Destiny, one of its popular monikers is "Jacob's Pillow." And then there is the theory that the Scots are, in fact, a "lost tribe of Israel." When historians, Biblical scholars, and adherents to British Israelism debate that theory, things get noisy.

But let's return to the Rosslyn bones, continuing to suppose that the remains belong to the jealous master and the slain apprentice. What better place for the apprentice to be buried than beneath the carved head of his grieving mother? And what greater insult to the master than to be condemned, forever, to be trod underfoot by God-fearing Scots?

As it happens, though, the head of the apprentice is also gazing at an exquisitely carved pillar—one attributed to the master's hands. Curiously, there is evidence that the Master's Pillar, as it is now known, had been concealed under a plain exterior for over 400 years and had been rediscovered by architect David Bryce during his 1860's restoration efforts. Might it not have been concealed because it was, after all, the work of an arch sinner? The Scots have historically done much more about a lot less, particularly over matters of morality.

Whether or not there is any truth to the slain apprentice legend, it is the height of coincidence that Rosslyn's most enduring legend involves the murder of one man by another, by a blow to the head, and that the murder has been memorialized by the carved heads of the murderer and the victim, on the wall above the unmarked grave of two recently discovered bodies, one of which shows indications of having been killed by a blow to the head.

But until the forensic experts release their findings, we must consider the possibility that the bones were put there more recently.

In 1846, during a lecture at London's Institute of British Architects, antiquary John Britton criticized the lines in Walter Scott's Lay of the Last Minstrel that suggest ten Rosslyn barons were buried, in full armor, below the chapel. Also in attendance was William Burn, architect in charge of the chapel's 1830's restoration. Burn supported Britton by claiming he had dug trenches up all three of the chapel's aisles, finding only one vault with a wooden coffin (presumably the vault long known to be accessed under flagstones in the north aisle, towards the rear of the chapel).

Burn makes no mention of having found human remains in the center aisle. But since his work was mainly concerned with the exterior of the chapel, there remains the possibility that Burn lied to support Britton's skeptical opinions, because the restoration of the chapel was the subject of a heated and ongoing debate. Thirty-four years later, in 1880, architect Andrew Kerr, under the direction of Robert St. Clair-Erskine, the 4th Earl of Rosslyn, added the baptistery to the chapel's west end.

If, as I suspect, the recently discovered bones stretched beneath the common threshold of both buildings, then there remains the interesting possibility that the bones were deposited there at that time, to be conveniently "discovered" at a later date. Kerr and the Earl have a well-documented conversation about the Slain Apprentice legend that appears on page 6 of the official Rosslyn Chapel guidebook, and it should be noted that both men were high-ranking Scottish Freemasons. The Earl, in fact, was the fraternity's 63rd Grand Master.

While this article has been hampered by the lack of more available evidence, further revelations may soon be made public.

At the time of this writing, I have learned that Ashley Cowie, "resident historian" for STV's The Hour Show, was recently seen at the chapel, shooting a new documentary series titled *Legend Quest*. Airing in July, the show is described as "an action-adventure series that follows real-life symbologist Ashley Cowie as he travels the world in search of hidden, mystical artifacts. Each episode is designed to combine Indiana Jones-style adventure and Da Vinci Code-type connections as theories are explored." While that description hints the show will do for archaeology what *The Deadliest Warrior* has done for the history of military warfare, perhaps Cowie will surprise us. Stranger things, as we will now see, have happened.

Late in my research for this article, I stumbled upon a curious tale connecting the 4th Earl of Rosslyn with yet a third skeleton. This one, though, was the property of his widow.

On March 15, 2002, Sotheby's auctioned the contents of Ken Paul's London theatrical-prop company. One paragraph of the Sotheby announcement reads as follows: "The ultimate conversation piece has to be the mystery clock in a full-sized inlaid mahogany coffin, dated c. 1900—complete with real skeleton—used in the opening scenes of *The Rocky Horror Picture Show*.

The skeleton is rumoured to be the remains of the young Italian lover and secretary of the Countess of Rosslyn. After his death she couldn't bear to be separated from him, so she immortalized him in the clock and took him everywhere with her!" Acquired by Ken Paul from an unnamed music-hall escape artist, the clock was won by an anonymous bidder for £35,000.

The Countess of Rosslyn at the time of the skeleton clock's manufacture had been married to the 4th Earl from 1866 until his death in 1890. Her own death, in 1933, would have provided the perfect opportunity for the rest of the family to offload Grandma's Italian paramour to the escapologist—at an eminently negotiable price, I'm sure.

Interestingly, besides appearing in *The Rocky Horror Picture Show*, the clock had most recently been hired to appear in a then-unreleased film about Jack the Ripper, *From Hell*, which presented the theory that Jack was a Freemason.

But the story of the clock's connection to the Countess of Rosslyn seemed suspect. I knew of only one Scottish luminary who was intimately involved with an Italian secretary—none other than Mary, Queen of Scots. On March 9, 1566, secretary David Rizzio was stabbed to death in Holyrood Palace for being the queen's confidant and lover and for being a Catholic. It has also been bandied about that he was the father of Mary's son, the future king of both Scotland and England.

Although a plaque in Edinburgh's Canongate Kirkyard reads "Tradition says that this is the grave of David Rizzio," who really knows? Could the countess and the queen have traded places in the telling of the tale over the years? Might not the bones in the clock be the bones of David Rizzio? Moreover, in a macabre concordance with the Rosslyn bones, there is an Edinburgh tradition that Rizzio's body was first buried at the threshold of Holyrood Abbey as a sign of disrespect.

My speculation that the clock's skeleton is David Rizzio's is not that outrageous.

It is well known that the Freemasons have made ritualistic use of skeletal remains. One short sentence in the 1896 minutes of Edinburgh's Mary's Chapel Lodge reads that "Brother Hay's presentation of a skull was accepted with thanks," and in the 1851 minutes we find an even more bizarre entry: "The Lodge was upon this occasion presented with two Thigh Bones of a Nun by Dr. Mc-Cowan."

The mind boggles ...

Just two years later, in 1853, the 4th Earl of Rosslyn is listed as Deputy Master of the Canon-

In the foreground is The Master's Pillar. The Apprentice's Pillar is farthest away.

gate Killwinning Lodge, still located on Edinburgh's St. John Street, just a hundred yards or so from Rizzio's Canongate Kirk grave. That's 1,750 miles closer than Prescott Bush, President George W's grandfather, trekked to bring the skull of Geronimo back to Yale University's most storied secret society, Skull and Bones.

Or could the escapologist have made the whole tale up?

Until the unnamed buyer steps forward and allows the bones to be studied, we can only speculate about the skeleton clock.

Tick, tock ... ○૨

Jeff Nisbet dedicates this article to his father, Bill, who passed away before it was finished.

Part THREE
Ancient Wisdom

21. CREDIT REPORT

☐ Excellent
☐ Very Good
☐ Good
☐ Average
☐ Poor

Meeting the Karmic Challenge

Have We Forgotten What the Ancients Once Knew?

Patrick Marsolek

D o you have good karma? If you live a happy life, with wealth, health, abundance, then maybe you do. In the West we've taken the concept of karma and simplified it to be a kind of fate—that which we have ended up with. If you've been cursed with ill health, disease, and misfortune, then using simplified Western standards, perhaps you have bad karma.

But the concept of karma from the Eastern traditions is much more complex, encompassing at its essence ideas about intentionality, life decisions, and most importantly, how we respond to what the world brings us. Modern psychological understandings of learning and emotional intelligence are now coming closer to an Eastern understanding of karma.

Consider karma in the context of your credit score. If you have a high credit score, you've likely learned the values of the modern financial system and play the financial game well. You might acknowledge that there's a relationship between your past financial actions and the score you have now. If you have a low credit score, there are things you can do to improve it. Even if you have bad credit, you are not fated to have bad credit forever.

In its most basic sense, karma refers to action or deed and how our previous actions affect us now and into the future. Karma is the universal principle of cause and effect, action and reaction, that is expressed in all life. The concept of karma has been recorded in India since the first millennium BC, although it is likely that the Indian Brahmins borrowed the idea from earlier aboriginal societies. For many, a belief in karma becomes a value system, since karmic beliefs tell us the results we experience are similar to the cause and the results of our actions are never lost. They stay with us. How often have you heard, "Violence begets violence," "One reaps what one sows", or the golden rule, "Do unto others as you would have them do unto you"? These are all expressions connected to karmic beliefs. We will reap the results of our actions, so we should live with those ideas in mind.

In Patanjali's Yoga Sutras, karma, rather than being fatalistic or mechanistic, is understood as a memory trace or disposition from previous thought or action—an impulse that can either be acted upon and reinforced or negated by other choices. In the Eastern traditions, as with many aboriginal cultures, karma is also interwoven with other metaphysical concepts such as reincarnation, the long-term development of the soul and its multiple worlds. An individual soul's actions in this physical world can affect the larger cycle of its path between Earth and other ancestral realms. A person might reincarnate in a lower world or even as a different form of creature, as a result of some "negative" action in this life. Though karma is present, there is no certainty that any aspect of personality or memory will come through different reincarnations.

In India, it is part of Hindu tradition that one's actions in this life will influence your rebirth in another life. This can result in the fatalistic view that one has no choice about one's position in the world. Similarly, because of karma, a kind person in a higher caste might understand that everyone in different levels of his society is on the same path of spiritual evolution. He might also judge people in a lower caste negatively as being less evolved. Some traditions believe that one God or many Gods play a role in dispensing karma or changing an individual's karma. For example, the events in the Book of Job in the Christian tradition show God's intervention. In many traditions though—Buddhism, Hinduism, and Jainism— only the individual himself can influence his own karma in either direction.

In Buddhism, all karma, good or bad, is seen as the force that holds us within the cycle of birth and death in this physical world. The conquest of karma and release from this wheel lies in intelligent action and dispassionate responses to life's experiences. Any action undertaken with raw emotionality, not tempered by the conscious intellect, will create more karmic actions and reactions. There is a folk tale from India of a Rishi, a realized being, who was in the process of leaving his body to merge with the divine. At the moment before death, he saw a deer and marveled at its beauty. This passionate act propelled him into another life as a deer.

His passionate attachment to the beauty of the deer was the expression of some lingering karma he carried. As long as some stored karma exists, the individual soul can not attain liberation from the veiling illusion of this physical existence.

Dalai Lama in Seattle in 1993

Some traditions believe one's karma is set and must be lived through. As the Dalai Lama says in his book, *Kindness, Clarity and Insight*: "Countless rebirths lie ahead, both good and bad. The effects of karma (actions) are inevitable, and in previous lifetimes we have accumulated negative karma that will inevitably have its fruition in this or future lives. Just as someone witnessed by police in a criminal act will eventually be caught and punished, so we too must face the consequences of faulty actions we have committed in the past, there is no way to be at ease; those actions are irreversible; we must eventually undergo their effects."

To Westerners this view might seem overly strict, yet these beliefs can lead to a life of virtuous action. Some traditions, though, do believe that one's karma is modifiable. It does not operate with mechanical rigidity but allows for a considerably wide range of modifications, a slow ripening of the soul's fruit. Karma is not fate, for humans act with free will creating their own destiny. A particular action now is not binding to some particular, pre-determined future experience or reaction; it is not a simple, one-to-one correspondence of reward or punishment.

In Jainism, karma refers to a kind of dark, negative subtle matter that pervades the universe and is attracted to the consciousness of a soul. When consciousness and this subtle matter interact, we experience life. It is also thought of as a mechanism, or innate quality of the universe, whereby we experience the important themes of our lives. We engage with these themes until we release our emotional attachment to them.

In Spiritism, karma is known as "the law of cause and effect." Individual spirits have choice in how they play out their past karma; and it is thought that disabilities, physical and mental impairment, or even being unlucky are due to choices that soul has made before coming into this life in order to release past karma. Thus the theme of reincarnation is strong and the effects of one's karma will stay with the spirit when it is not in a body, and even when it incarnates in other worlds.

Some people in the New Age movement have used karma to explain why everything happens, labeling events as positive or negative karma depending on how each event affects the person at an ego level. These popular views don't take into deeper consideration the complexity of an individual's experience, what they're learning, and what the "right" path may be at a soul level. On the flip side, movies like *The Secret* promote the "Law of Attraction," a kind of visioning/imaging where one is able to manifest good karma when one focuses correctly. These overly simplistic views assume that intention and desires at the ego level have an affect on the soul of a person.

Psychologists are now using the term karma without the metaphysical trappings. Here it is an expression of human emotionality, whereby one's volition is the primary instigator of karma. Any conscious expression or thought that arises from cognitively unresolved emotions results in karma. Practically, this effect may manifest as physical, mental, or emotional learned behavior that has been dysfunctional and which a person may continue to relive. In this model, any practice that enhances emotional awareness, such as meditation, counseling, or other chosen therapies, can serve to release a person from his emotional karma. This psychological approach is appropriately grounded in brain research studies that show changes in the chemistry and functioning of the brain as a result of such practices as well as long-term psychological improvement.

The transpersonal theorist Ken Wilbur described karma as the influence of yesterday's feelings on today's feelings, a kind of habit. He suggests that our lives are not determined by our past feelings. We can transcend the past with our own creativity. Each moment has a spark of novelty, the possibility of something that hasn't been before, and a chance for transcendence, the ending of the trance of this life. This idea resonates with the experiences of realized beings who've tasted Satori, or enlightenment, and, on coming back into day-to-day experience, have described how this physical world is the dream. To wake from the dream, one only has to cease being attached to it. It's the emotional attachment that generates the karma that keeps us asleep.

Transpersonal Theorist
Ken Wilbur

Wilbur also describes a kind of collective and even global karma that can act to keep the consciousness of large groups of people in a kind of rut or groove. As an analogy, he described the deep valley of the Grand Canyon. It is far easier to go with the flow down the river than to try to travel any other direction. On a collective level, our understanding and perception of the world is also shaped by similar deep grooves and habits. The way scientists and the public view an atom is channeled by all the collective beliefs that have gone before this time in history. On a more personal level, the way we view our hometown, our cultural heritage, even our family of origin, may be a groove that we've inherited from a collective group of people. He also suggests that most collectively inherited karmic views are not universal but rather confined to one small group, subculture or culture.

The Swiss psychiatrist Carl Jung had a dream late in his life that helped him shift out of a groove, opening his mind to the concept of the waking dream and reincarnation. He wrote, "... I came to a small wayside chapel. The door was ajar, and I went in. To my surprise, there was no image of the Virgin on the altar, and no crucifix either, but only a wonderful flower arrangement. But then I saw that on the floor sat a Yogi—in lotus posture, in deep meditation. When I looked at him more closely, I realized that he had my face. I started in profound fright and awoke with the thought: 'Aha, so he is the one who is meditating me. He has a dream, and I am it.' I knew that when he awakened I would no longer be."

Through much of his life, Jung had considered his dreams to be a valuable, clear source of information from his higher self, through his unconscious. He said "Our unconscious existence is the real one, and our conscious world a kind of illusion, an apparent reality constructed for a specific purpose, like a dream that seems a reality as long as we are in it."

It was often through the unconscious that Jung experienced direct contact with the archetypes that guided his life. Starting as early as the 1930's, Jung developed his idea of archetypes after reading about karma in the Yoga Sutras. These archetypes, Jung proposed, are a kind of universal psychic form that inform people's lives in meaningful ways at the unconscious level. He described archetypes as eternally inherited forms and ideas that have at first no particular content. As a person lives, he inhabits these forms with his own experiences. An individual may also carry some forms with particular content that is inherited from the collective karma of one's ancestors. For example, I have personally felt an attraction to the spirit world and the spirit of the land and wonder how much of my attraction is an archetypical karma from my Irish heritage.

Jung initially proposed that these archetypes were an expression of the karma of the individual. Karma might be a kind of psychic heredity of particular characteristics, like eye and hair color are on a physical level. On the psychic level these are universal qualities, the archetypes. He proposed that the bulk of our life is shaped by qualities that are unconscious and not even specific to our personality. He even suggested that complexes could "start a century or more before a man is born."

It was through this dream and other dreams that Jung started to welcome the metaphysical idea of reincarnation and the idea that one could inherit personal karma from previous lives. He felt that his personal karma had to do with a pursuit of knowledge, specifically around the development of the divine triad and its confrontation with the feminine principle. In his own inquiry, he wondered if his karma was from his own past lives or if it was from the heritage of his ancestors. He wrote, "I could well imagine that I might have lived in former centuries and there encountered questions I was not yet able to answer. I had to be born again because I had not fulfilled the task given to me. When I die, my deeds will follow along with me—that is how I imagine it. I will bring with me what I have done."

Bert Hellinger is another modern psychiatrist who built on this idea of family karma with his experiential therapeutic process of Family Constellations. In a constellation, a participant's family members and ancestors are placed in a room, with workshop participants standing in. As people embody these roles, they seem to be able to access unconscious and archetypal energies that the person's family members are carrying. Making these energies conscious and physically shifting the positions of these actors is thought to shift their relationships and release karma that is carried down through the participant's family. Entangled karmic relationships in a family system may manifest in a person as a psychological condition, a physical illness like cancer, or other negative habits and addictions. The acting out of a constellation uses a kind of shamanic container that allows individuals, who might not even know which person they are representing, to bring into consciousness these damaging karmic forces and release them.

Whether interpreting karma spiritually or psychologically, we live with gifts of our past, which will influence our future. Jung suggested that what is needed is a shift of the karmic center of gravity from the conscious towards the unconscious, from the ego to Self, that which is more aligned with the Soul. The problem with popular views of karma is that they focus on the ego level of desire and fulfillment. Some of the older, Eastern traditions can bring us valuable perspectives about karma and help us focus on the deeper unconscious part of ourselves that is expressing itself through our embodiment in this life. To touch that deeper part you might ask, "What is the path along which my soul is traveling in this life? How can I pay attention to it and follow it? Am I following the emotional passions I have been gifted by my family, tribe or culture, caught up in these collective trances? If I am caught up, how can I free myself?"

ରଃ

22.

Madurai Meenakashi Tower, Tamil Nadu

Places of the Builder Gods

Understanding the Ancient Science of Temple Creation

Freddy Silva

If we had been given the choice of incarnating in a period such as 16,000 BC, the world would have looked a lot different than it does today. This was the time of the last glacial maximum, when more of the Earth's landmass was exposed. During this period Australia and New Guinea formed a massive continent; the British Isles were joined to each other and to Europe; the Black Sea, the North Sea, and the Persian Gulf were dry land; the Mediterranean was a lake, and the Indonesian archipelago and Asia were one.

Southern India was also much more vast and incorporated Sri Lanka, which is now an island. Together they comprised the kingdom of Kumari Kandam, "the Land of the Virgin"—an interesting correspondence to the name given to ancient Egypt, Ta-Mery, "the place of Mary." As with Heliopolis and Tiwanaku, Kumari Kandam is described in the Tamil texts as a high civilization, part of a "Golden Age," where the pursuit of knowledge was held in the highest esteem; and cities of knowledge were created by men of great stature, both physically and mentally, who possessed exquisite skills in temple building and sacred knowledge that compared them to gods.

Tamil traditions describe this age as a time when "kingship was lowered from heaven" at the sacred hill of Arunachala, whereupon it became a repository of a creator god's power and knowledge.

Arunachala lies in the land of the Dravidian culture, which is at least 10,000 years old, and the origin of today's Tamil culture. The hill is mentioned in the oldest Tamil sacred literature, the Tolkappiyam, which itself refers to an even older work that was based on a library of archaic texts said to have been compiled more than 10,000 years earlier. We are therefore talking about an extremely old scripture spanning unimaginable eons of time, much like the oral traditions of the Aborigines.

The theme is repeated in Central America. Of all the interesting things about the Mayan corpus named Popul Vuh, two items in particular stand out. First, its depiction of life during a "Golden Age" before a catastrophic global flood swept the earth sounds remarkably like most gnostic texts compiled by other civilizations with whom the Maya supposedly had never interacted. Second, it describes how the "First Men" possessed clairvoyant ability: "Endowed with intelligence, they saw and instantly they could see far; they succeeded in seeing; they succeeded in knowing all that there is in the world. The things hidden in the distance they saw without first having to move… they were formidable men."

The Flood and the End of the Golden Age

Certainly makes one yearn for those times, but all good things come to an end. The Tamil Puranas state that there came a great pouring of the waters that submerged vast tracts of land, including the ancient academies, beneath gigantic waves. In fact there are at least 12 identical worldwide legends of great lands swallowed by rapidly encroaching oceans, and with them, the folding of the "golden age" of the gods.

Such written accounts are hardly the product of a fertile imagination. Off the coast of India there have been found no less than five sites of pre-diluvial cities, such as the former Mahabalipuram ("The city of the giant Bali"), along with the Temple of the Seven Pagodas whose golden tips are seen by fishermen during a calm sea. On the northwestern coast of India, out across the bay from the present city of Dwarka, lies the original city of Kushasthali and its temple presided by Khrishna, now submerged beneath 50 feet of murky ocean.

To the southwest of India lie submerged staircases in what are now the Maldive Islands, while in the Micronesian island of Pohnpei ("upon a stone altar"), 100 artificial islands comprise the pentagonal temple of Nan Madol ("reef of heaven"). Within it sits the basalt temple of Nan Dowas and its central pyramid, wherein megalithic foundation stones are said to have been erected by two antediluvian gods who came by boat from a sinking land to the west, and "by their magic spells, one by one, the great masses of stone flew through the air like birds, settling down into their appointed place." Traditionally called Sounhleng, "reef of heaven," it's built as a mirror image of its sunken counterpart Kahn-imweiso Namkhet ("city of the Horizon"). Indeed, undersea ruins of two cities have been discovered here, lying at great depths and complete with standing columns on pedestals rising to 24 feet.

Off the Japanese island of Yonaguni lies an entire citadel complete with deliberately cut and purposefully angled platforms and columns. It, too, now lies beneath 100 feet of ocean water following a catastrophic rise in sea level.

So, what does science have to say about this event so unanimously experienced around the world?

There are 175 global flood myths sharing near-identical descriptions, and mostly in cultures that allegedly had no contact with one another. Professor of Geology, Alexander Tollman, compared several flood myths in which the Earth was described as hit by "seven burning suns" before being overwhelmed by floods. He compared these with geological anomalies of molten rock thrown up by impact sites and proved that around 10,000 BC the Earth was indeed hit by seven comet fragments whose impact generated an increase in radioactive Carbon-14, which has been found in fossilized trees dating to that period.

Another impressive study into terrestrial comet impacts concluded that "the environmental data in the flood myths fit remarkably well with the modeling for a large, oceanic comet impact, above the threshold for global catastrophe at or greater than 100 gigatons." The geologic and atmospheric report of the impacts pretty much synchronizes with the description of conditions in myths: six or seven days of intense rain and hurricane-force winds, generated and sustained by the air pressure blast wave and the impact plume, not to mention the thick, muddy rain filled with submicron debris generated by the impact itself. The Maya described it as "heavy resin fell from the sky... a black rain began to fall by day and by night."

There is certainly evidence that both animal and human survivors found shelter on tops of mountains as high as 1,430 feet, only to be overwhelmed by advancing water. On the peaks of mountains in France lie the splintered bones of humans violently mixed with that of mammoth, reindeer, carnivores, and birds that became extinct shortly thereafter. Whale skeletons and Ice Age marine life can even be found 600 feet above sea level—inland in Vermont!

If a comet, or fragments of one, collided with the earth and generated this kind of unparalleled destruction, the soot and particle debris from the event—which according to world legends seems to have blanketed the entire globe—would be sealed in the geologic record as sediment in ice. In 2008 a team of Danish geologists conducting an extensive examination of ice cores in Greenland secured the precise date of the event to 9703 BC. Startled by the layer of soot in the ice, they remarked that "the climate shift was so sudden that it is as if a button was pressed."

The Tall Ones

Various traditions state that "the knowledge" and other important records of "men of high learning" not only survived the flood but were promulgated by groups of adepts, the most notable being the Seven Sages, and the Akhu Shemsu Hor, "the shining ones, followers of Horus." In the Edfu Texts they were the only divine beings who knew how temples and sacred places are to be created.

The Tamil Puranas also mention how seven sages visited the sacred hill of Arunachala after the flood to collect 'the knowledge' and embark on reconstructing the area between the Indus and the Ganges, creating new temples and sowing the seeds of civilization. Likewise, Andean traditions describe the megalithic monument builders as the Huari, a race of unusually tall, white-skinned, bearded giants, the most celebrated of which was a builder god named Viracocha. Together with seven "shining ones," he set about rebuilding the temple complex of Tiwanaku, from whence they set out to promulgate the knowledge throughout the Andes.

The same story is repeated over and over by cultures seemingly disconnected from one another. And it is due to their efforts that we have inherited this legacy of temples and places of veneration.

The initiates at the temple of Edfu were instructed to "stand up with the Ahau" who measured nine cubits tall. There is evidence that such beings not only existed but their descendents survived well into historic times. In the Pacific Ocean, the first European explorer to reach the island of *Te Pito o Te Henua* ("Navel of the World") was Jacob Roggeveen, who did so on Easter Sunday, 1722, hence its recent, anglicized name of Easter Island. He faithfully recorded the experience along with some of the islanders' traditions; one of them states that the population consisted of two types of races—the Short Ears and the Long Ears.

The Short Ears referred to the typical homo sapiens. As for the Long Ears, Roggeveen and his crew had direct interaction with them: "In truth, I might say that these savages are as tall and broad in proportion, averaging 12 feet in height. Surprising as it may appear, the tallest men on board our ship could pass between the legs of these children of Goliath without bending their head."

Are we dealing here with the same Ahau associated with ancient Egypt? Possibly. Like so many other lands and their flood myths, Easter Island is said to have been part of a larger landmass before a giant cataclysm and a subsequent rise in sea level claimed much of it. Ocean maps validate this to be the case: what is now Easter Island was once a longer ridge of mountain ranges. The natives apparently received survivors from the drowned land of Hiva, and seven sages, "all illuminated men," carefully surveyed the island before setting up sacred mounds at specific locations. Here we find several linguistic associations with Egypt and its builder gods, the Ahau, for the sacred platform constructed at the original landing place is called ahu, upon which seven moai were subsequently erected in commemoration of the original seven extraordinary builder gods.

There is also the word *akh*, "everlasting spirit," not a far cry from the

Egyptian ankh, meaning "everlasting life."

The magician-builder gods of Easter Island were called Ma'ori-Ko-Hau-Rongorongo, "master of special knowledge," and they are claimed to be the ancestors of the Long Ears. According to oral tradition they moved the moai with the use of mana, a kind of psychic force where matter yields to the focused intent of a person skilled in the subtle arts. Legend states that by "words of their mouths" the enigmatic stone heads were commanded to walk through the air.

Easter Island statue

There is an echo of this in Central America. Just as the Popul Vuh represents the oral history of the Quiche Maya, so the Codex Vaticanus records faithfully the very ancient oral traditions of Central America. In one curious passage it states that "in the First Age, giants existed in that country [Mexico]. They relate to one of the seven whom they mention as "having escaped from the deluge... he went to Cholula and there began to build a tower... in order that should a deluge come again he might escape to it." Indeed the pyramid of Cholula still stands, partly because a newer, Spanish church now resides on top of it, and mostly because it's the largest pyramid ever constructed in the world—its volume is greater than that of the great pyramid at Giza. In Nahuatl language it's named Tlachihualtepetl, also known as the "artificial mountain." Originally it was named Acholollan, meaning "water that falls in the place of flight."

Certainly these builders were physically and intellectually endowed, as one account after another credits these unusual individuals with achieving the seemingly impossible, using techniques that bend the presently-known laws of physics. At the temple complex of Uxmal, the Pyramid of the Magician is said to have been raised in just one night by a man of magical disposition who "whistled and heavy rocks would move into place." Compare this with the traditions of Tiwanaku, in which "the great stones were moved from their quarries of their own accord at the sound of a trumpet… taking up their positions on the site." Similar attributes are common to the creators of Teotihuacan and Stonehenge, as well as the original Egyptian temples, which are described as "speedy at construction."

Such legends are consistent with the use of mana by the magician builders of Easter Island.

The Purpose of the Temple

The primary purpose behind the temple and the builder gods who restarted this legacy was to go on promulgating the knowledge over an enormous span of ages, by which I mean 4,000 years at a stretch. This is an incalculable reach of time by modern standards, particularly as we in this computer age can barely cope with planning a quarter of the year at a time; even a week in the world of e-mail seems like a century. Physical evidence of the multiple layers of structures beneath present temple buildings suggests the original sites were maintained, improved, and expanded over the course of thousands of years. Ancient Egyptian traditions assert beyond their 3,000-year recorded history that no site was considered sacred unless it had been built upon the foundations of earlier temples, particularly those connected with Zep Tepi.

A temple built during the historic period and superimposed on the foundation of another was determined by a pre-existing entity set in the time of myth, so that this new structure became a concretization of its ancestral predecessor, or as the Pyramid Texts inform us, "…made like unto that which was made in its plans of the beginning." Thus, the foundation mound of the Great Pyramid at Giza dates to 10,500 BC, but the additional final courses of outer casing stones over the inner core of the building features shafts that reference specific stars in 2,500 BC.

Aside from the visual impact of the sight of Tiwanaku on the eyes of Spaniard Pedro Cieza de Léon in 1549, it's not unusual that such places should still exert a tremendous influence on the pilgrim like a master hypnotist's pass of the hand. The art of creating temples was serious business involving the synthesizing of universal laws and the harnessing of natural forces to create spaces where the veil between worlds is thinner.

As a testament to the skill of the builder gods, their practical magic is still palpable across the face of the earth; their creations remain sentient, living and breathing, like organisms. Their structures are mirrors of the universe. When we stare at them, we see our own image reflected back in stone. The experience is commonly shared from generation to generation. This may not seem so far-fetched because the locations chosen by the builder-gods for their "cities of knowledge" are places where planetary electromagnetics behave differently. And being electromagnetic by nature we pick up on these subtleties.

The Edfu Pyramid Texts—as well as inscriptions at Teotihuacan and instructions in the sacred texts of the Tamil—describe how the temples were to be designed as places where the individual could be "transformed into a god, into a shining star." In other words, the purpose of these mansions of the gods was nothing less than the transfiguration of the human soul, through which it was believed the individual achieved complete self-empowerment. Their craftsmen wished to remind us of this someday, lest we forgot. Thus when they built temples, they also created myths and rituals to preserve the knowledge, so as to survive whatever cataclysm the Earth cared to brew.

The Gnostic Gospels unearthed in 1947 at Nag Hammadi, near the temple of Dendera, offer a graphic reminder of this aim and why the tradition was maintained from age to age. The papyri state that temples were built "as a representation of the spiritual places," and in doing so, created an antidote against forces of darkness that "... steered the people who followed them into great troubles, by leading them astray with many deceptions. They died not having found the truth and without knowing the God of truth. And thus the whole creation became enslaved forever from the foundations of the world." ❧

The Nag Hammadi codices

© 2010, 2011 Freddy Silva. Adapted from the new book, Common Wealth: The Origin of Sacred Sites and The Rebirth of Ancient Wisdom, by Freddy Silva. Available from the author's website Invisibletemple.com.

23.

Inscriptions in Egyptian temples describe the buildings as places where initiates can be "transformed into a god—into a bright star."

The Seven Gates of Paradise

Another Take on the Meaning of Ancient Temple Science

Freddy Silva

Temples have long been associated with a state of bliss. Through a combination of stone and geometry, and the cunning harnessing of natural forces, they became places of power where a person is enabled to pierce a veil into worlds and levels of reality that access a vast sea of information and expanded potential. In Egypt and Central America these sacred buildings are even described as living entities, as a god, and where the initiate can be "transformed into a god, into a bright star." For this singular reason, then, the temple has occupied a central stage in human spirituality.

Human-constructed temples have their origin in the landscape. They are mirrors of natural forces at play, forces that once upon a time were perceived, then synthesized and concretized into structures that represent the perfection of the universe. The most ancient of temples—particularly

171

the stoic men-hirs ("standing stone")—are reflections of the sacred mountain which, even in the oldest of scriptures, such as the Tamil Puranas, was considered to house the energy of the god Siva. The sacred mountain was a Sivalingam, a sacred stone, the effulgent power of a creator god descended from the sky and manifested on Earth. As such, sacred mountains have been magnets for pilgrimage and veneration for thousands of years.

A men-hir, the simplest of all temples, is a mirror image of the sacred mountain in which the effulgent power of a creator god resides. (Note its size in relation to the child sitting next to it.)

In Eastern religious lore, the best known example of a mountain as a sacred site is Su-meru, or Mount Meru, which represents at the same time an allegorical structure of the universe as well as the highest spiritual achievement sought by adepts in the physical, spiritual, and metaphysical cosmology of Hindus, Buddhists, and Jains. The roots of Jainism, in particular, are as old as mountains themselves, and its influence is noted in many other religions.

Interestingly, these faiths share similar spiritual philosophies: the practice of self-effort in progressing the soul towards divine consciousness through non-violence, and the conquering of inner struggles (commonly known as the seven deadly sins). To overcome these conditions, devotees have traditionally sourced the energy of places of power, such as making pilgrimages to sacred mountains, and later, temples, where meditation and integration with the spirit of place has helped countless individuals disentangle themselves from such negative limitations as fear, anger, envy, and so forth. And once enlightenment is reached, one attains a state of bliss. Or as many of us prefer to call it, we reach paradise.

"Paradise" originates from the word pairidaeza in Avestan—the sacred language of Zoroastrianism—and literally means "a walled enclosure."

A Jain who has mastered discipline over the physical world and achieved the state of godliness is called a Jina. As this word traveled west it became the Arabic Djinn, along with its derivative Allah-Djinn, and finally, the Latin genius—a kind of tutelary spirit, like one's personal guardian angel. By the seventeenth century it appears as genie, later known in the West from the story of Aladdin.

Back in the days when Asia Minor was Assyria, this Djinn was a supernatural being. And rightly so, since the root j-nn means "hidden"; it is also the root of jannah, the Islamic concept of paradise. Its derivative in Portuguese—a language brimming with Arabic—is janela, "a window, an opening in a wall."

In other words, paradise is a hidden space that is demarcated and separate from the ordinary and troublesome world. And if we follow this dizzying etymological trail, it seems we can get into this "walled enclosure" through "an opening in the wall."

Paradise is, admittedly, what every living human being strives for, be it in the now or in the afterlife. As far as the temple builders were concerned, there was no better time than the present; and by erecting stone circles, pyramids, and other formidable structures, they essentially created "walled enclosures" demarking this world from the next. Could these temples be windows into paradise?

They may just be. We already know that such places concentrate measurable levels of electromagnetism, particularly the entrances, where electromagnetic and geomagnetic forces are directed, by design, into the inner sanctum of the temple. For lack of a better word, the entrance is the window into the walled enclosure, and the main beneficiary being the human body, which is suitably entranced.

Being electromagnetic by nature and composed of two-thirds water, when a person walks into a temple he is effectively walking into a highly charged version of himself. For one thing, every temple is also sited above or beside water; and the local magnetism, when rotated or spiraled, charges this fluid. Samples of water from holy wells and other sacred places do show an increase in the liquid's vorticular motion as compared to ordinary water. By implication, the process produces a corresponding effect in the human body.

Furthermore, the temple stimulates the iron that flows through the blood in the veins as well as the magnetite suspended inside the skull.

Any excitation of the local electromagnetic field can also influence the body's state of awareness, primarily through stimulation of the pineal gland, leading to visions, heightened imagination and altered states. In other words, the stimulation of the human energy field in a temple allows the recipient to be able to receive information more readily from more subtle levels of reality.

Which was precisely the purpose the temple builders had in mind: the transformation of the ordinary human into a god, into a shining star. Such effects induce oneness between mind, body, spirit, and God, a shamanic experience that leads to a blissful state of oneness with all levels of creation.

That is what we call paradise.

So, in creating places of power, the ancients created sanctuaries where paradise can be experienced on Earth.

It is natural to assume that the builders of such elaborate and sensitive environments would also invest a significant amount of effort in protecting them from harm. It appears they did. In the Funerary Texts at the temple complex of Saqqara, there is a curious passage in which it is stated that "seven degrees of perfection enable passage from earth to heaven." This instruction is widely interpreted as referring to a series of challenges the soul needs to pass before gaining entry into the otherworld.

Then again, with Egyptians being so fond of allegory and metaphor, I wondered if the phrase alludes to some doorway or protective barrier the individual crosses when entering the temple; a passage from earth to heaven suggests a crossing from the profane, material world into a heavenly otherworld, which is precisely the purpose of the temple. But why should there be "seven degrees of perfection": does the visitor undergo a process of purification? Possibly. If you recall, the temple was considered a mirror of heaven on Earth, the material dwelling place of a god as well as its physical embodiment. Consequently, the purity of energy of the temple was everything; and defilement of the sanctum, physically or otherwise, was seen as a precursor to the downfall of the spirituality of the individual, and hence, the collapse of the entire tribe.

The more I looked at the "seven gates" as an allegory, the more the idea of a protective device made sense. Besides, energy measurements conducted in and around stone circles in Britain have proved the existence of a force field around such temples—in essence, there exists an invisible yet defined threshold between profane and sacred space.

There is further evidence to support this possibility. There exists a kind of woven electromagnetic grid over the entire face of the globe. Discovered by the man whose name it bears, Dr. Ernst Hartmann, this network is composed of small rectangular "nets" and appears as a structure rising from the earth, each line 9 inches thick and spaced at intervals of 6 feet 6 inches by 8 feet, magnetically oriented; the dimensions are very close to the mathematical roots of the Great Pyramid. Hartmann noticed that the intersecting points of the network—the knots—are influenced by underground veins of water as well as magnetic forces emanating naturally from the earth.

Consequently, he found that the knots alter in strength from time to time and that a relationship exists between the location of the knots and the adverse health of people who work or sleep on them. Dowsers have been aware of this geopathic stress for centuries, and it is not uncommon for them to be hired to alter the location of the Hartmann net on a property by embedding conductors such as metal rods into the ground, which stretch the electromagnetic net away from desired locations. It is the dowser's equivalent of what ancient Egyptian temple builders used to call "the piercing the snake," the practice of anchoring or moving the earth's electromagnetic lines of force to achieve a desired energetic effect on a specific location, particularly the site of a future temple.

Conversely, the holes of the Hartmann net are places of neutral space where the weather is perfect. Could a relationship exist between temples and the stretching of this net?

Nothing more came of these musings until I read a fascinating research document by the geobiologist Blanche Merz, in which she conducted readings at temples in Europe, Egypt, and India, and found the Hartmann net to be stretched around the temples like a protective membrane. As Merz wrote: "The gigantic Pharaonic structures have this in common: the Hartmann network forms a veritable dam of 18 geomagnetic lines around the perimeter of the buildings." Celebrated temples such as Saqqara, Karnak, Luxor, Kom Ombu, as well as the pyramids, enjoy an immense neutral zone, much in the same way as the henge monuments in Britain circulate electromagnetic forces that concentrate the energy inside the temples and in a controlled manner that is beneficial to people. All these places are listed in the Edfu Building Texts as the original primordial mounds of the gods. Merz went on to find other energy hotspots

175

at Chartres cathedral, the cathedral of Santiago de Compostela, and a plethora of Indian sacred sites; in Tibet she found that stupas marked with nagas (serpents) identify the position of Hartmann knots and that telluric energy is transmitted via these upright stones.

Naturally, this revived my interest in the "seven degrees of perfection" and the possibility they might be referring to thresholds of some kind. As it happens, in Egyptian mythology, the passage of the soul into heaven is made through a place called Sekhet Ianu, the "Field of Reeds," a land of paradise where the spirit spends eternity; we simply know it today as the Elysian Fields. Egyptian mythology states that to reach this much-desired land one must pass through a series ofgates.

During a visit to the temple complex at Saqqara, I had the opportunity to study the passageway leading from the profane world into the grand courtyard and its evocative stepped pyramid, engineered by Imhotep, an architect of the gods. This passageway is unique in that it is a colonnade of 18 reeds separated by narrow alcoves. Each of the alcoves discharges an alternating field of positive—and negative—charged force, which serves both as a barrier into the temple while at the same time influencing the body's electromagnetic circuitry. In essence, as one walks down the preparatory hallway into Saqqara, one is suitably entranced prior to mak-

Seven positive nodes along the entrance to Newgrange

ing contact with the courtyard of the temple and the mansion of the gods. In its time, this was the procedure necessary for dispelling negative thoughts and feelings one may be harboring before entering the sacred abode.

Or as the Funerary Texts put it, one had "to master oneself before crossing the threshold of each gate."

The numerical relationship between the 18 reeds and the 18 Hartmann lines protecting the perimeter of the temples is unmistakable. But for me, the revelation lay in the readings of the alternating energy field along the passageway, for they consisted of exactly seven, positive-charged currents. Suddenly an answer to the "seven degrees of wisdom" loomed near. Merz's own research revealed that at the very wide thresholds preceding the initiatory rooms of the temples, the Hartmann net traverses the entrances with seven, tightly-packed grid lines that protect "the passage from the known to unknown."

I found this spiritual engineering isn't reserved just for Egyptian temples. In Ireland, the entrance to the ceremonial chamber at Newgrange is similarly protected by alternating energy currents, with seven positive-charged lines anchored on either side of the chambered passageway before reaching the inner sanctum.

It seems these precautions were undertaken in different parts of the world not just for the protection of the site but also as a preparatory area for the initiate prior to crossing the threshold between visible and invisible, much like the ritual a Muslim pilgrim undertakes as he winds seven times in an ever-decreasing spiral around the Ka'Ba before touching this stone called the "Soul-Body."

The greater purpose of the temple builders was to induce a closer bond between the initiate and the unseen universe. Temples were designated as repositories of the knowledge of the gods, and 'imbibing' such knowledge empowered the individual to be free—that is, free from the illusions of the world of matter. Under such conditions any individual is able to live life fully aware, precisely as the Rig Veda states—total self-empowerment through total self-realization.

This ideal would eventually bring the original temple builders and the benevolent guardians of the temple into direct conflict with organized religion, which abhors anyone savoring direct contact with the divine. Few tales portray the fight for the domination of the human soul better than the biblical story of Adam and Eve, their own sojourn in paradise, and that apple they ate from the Tree of Knowledge. Anyone raised in the Christian faith knows the story all too well. But in the account of Genesis given in the Gnostic gospels of Nag Hammadi, which precede the four canonical gospels selected by the Catholic Church, the serpent appears as the benevolent hero of mankind, and the god portrayed in the story is a shadow of the god of Light: "What did God say to you?" the serpent asked Eve. "Was it, do not eat from the tree of knowledge?"

Eve replied, "He said, not only do not eat from it, but do not touch it lest you die."

The serpent reassured her, saying, "Do not be afraid. With death you shall not die; for it was out of jealousy that he said this to you. Rather your eyes shall open and you shall come to be like gods, recognizing evil and good."

The Gnostic writings then describe that once Adam and Eve had eaten of the Tree of Knowledge they experienced enlightenment, precisely as one does, and the knowledge empowered them to discover spiritual transfiguration.

All of this is in stark contrast to what many have been traditionally taught. Thanks to the machinations of the Church, the attainment of knowledge gets Adam and Eve booted out of paradise, the apple is labeled forbidden fruit, and worse, the whole episode is presided by a serpent who was doing fine as a symbol of telluric forces until the Church turned it into a tool of the devil. And just like that, knowledge becomes evil, and coming into contact with it removes you from a state of bliss.

And yet "drinking" of this knowledge and applying it was precisely the reason why we sought out places of power on the land to begin with and why creator gods with benevolent intentions would later imprint "the knowledge" at sacred places, so we can travel to them whenever we forget that we too are gods, by experiencing, even if for a few moments, the taste of paradise. ❧

© 2010, 2011 Freddy Silva. *Read his new book,* Common Wealth: The Origin of Sacred Sites and the Rebirth of Ancient Wisdom.

24.

Buddha, with his hands
in the *Abhaya Mudra*,
representing protection,
peace, benevolence,
and the dispelling of fear.

The Mystery of Mudra

*Is There Hidden
Meaning in the Gestures
of the Saints?*

Patrick Marsolek

For centuries yogis, martial artists, and spiritual seekers have used ritual hand gestures as part of their spiritual practice. Their belief is that these positions help them attain the mental and physical discipline or spiritual transformation they seek. We all use common gestures to reinforce certain ways of feeling and thinking. What do you feel if you cross your arms across your chest when you are in conversation with someone? What happens if you open your arms and hold your hands out in front of you with your palms facing up? The first posture may show psychological closing off, suspicion, and even possibly defensiveness. The second posture is more open, accepting, and vulnerable. In India, the palms pressed flat together in front of the chest is used with the greeting "Namaste." One translation of Namaste is "the divine within me salutes the divine within you." It is thought that if you practice this palms gesture, you will see the divine more readily. Are there such connections between our physical bodies and our inner mental or spiritual terrain?

Mary, the Mother of Jesus, depicted in the *Orans Prayer Posture*, as depicted in this painting from Medjugorje, a village in the former Yugoslavia where miraculous apparitions have been reported since 1981.

These gestures—or to use the Sanskrit word—mudras are an important part of many different spiritual disciplines. Yogis claim that mudras possess healing and transformational powers and can even activate paranormal abilities. They are gestures of delight, meaning a 'mark' or a 'seal' of an inner transformation. If you were sitting and you had your palms open on your knees, then closed your thumbs to touch your forefingers, you'd be doing a form of the Jnana Mudra. This posture has been used for thousands of years by meditators to heighten concentration. The use of mudras such as this one has evolved into a complex form of language that transmits esoteric concepts and embodies spiritual ideals. The tradition of using gestures as a way of sacred expression is not limited to Indian traditions. Egyptian priests used mudras to communicate with their gods. The Greeks, Indians, and Chinese used them as part of the elaborate choreographies of their religious plays.

If you look at sacred art from all over the world, you can see figures expressing specific gestures. Jesus is often depicted with his right hand in *Prithvi Mudra*, with his palm facing outward and the tips of the thumb and ring finger joined. *Prithvi mudra* is said to provide stability and cure weaknesses of the body and mind. Mary is often depicted in the *Orans Prayer Posture*, a female standing with the hands outstretched sideways with the palms up. Many think this posture was used to signify the departing feminine soul. The Buddha is also pictured in works of art expressing a variety of different mudras in his hands.

Some scholars believe that mudras may have originated from primitive Shamanistic expressions or dances, in which a Shaman was in contact with and expressing the spirit of an animal or a spirit. In this trance, the Shaman would spontaneously adopt a certain hand position, or even an entire body posture, as an expression of the energy of that spirit. The assumed posture would help the Shaman channel the powers of that spirit for healing or divination.

Other scholars think that the first mudras evolved spontaneously as meditators chanted the earliest recorded vedas, the early Hindu scriptures. The mudras are thought to have spontaneously begun with the realization of the states described in the scriptures. Some researchers go further to suggest that the all of the physical postures or asanas in yoga also evolved from simple hand gestures into the complex system of full body practices that we know today.

Some indigenous Shamanistic practices today still involve a kind of spirit possession. In an African trance dance for example, a person or even a whole group of people will start expressing different postures and movements. The specific spirit can be identified by the postures and movements the person makes. The elders watching over the trance dance will know from their cultural experience how to properly engage with each spirit.

The modern day practices of Tai Chi and Chi Kung are still connected to their Shamanistic animal origins. They embody specific animal totems such as the forms of Soaring Crane or Turtle Longevity. The early practitioners learned that adopting the posture or gesture would help them connect with the state of consciousness or the spirit with which it was associated. Probably in each different form of these martial arts, an individual had an initial spontaneous expression of that spirit. That individual and their followers continued to access that spirit or energy by recreating the discovered form. Each form has its own characters and qualities. In a shamanistic sense, the spirit dance can imbue the individual with super-human strength, healing abilities, or spiritual clarity. In the case of the group trance dance, those that embody the spirit might bring back some vision or wisdom for the tribe.

There is some interesting research that explores some of the mechanisms of gesture and posture. Certain nerve cells in the lower temporal lobe of our brains are dedicated exclusively to responding to hand positions and shapes. This area of the brain is very active in infants. The site of these cells, deep in a relatively primitive part of the brain, suggests that the gesture may predate words in evolutionary history as a means of human expression. Evolutionary linguist Sherman Wilcox speculates that "Language emerged through bodily action before becoming codified in speech." Other researchers have shown that when people perform actions, they remember those actions better if they gesture while they are talking about the actions they did.

The neurological cluster becomes less important as our ability to talk increases in early childhood, but it remains connected to the expressive movement of our bodies. Gestures precede our speech, even before we are conscious of our own thoughts or what we're going to be saying. Hand movements and, for that matter, all matter of body movements, occur first, as thoughts in the brain emerge as images and feelings. Because gestures don't pass through the left-brain language filters, they can be connected to deeper, unconscious expressions, perceptions and capacities, which would explain their use in spiritual practices.

We often use gestures to bring thoughts, feelings, and memories more to the surface of our awareness, just as a meditator might use them to invoke a state of awareness. Have you ever held the palm of your hand open when trying to express something verbally or squeezed your hand or your fingertips together trying to formulate a thought? You might also pull your head back with a jerk, saying "No" physically with the body before being able to say "No" verbally.

Researchers have noted how gestures help speakers formulate coherent speech by aiding in the retrieval of elusive words from their memory. The linguist David McNeill refers to gestures as an actual form of thought, not just an expression of thought but as a cognitive process whereby we can realize meaning without ever expressing it verbally. The experience of the physical might be critical to rounding out the fullness of what is being learned.

The embodiment is what is being actualized by the Shaman, the Chi Kung master or the Yogi. There is an intention in these practices to embody and communicate certain ineffable spiritual ideals that cannot be understood just from verbal language. Can you feel a change in your being when you shift from arms crossed on your chest to the palms together Namaste gesture? In that felt sensation you may be tapping into something that can't be grasped cognitively. If you notice how it calms your mind and puts you into a state where you are more connected with 'the divine within,' then you may choose to use this gesture when you are in conflict with someone.

Another way you can experience the mystery of this body/mind connection is when you awaken from sleep in the morning after dreaming. Often when we wake, we lose the memory of our dreams. This can be frustrating when you are trying to recall your dreams. You can notice, though, if you change your body position when you wake. You may be lying on your side when sleeping, then roll to your back when you awaken. If you want to remember the dream you can simply turn your body back to the position you were in when sleeping and let the felt sense of that posture come back. Often, dream images and memories will return with this shift.

The intention of the mudras and some of the asanas in yoga is to place the body in a configuration that induces and reinforces a specific state of consciousness. The shape of the pose or posture acts as a doorway into the expression of that awareness. This is something many people do unconsciously. You might cross your arms over your chest to feel more safe and secure, or you might hold your palm to your heart when you want to feel more compassion. These seemingly spontaneous gestures shift your consciousness. This is one reason teachers suggest you sit with your spine straight when you meditate. The collective wisdom of meditators from many countries suggests that posture helps to calm and clear the mind.

A kind of morphic resonance may also be present in sacred mudras and postures. Rupert Sheldrake proposed the idea of morphic fields of information. These are fields of information that are created any time organisms do a specific kind of behavior. With these fields, the experience becomes accessible by the same kinds of organisms at a later date. If enough people have sat straight in meditation or held a particular mudra in their hands while having a spiritual experience, then it may be that others tap into this powerful field of information when they assume the same posture. This collective memory might partially explain why specific postures and mudras evoke certain experiences. There may also be an activation of the nervous and energetic systems in our bodies when we take specific postures. Although we have the higher intellect and self-reflective consciousness of humans, we are still housed in animal bodies with concrete physical systems.

Gestures and mudras can also express themselves spontaneously. In India, individuals have been known to suddenly drop from walking into the seated pose and lapse into a unified state. Some say that it is the awakening of the Kundalini energy at the base of the spine that causes a meditator to suddenly assume an erect posture or even visibly shake. An interesting correlate to this expression of kundalini occurs in some people who are experiencing Grof's Holotropic breathwork. In this process that induces a transformative altered state, it is common to have a regressive experience where a person can physically revisit early birth experiences. When this happens, their hands and feet constrict in ways that babies do at that phase of their development.

In a more overt way, we communicate through our gestures much more of what we are thinking and feeling than we are consciously aware. Recently some researchers have studied the speech of politicians and noted how they gesture with their dominant side more frequently when they're speaking about something they judge as 'good' or 'positive.' It seems the dominant side is used more to say "Yes." Psychologically, this may be related to the Jungian concept of shadow, where our unexpressed or negative parts are expressed in less dominant ways. People who are good at reading others have learned to watch these subtle subconscious cues to determine if someone is lying or telling the truth. Body workers refer to this connection when they say, "the body never lies."

Researchers have also found that simply observing a gesture can stimulate the same patterns of neural firing as when actually performing it. We have mirror neurons in our brains. These neurons stimulate your body in the same way as if you were actually doing what you are seeing. These mirror neurons might explain why just seeing a particular mudra or posture can trigger the observer to activate some of the same spiritual awareness, especially if the gesture was originally con-

Christ, as painted in this Eastern Orthodox Christian icon, with his right hand in *prithvi mudra*.

nected to a powerful, transformative state of consciousness. The artists who portrayed saints, teachers, and spiritual seekers through history in specific postures and mudras may have transmitted more than just a beautiful image. These images may serve as a tangible way to activate us today, helping us touch the ineffable in ourselves.

Seeing the posture is a beginning; physically doing it allows further embodiment. The different yogas, Tai Chi, Chi Kung, other martial arts, and even meditation and prayer are all technologies to attain some kind of spiritual awakening. They all have physical embodied components that can't be cognitively comprehended. Seen in this light, these practices are not intended to subvert the physical body in service of spirit or conscious-ness. Rather the interconnection of posture and awareness highlight how the mind and body may be equal partners in the realization of higher lev-els of consciousness.

The ecstatic experience of the realized state is in part possible because of full physical embodiment. Many of the sacred texts of the world have hand gestures that accompany them. For example, Stan Tenen of the Meru Foundation has proposed that the meaning of the Hebrew texts may be secondary to a set of hand gestures and mental movements that accom-pany them. Like the Sanskrit Vedas, these hand gestures are thought to be integral to the transmission of the meaning of the Hebrew texts.

Another interesting corollary here is what have been termed "Ecstatic Trance Postures." The Cuyamungue Institute, which was founded by the late Felicitas Goodman, has been researching how certain whole body postures, when held in trance states, produce very predictable and specific experiences. Looking through historical and prehistorical archaeological artifacts and artwork, Goodman catalogued over 80 postures that were portrayed in art dating back to the early Neolithic period. Goodman pro-posed that it is the physiology of the human body, which has remained unchanged for the last 30,000 years. A modern person may have an ex-perience in trance that would be very similar to a Neolithic medicine woman's experience. ∞

25.

Temple Ruins
at Luxor, Egypt

How Modern Is Modern Science?

*Did Quantum Physics First Appear
as Ancient Egyptian Temple Wisdom?*

Edward F. Malkowski

You might think that since quantum physics is a relatively new branch of science, this burgeoning "new science" philosophy is also new. It is not. These new insights into nature and reality are very old but have been masked by modern attempts to characterize the ancient Egyptian culture and religion as primitive. The concepts of mind and consciousness, as well as reincarnation and evolution, were expressed long ago in what historians have labeled the "ancient mystery school"—what Schwaller de Lubicz termed "sacred science." Although shrouded by the secrecy of the temple and rites of initiation, ancient Egyptian schools taught this secret wisdom through myth and symbolism, an approach that leads to an understanding of the world that is virtually identical to today's new science philosophy.

In fact, the sacred science of the ancient Egyptians, best described as a philosophy of nature's principles, inspired the Hebrews, the Greeks, the Romans, and the Christians, which led to the emergence of what we call Western civilization—but for us, thousands of years later, the founding knowledge of our civilization is all but lost. However, there have always been people who have handed down the secret wisdom and the sacred science of the ancient Egyptians: Kabbalists, Hermeticists, Gnostics, Sufis, Buddhists, and Alchemists. It is secret only in the sense that this wisdom must be understood through esotericism and symbol, and it's sacred only in the sense that scientific investigation inevitably leads to an understanding of Man, Divinity, and a unique knowledge of "Self."

Leaving behind modern biases and looking deep into ancient Egypt's civilization, there can be found a brilliance and understanding that rivals our knowledge today. Their "gods" were of a different order than our Western concept of God. They were not "gods" at all, but principles of nature that represented concepts like digestion and respiration. They also represented intangible qualities found in mankind, such as knowledge and personality. This ancient view of nature has been mistaken as religious and cultlike, but is, in fact, technical and philosophical.

For example, the king's diadem, with its serpent and vulture, symbolized the principles of life and form. The serpent represented the concept of the Source for all that exists and its manifestation as the cosmos; and the vulture, man's spiritual immortality. Like a spirit, the vulture, soaring high in the sky, escapes this world to an existence beyond the bounds of Earth. Thus, the pharaoh's diadem symbolized man's kingship in a cosmic sense and the mystery of life's essence, where the mystery is the reality of Cause and Effect. This mystery, which defines the human experience, is abstract but operates through the concrete court of three dimensions to create another abstraction—what we experience as consciousness and self-perception.

How the ancient Egyptians developed such a refined philosophy is a mystery in itself. Scholars such as Samuel Mercer, who translated Saqqara's Pyramid Texts during the 1950s, have noted that the tenets of this philosophy appear to have emerged fully-fledged nearly five thousand years ago, without historical precedent. It is ironic that ancient Egypt's technical capabilities—so ambitious, so precise—also appear to have emerged, fully-fledged, without precedent; although we shouldn't be surprised, since the development of a sophisticated philosophy does not occur without sophisticated technology.

Schwaller de Lubicz

Such insight into ancient Egypt's earliest traditions moistens the seeds of doubt for history's linear model of man and civilization—particularly so when today's emerging "new science" philosophy parallels concepts described long ago in Ramses' Temple of Amun-Mut-Khonsu, so meticulously described by Schwaller de Lubicz in his two volume work, *The Temple of Man.*

In 1937, alchemist and Hermetic philosopher René A. Schwaller de Lubicz was drawn to Egypt by an inscription at the tomb of Ramses where the pharaoh was depicted as the side of a right (3:4:5) triangle. For Schwaller de Lubicz, this meant that the ancient Egyptians understood geometry's Pythagorean theorem long before Pythagoras was born. Intrigued, he moved to Luxor and studied ancient Egypt's art and architecture for thirteen years, concluding that the temple architecture was a deliberate exercise in proportion. The temple, in its detail, described the nature of man as a science, a philosophy that Schwaller de Lubicz termed the "Anthropocosm" or "Man Cosmos."

Philosophy of the Anthropocosm

The question of who we are and why we are here will likely remain the ultimate mystery. Intuitively, however, this mystery can be understood upon the realization that our existence as a conscious biological form can be traced to cosmic events, and that the prerequisites for our existence can be traced to a universal state. Our Earth is dependent on the sun and the solar system in which it is gravitationally trapped; which is dependent on the Milky Way galaxy, in which it is gravitationally trapped; which is also held in place by other forces including, but not limited to, our neighboring galaxies. Any interruption in this line of cosmic dependency would likely result in the cessation of our existence. Thus, it can be said that the cosmos is the true nature of man, and form is the sole means of its expression.

Although it seems as though we are insignificantly small compared to the rest of the universe, there is a single truth to our existence that cannot be denied and that lends credence to the abstract nature of man—the reality of the observer. We observe and perceive an ordered, yet dynamic, arrangement of energy that we naturally translate into sight, sound, smell, taste, and touch. To take away the measures of this reality means reality's destruction, which suggests that the universe was never concrete in the first place. We only perceive that it is. Therefore, like Plato in his cave, we can conclude that the concreteness and form in which we live are really only the knowledge of such things. Einstein agreed implicitly in one of his famous statements: "Reality is an illusion, albeit a very persistent one."

The most interesting question is, where does our ability to observe and perceive come from? According to physicists, it comes from an event called "state vector collapse" where all possible states of the system (the universe) collapse into a single observed state.

During the 1920s, while Werner Heisenberg and Neils Bohr were further developing quantum theory, they realized that a new viewpoint had to be created to achieve a proper understanding of the quantum world. The classical view of a discrete world would simply not work. To accomplish this,

Niels Bohr

they embraced the idea that the world is fundamentally not a collection of discrete objects, but an indistinct, unified world of energy where, at times, discrete objects are perceived. Heisenberg developed his wave matrix theory, and Schrödinger his wave mechanics, to explain their insights. Although slightly different in their approach, these two theories offered a more accurate description of the atomic structure than did classical physics.

What their theories state is that all matter exists as a wave structure that we cannot directly see. What we do see is the localization of the wave structure with its release of energy, which is a simple way to explain state vector collapse. The energy released is what physicists call a photon (a particle of light). We perceive the released energy as a particle, even though it is really a wave. This occurs for us because that is how the human brain works.

Without state vector collapse there would be no perception of separation, no form to experience and, consequently, no expression. The cosmos would remain in an undefined state of absoluteness, a potential of all cosmic possibilities.

All matter that makes up the cosmos is actually configured energy that now exists as a result of stellar nucleosynthesis and supernova. Carbon, nitrogen, oxygen, and other heavy elements—the building blocks of life—were created as a result of large stars collapsing under their own weight and then exploding with tremendous heat, spreading newly created elements into empty space to form interstellar clouds. New research suggests that even amino acids, important for protein synthesis, were formed in interstellar clouds. Thus, scientists argue that since the elements that make up our bodies are the results of a cosmic process, then we are made from stardust and are literally children of the stars.

The big bang origin of the universe has been the model of choice for cosmologists for many decades now, but it has always been a scientific paradox. Our known laws of physics are not valid until after the moment of the big bang. So, how do we arrive at a universe that we experience, which sprang from nothing? Perhaps the big bang is only a perspective to explain the current body of scientific data and does not accurately represent actual events. As is all of nature, perhaps the universe is cyclical and oscillates between the never-ending destruction and creation of galaxies. No one really knows.

However, what we do know and can be certain of is our conscious experience. It is the one thing all six billion of us can agree upon, and the key to understanding nature. According to the anthropocosm theory, consciousness creates a venue in order to experience, and does so through the unique quantification of its qualities. This cosmic and anthropic "new science" understanding of man puts forth the same principles that were built into the architecture of Luxor's Temple of Amun-Mut-Khonsu.

The temple was not about the piety of a man but our solar legacy as the philosophical "Divine Man" portrayed in the great statues of Ramses—the birth of the sun. The temple was (and is) a form of communication, a lesson, and at its core its builders' philosophy is carved in stone. Amun, Mut, and Khonsu were not "gods" in the Western religious sense, but principles that form and explain the nature of mankind as coherently as such an abstract subject can be explained.

The definition of man and the story of the human experience were built into the temple architecture. Physically, the temple describes the structure of man, from the importance of the femur in the creation of blood cells, to the role of the pineal gland in the brain. Spiritually, the temple conveys life's cosmic drama and man's spiritual immortality. Amun was the "Hidden One" or the "Invisible One," best described today as the Western concept of God, omnipotent and omnipresent, or, from a scientific viewpoint, the energy field that pervades all that exists. From the ancient Egyptian point of view, Amun was self-created, the creative power and source for all that exists. Mut, which means "mother," was Amun's cosmic wife and the mother of the "Son" Khonsu, who represented the king.

However, the kingship of Khonsu was not a physical kingship but refers to a cosmic (or spiritual) ruler made flesh through the principles of nature. Thus, Khonsu the King represents the essence of mankind—the archetypal "Man"—and essence of all who ever lived, is alive now, and will live in the future. Khonsu, by being associated with Ra and Thoth, represented the essence of life's energy and man's wisdom and knowledge, where mankind is a consequence of the universe's evolution culminating in the physical endowment of the universe's self-perception. In myth, Khonsu was a lover of games but was also the principle of healing, conception, and childbirth. Literally, he was "the king's placenta."

Just as the ancient *Uroboros*—the circular serpent biting its tail—symbolizes cyclicality, through our modern scientific endeavors we have come full circle in understanding ourselves. No one knows for sure in what culture or at what time the Uroboros was first fashioned as a symbol, but it is one of mankind's most ancient ones.

Plato tells us in the Timaeus that since nothing outside of the serpent existed, it was self-sufficient. Movement was right for his spherical structure, so he was made to move in a circular manner. Thus, as a result of his own limitations, he revolves in a circle, and from this motion the universe was created. From Egypt's Ptolemaic period, the artist who drew the

"Chrysopoeia [gold making] of Cleopatra" wrote within the circular serpent: The All Is One. Thus, the serpent is the ancient Egyptian symbol depicting self-creation and the source of life: "It slays, weds, and impregnates itself," writes Erich Neumann in The Origin and History of Consciousness. "It is man and woman, beginning and conceiving, devouring and giving birth, active and passive, above and below, at once."

For the ancient Egyptians, the Uroboros—the serpent—represents the creative principle of the cosmos, as well as the cosmos itself. Since the serpent's form is singular, without appendages, but has a forked tongue and forked penis, its form is an apt symbol of creation's initial movement from an undifferentiated state into a world of multiplicity, a movement from one to two. Schwaller refers to this as the "Primordial Scission."

Uroboros, ancient symbol of the serpent devouring its tail

The Uroboros, however, is not just an ancient mythical symbol, nor is it the fabricated imagery of the primitive mind. Rather, it is man's identification with the seamless, eternal state of oneness whose essence is a deep memory of an origin that words cannot explain and has to be understood through esotericism. As such, the Uroboros' esotericism is as valid today as it was at the dawn of man.

Spiritual Technology of Ancient Egypt

The Western worldview has a long history of separating the physical from the conceptual, the scientific from the religious. So together, spirituality and technology appear contradictory. This contradiction, however, is based on a naïve and exoteric view of "spirit" and "technology."

Spirit is not some immeasurable, metaphysical thing. Rather, Spirit is the driving force behind the human experience, the quest for knowledge, and the building power of civilization that can be measured by achievement. Technology is mankind's application of knowledge into industry that provides for the civilization's well being. Technology, which is the application of science into civil practicalities, is also the building power of civilization.

Even though technology's final product is most evident, it is the spirit of man that turns ideas into concepts, and concepts into knowledge, which through engineering brilliance, turns science into technology and makes life more efficient and comfortable. Every product ever made began with someone's inspiration and creativity. So, spirit and technology are really different aspects of the same human endeavor.

The desire to know inspires us, and the ever-increasing level of knowledge and technology has allowed us to reach new levels in understanding our state of existence—but what might have inspired the ancient Egyptians? Schwaller de Lubicz believed that ancient Egypt was the legacy of a technical civilization of which there is no history or knowledge in today's world, a civilization for which spirit and technology were integrated into a worldview that embraced life's mystery. For me, it is this technical and spiritual legacy that is so evident in the art and culture of ancient Egypt.

The spiritual technology of ancient Egypt expounds upon the works of Schwaller de Lubicz and tells the untold story behind the birth of the Western religious tradition. The Egyptian Mysteries, as they were called, inspired greatness in men who instilled the concept of the anthropocosm into our own sacred literature, and it is the same philosophical understanding of nature that is at the forefront of today's "new science"; whether symbolized by the Uroboros or Schrödinger's wave equation, human consciousness exists as a local manifestation of a self-perceiving universe. ❧

Excerpted, with the publisher's permission, from Lost Knowledge of the Ancients, *edited by Glenn Kreisberg (Inner Traditions, 2010).*

Lost Tradition of the Sacred Bee

Today's Threat to the Honey Bee—
A Reminder of Forgotten Wisdom?

Andrew Gough

Washington's Monument, arguably the most enigmatic testament to America's hope and vision for the future, also contains a powerful reference to its past: "Holiness to the Lord. Deseret," it states, meaning 'Holiness to the Lord, the Honeybee.' The word 'Deseret' translates as Honeybee in the language of the Jaredites, a mysterious tribe that is believed to have migrated to the Americas during the time of the construction of the Tower of Babel, according to Mormon tradition. The existence of this peculiar dedication to a bee, let alone its meaning, has largely been forgotten; but those with eyes to see know that it hails from a time when civilizations that understood its contribution flourished and those who did not perished.

Quite simply, the bee is Earth's most industrious pollinator of plants and trees, a vital function for sustaining life on Earth. They also provide important ritualistic, medicinal, and health food by-products, such as honey. To understand the bee's importance is to appreciate how crucial these essentials were—still are—to any advanced society. When we look to the dawn of civilization and trace the veneration of the bee over time, only then do we realize how this diminutive creature may represent the greatest lost tradition in history.

Honey hunting

Incredibly, bees over 100 million years old have been discovered in amber, frozen in time, as if immortalized in their own honey. The Greeks called amber Electron, associated with the Sun God Elector, who was known as the awakener, a term also given to honey—which resembles amber—a regenerative substance revered across the ancient world. This association led to the bees' illustrious status amongst ancient man, exalting their fossilized remains over the preserved vestiges of all other insects.

Prehistory is full of clues that hint at ancient man's obsession with bees. In the Cave of the Spider near Valencia in Spain, a 15,000-year-old painting depicts a determined looking figure risking his life to extract honey from a precarious, cliff-side beehive. Honey hunting represents one of man's earliest hunter / gatherer pursuits—its very difficulty hinting at the genesis of the bee's adoration in prehistory. And, of course, it was the bee that led ancient shamans to the plants whose hallucinogens transported their consciousness into the spirit world of the gods. Curiously, recent research has revealed that the sound of a bee's hum has been observed during moments of change in the state of human consciousness, including individuals who have experienced alleged UFO abductions, apparitions, and near death experiences. Was this phenomenon known by the ancients and believed to have been one of the elements that made the bee special?

Honey Hunting in Spain

In Anatolia, a 10,000-year-old statue of the Mother Goddess adorned in a yellow and orange Beehive-style tiara has led scholars to the conclusion that the Mother Goddess had begun to morph into the Queen Bee, or bee goddess, around this time. At the Neolithic settlement of Catal Huyuk, rudimentary images of bees dating to 6540 BC are painted above the head of a Goddess in the form of a halo; and beehives are stylistically portrayed on the walls of sacred temples. Not surprisingly, it was the Sumerians who soon emerged as the forefathers of organized bee keeping. Mesopotamia—modern day Iraq—flourished from the early sixth century BC and is known as the cradle of civilization; and it is here that the Sumerians invented Apitherapy, or the medical use of bee products such as honey, pollen, royal jelly, propolis, and venom.

Sumerian reliefs depicting the adoration of extraordinary winged figures have often been interpreted by alternative history writers as proof of extraterrestrial intervention. In the context of the benefits of beekeeping, it is more likely they depict the veneration of bees. Significantly, the Sumerian images gave rise to the dancing goddess motif, a female dancer with her arms arched over her head that scholars believe represents a bee goddess priestess or shaman. The motif, which would become central to Egyptian symbolism, appears to allude to the bee's unique ability to communicate through dance, the waggle dance as it is known, or the ability to locate food up to three miles from home and return to communicate its whereabouts to the hive through dance, sort of prehistoric satellite navigation.

So, society had discovered the immense value that bees provide, ten thousand years ago or more, back in the mist of prehistory. As life along the River Nile evolved and Dynastic rule in ancient Egypt slowly developed, the seeds of bee veneration had already been sown. But the tradition was about to be embraced like never before, or since.

The Bee Goddess in Ancient Egypt

Egyptologists, such as David Rohl, believe that Sumerian culture migrated across the Eastern Egyptian Desert and into the Nile Valley. This desolate expanse of Wadis is renowned for its predynastic rock art depicting exalted-looking figures with exaggerated plume-like decorations. The unusual lines extending upwards from the main figures' heads recall the antenna of the bee while hinting at the shape of the plumes that would characterize the headdress of Egyptian Kingship for thousands of years to come. The images also depict the Dancing Goddess motif, a woman with her hands bowed over her head just as the 'dancing' bee Goddess had been depicted in Sumerian and Central European reliefs thousands of years earlier. The icon is widespread in Egyptian mythology and appears to have originated from an understanding of the bee's unique ability to communicate through 'dance.'

Another clue to the bee's artistic influence can be found in ceremonial Egyptian dress, which has certain stylistic similarities with the bee, namely the headdress, or nemes, which consists of alternating yellow and dark horizontal stripes. This visual synchronicity is discernible in many reliefs and sculptures but is perhaps best illustrated in the death mask of the 18th Dynasty Pharaoh, Tutankhamen, which famously depicts the Pharaoh adorned in alternating black and yellow stripes or bands, just like a bee.

The Egyptian Death Mask

Image of a bee placed next to the Pharaoh's cartouche

Egypt's fascination with bees stems from the earliest of epochs. Northern Egypt, or the land stretching from the Delta to Memphis, was known as "Ta-Bitty," or "the land of the bee." King Menes, founder of the First Egyptian Dynasty, was bestowed with the office of "Beekeeper", a title ascribed to all subsequent Pharaohs, and an image of the bee was positioned next to the Pharaoh's cartouche.

The Egyptian God Min was known as the 'Master of the Wild Bees' and dates to 3000 BC or earlier. Similarly, the Egyptian Goddess Neith was a warrior deity also possessing fertility symbolism and virginal mother qualities, all attributes of the Queen bee. In Sais, Neith was regarded as the Goddess of the 'House of the Bee' and the Mother of RA, the 'the ruler of all'. Egyptian mythology contains countless references to bees, including the belief that they were formed from the tears of the most important god in its pantheon, RA. The bee is even featured on the Rosetta Stone.

Bees are portrayed on the walls of Egyptian tombs, and offerings of honey were routinely presented to the most important Egyptian deities. Indeed, honey was the 'nectar of the gods,' and like the Sumerians before them, Egyptian physicians relied on its medicinal value for many important remedies and procedures, including early forms of mummification.

One Egyptian monument that exhibits a peculiar form of bee symbolism is the Saqqara step pyramid, which recalls the six-sided shape of a bee's honeycomb, with six levels above ground and one very special level below—the Apis bull necropolis known as the Serapeum. Egyptologists believe that the Apis bull was bestowed with the regenerative qualities of the Memphite god Ptah—the Egyptian god of reincarnation. They also believed that those who inhaled the breath of the Apis bull received the gift of prophecy; and perhaps most importantly of all, the Egyptians believed that the bull was transformed into Osiris Apis, after death. 'Bee' in Latin is 'Apis', which may have derived from Sipa/Asipa in Mesopotamia; Sipa meaning 'Great Shepherd in the Sky' and Apis mean-

King Tut's Death Mask

ing Osiris. This relates to the belief that after death, the Pharaoh's soul joined Osiris as a star in the constellation of Orion.

Legend tells us that an Apis bull produced 1000 bees, and that the bees represented souls. Intriguingly, the Egyptian Goddess Nut was the goddess of the sky—the domain of bees—and keeper of the title She Who Holds a Thousand Souls, which appears to refer to the 1000 bees—or souls—that are regenerated from the body of an Apis bull.

Similarly, the Hebrew letter Alef | Aleph carries the meaning 'thousand' and both the Proto-Sinatic Hieroglyphic and its Pro-Canaanite symbol depict a bull's head, alluding to the fact that 1000 bees—or resurrected souls, are produced by the sacrifice of an Apis bull. Additionally, Christ—the saviour archetype of Osiris, renowned for his resurrection, is written in Hebrew as 'QRST' and carries the value 1000.

The ancient belief that bees were born of bulls leads me to think that the underground necropolis known as the Serapeum may have been a ritual center of regeneration designed to recycle souls from the heads of bulls, and not simply a mausoleum for bulls. Might the rituals carried out in the Serapeum represent the earliest form of Mithraism, the Roman mystery religion involving the ritualistic slaughter of bulls?

Another ancient culture influenced by the ancient Egyptians was the Minoan, a civilization with close ties to the ancient Egyptians who were experts in beekeeping, a craft they later imparted to the Greeks. This leads us to another fascinating aspect of Egyptian bee symbolism; the Sphinx, the famed rock-hewn statue known by the Egyptians as Hun nb, but renamed Sphinx by the Greeks. How does all this relate to the bee? Quite simply, the Minoan word for bee was 'sphex.' (Hilda Ransome, *The Sacred Bee*, P. 64, 1937)

So what can we conclude from this revelation? The civilization that educated the Greeks in the craft of beekeeping used the word 'sphex' to describe the bee—and the Greeks named the goddess-like rock statue 'Sphinx'. Was the Sphinx already present when Menes first established Kingship and was it known that the Sphinx represented a bee goddess, hence the Pharaoh's title, Beekeeper? The possibility is tantalizing, and given the Egyptians fascination with bees, not altogether far-fetched.

The Lost Tradition

The influence of Sumerian and Egyptian bee veneration spread to Greece, where Greek mythology depicted bees on the statues of their most important gods and goddesses and evolved the notion of bee Goddesses into the honored position of female bee shamans called Melissa's, which later morphed into the sacred status of Sybil's. In fact, the second temple at Delphi is said to have been made entirely by bees, and the great oracle stone resembling a hive encircled with bees.

The Omphalos and Bee Veneration?

The Romans practiced Mithraism, a secret religion predicated on the ritualistic slaughter of bulls that is reminiscent of Egyptian bull/bee rituals that were performed in the under-

Bas relief depictions of Mithraic ritual bull sacrifice (Louvre)

ground temple known as the Serapeum. Curiously, the practice appears to have been preserved in modern times in the controversial sport of Bull-fighting, and many of Spain's oldest bullrings are built on or near Mithras temples, confirming the association.

Mayan culture venerated the bee and depicted gods in its image in their most sacred temples; and as far away as India religions adopted bee gods and goddess into their mythology. Even the Catholic Church incorporated the bee as a symbol of the Pope's authority; evidence of which can be seen in Vatican City today.

Beehive-styled stone huts were constructed in antiquity from Ireland to Africa, and many places in-between, such as Germany, where Heinrich Himmler, the most powerful man in Germany after Adolf Hitler, constructed the SS's most sacred ritual chamber in the shape of a beehive in the basement of the seventeenth century Wewelsburg Castle.

Political movements, such as Communism, drew upon the altruistic behavior exhibited in a beehive as a blueprint for their ideologies; while rulers such as Napoleon followed the tradition of their ancestors, in this instance, the long-haired Kings of France known as the Merovingian's—believed by some to represent the bloodline of Christ—whose famous King Childeric was discovered buried with 300 bees made of solid gold.

Precursor to the Fleur-de-Lis

Not only did Napoleon ensure that the symbol of the bee was infused in the decor and style of the royal court, and greater society, he adopted 'The Bee' as his own nickname. It is also believed that the bee was the precursor to the fleur-de-lis, the national emblem of France. The theory is supported by many, including the French physician, antiquary, and archaeologist Jean-Jacques Chifflet. In fact Louis XII, the 35th King of France, was known as 'the father of the pope' and featured a beehive in his Coat of Arms.

And then there is the strange tale of Pierre Plantard, a Frenchman who in the later half of the twentieth century promoted his association with the Merovingian's and was regarded by some as the last direct descendant of Jesus Christ. Plantard claimed to have been a Grand Master of the Priory of Sion, a controversial society with considerable interests in the Merovingian lineages commissioned by Napoleon. Curiously, Plantard's family crest featured both the fleur-de-lis and the bee, and he is purported to have written, 'we are the beekeepers' in his private correspondences.

French Freemasonry soon spread to the United States of America, aided by early American forefathers such as Thomas Jefferson, who wrote passionately about the importance of bees, while others such as President George Washington featured the beehive on his Masonic apron. In no uncertain terms, early American society borrowed many of its philosophical principles from Freemasonry, which had incorporated bee symbolism and themes into its rituals, and established its government on the orderly, stable and altruistic behavior exhibited in a beehive, like societies and movements before them had for thousand of years.

An indication of the bee's importance to early American forefathers is expressed in the fact that the entire Western Region of the United States was originally named Deseret (honeybee). Not surprisingly, folk culture embraced the bee, and the concept of 'telling bees' about the death of a loved one became common practice. The Austrian philosopher and esotericist Rudolf Steiner (1861 – 1925) wrote and lectured extensively on the bee and predicted its demise in just under a 100 years time, right about now. So too did Albert Einstein (1879 – 1955) predict the demise of the bee. The famed physicist is attributed with having said:

"If the bee disappeared off the surface of the globe then man would only have four years of life left. No more bees, no more pollination, no more plants, no more animals, no more man."

In 2008, bees began to die in alarming numbers; and four years after that—as Einstein is said to have predicted— is 2012, the date of an alleged new age brought about by a spiritual reawakening, or life-ending cataclysm, depending on which theory you believe. Curiously, the fate of the bee, like so many aspects of the world today—i.e. the economy, politics, etc.—is showing signs of recovery, as if echoing the fate of man, mirroring life as if it were part of our DNA and an element of our consciousness. And who knows, perhaps it is. After all, the bee has been held sacred since time immemorial for a reason, and that alone is a tradition worth remembering. ❧

Ancient Keys to the Future

*What's to Be Learned from the Changing
Seasons of Human Evolution?*

Walter Cruttenden

Textbooks tell us that civilization is about 5,000 years old. At least that's about as far back as we find the first writing and the first significant man-made structures such as ziggurats and pyramids. Before that was a period called 'prehistory.' Unrecorded, it was a time assumed to be far more primitive than our own.

No one would argue that a lot has happened since "prehistoric" times; useful things like the invention of the television remote control, escalators, and computer dating services. O.K. maybe some of these aren't essential, but they do show how different life is now from 5,000 years ago. In fact, most of the products and services that fill our lives today were absolutely inconceivable to our distant ancestors; and that's the point. Just as our great great grandfather could hardly envision our present, so, too, is it exceedingly difficult for us to see our distant future.

Just one hundred years ago, few could have imagined we would now be sending robots to the surface of Mars, cloning plants and animals, and carrying around little cellular devices that enable us to instantly talk to or text someone halfway around the world. If we could go back in time and query a nineteenth century farmer about these things he would probably say, "What's a robot and how did it get to Mars?" Or, "why do you want to talk to someone in China?" Could they have understand you? Cloning would probably sound downright scary to them—if they believed you. Relevance is a prerequisite for understanding the future—without it, it is hard to conceive of where we are going.

While predicting specific technologies might be very difficult, our distant ancestors did leave us a key to comprehending the future—at least in broad terms. They talked about it in myth and folklore and ancient texts; Plato called it The Great Year.

Ancient cultures around the world believed that history or consciousness moved in a vast cycle of time with alternating Dark and Golden Ages. Of course most scholars consider this just a myth nowadays and assume there was no fabled Golden Age. But an increasing amount of evidence suggests our remote ancestors (long before the classical Dark Ages) possessed tremendous knowledge.

For example, we find evidence of precision engineering in the pyramids and canal systems of ancient cultures in both Mesopotamia and South America. There are also tell-tale signs of a massive agricultural society in Brazil where we find the famed Terra Preta de Indio soil. It is self-replenishing, containing billions of living organisms per cubic centimeter, and plants thrive in it. It is found all over the Amazon basin, in measured plots averaging 2 to 4 hectares and laden with pottery shards, so we know it was used extensively by some unknown culture. This remarkable soil has been studied at Cornell University, but still no one knows how to recreate it. Scientist John Burke (see sidebar, page 61) has shown us that the megalithic stones at Avebury are neatly aligned by polarity.

The amazing non-random pattern tells us the unknown ancient builders could somehow detect the subtle magnetism in these stones thousands of years before we developed the instruments to do the same. All these things were thought to be impossible for ancient civilizations according to most twentieth century textbooks. Yet, here they are popping up left and right. Most of us are familiar with the more mundane examples:

Schools teach that Volta invented the battery in the early 1700's, but ancient batteries have been found in Babylon dating to the BC era (Baghdad Battery).

Textbooks state that complex geared devices were not developed until the great clock making era around AD 1300 to AD 1400 yet highly sophisticated gears were found in a Greek shipwreck that dates to the BC era (Antikythera device).

Orthodontics and dentistry were thought to be developments of a modern society, but now we find the Egyptians wore orthodontics 4,000 years ago and some skulls in Pakistan show neatly drilled rear molars that date to almost 8,000 years ago.

We were taught that Copernicus discovered the heliocentric system (Earth goes around the sun) in 1543, but it has recently come to light that Aristarchos of Samos and Archimedes knew of such a system almost 2,000 years earlier.

This story repeats again and again with engineered structures, metallurgy, plant hybridization, mathematics, and many other sciences. It seems we are just rediscovering that are ancient ancestors weren't so primitive after all.

Therefore, if we read repeated myths that our ancestors saw an ebb and flow of the ages, wherein history or consciousness moves in a vast cycle of time, should we not at least consider they might be right—even if we have not yet noticed such a phenomenon?

It should be noted that more than a few pre-Dark Age cultures (including Ancient India, Egypt, Babylon, and Greece) predicted their own decline as a natural process of the Great Year. And they were right! Every last one of them slipped into a worldwide Dark Age that obscured the ancient knowledge and nearly destroyed the culture. Many ancient discoveries, from the heliocentric system of the Greeks to the Babylon battery, were lost for millennia and not rediscovered until the "renaissance" (French for "rebirth") or later.

So how did these people know they were headed for a decline? Hesiod and the Greeks spoke poetically of the long lost Golden Age but knew their own time was in a lower age and descending era. They had hundreds of stories about the amazing course of life and history, tales that we now call myth and folklore, but they believed them to be true.

Our very distant ancestors lived much closer to nature than we do today. Their view of time goes like this: Just as the earth spins on its axis and gives us the cycle of night and day, and just as the earth goes around the sun and gives us the cycle of the seasons, so too is there an even larger celestial motion that results in a larger cycle. This cycle, their Great Year, a.k.a. one precession of the equinox, is said to have its own type of seasons or "ages of man."

The Greeks broke the cycle into the Iron, Bronze, Silver, and Golden ages. In one phase, we are said to progress upward and everyone and everything evolves to great heights. They implied consciousness would expand when they said humanity goes through the following stages: age of man, to the age of the hero, to the age of the demi-god and finally to the age of the gods (Golden Age) before the cycle slowly reversed itself.

The ancient people of the Indus Valley (whom Alexander the Great called the "Indoos," the writers of the Vedas) called it a "yuga" cycle and broke it into the Kali, Dwapara, Treta, and Satya yugas, corresponding to the Greek ages. Other cultures from the Hebrew to the Hopi also spoke of it although it was often in obscure language.

Giorgio de Santillana, the former professor of the history of science at MIT, states in his book *Hamlet's Mill* that this thought was embedded in several hundred myths from over thirty ancient, diverse cultures. This is how universal the cycle of the ages once was. Giorgio suggested that we should try to understand why the Great Year and its attendant motion of the heavens, the precession of the equinox, held such importance to the ancients.

There is an increasing body of modern work that examines the cycle, its nuances and possible causes, and it is gaining in scientific merit. In fact, the 6th annual "Conference on Precession and Ancient Knowledge" will be held this year at the National Academy of Sciences Beckman Center on the University of California campus where a host of scientists, historians, and students of ancient history will address the topic. But our interest here is not to discuss the merit or mechanics. Our focus now is if the ancients are right, then understanding the ebb and flow of the cycle can give us a glimpse into our own future.

Back to the Future

According to the Vedic scholar, Swami Sri Yukteswar, the cycle takes about 24,000 years (which is within 7% of the currently accepted periodicity for one precession of the equinox). By his reckoning, the last Golden Age peaked in 11,500 BC and consciousness slowly declined from this time until bottoming out around AD 500. We can see from the historic record that most of the world's great ancient civilizations are indeed in decline leading up to this point in time. In particular, Egypt, Sumer, Akkad, Babylon, and many of the cultures in the Mideast region have fallen to the point that they are almost nomadic societies, unable to build any of the ziggurats or pyramids of their ancestors. In Europe, too, Greece and Rome had fallen to very chaotic and brutal states, with most of the world's historians calling the final fall of Rome, and the shuttering of Plato's Academy (in AD 519), the beginning of the "classical Dark Ages." China went through a similar process losing much knowledge and turning fierce with the Han Dynasty. Many of the cities of the early Americas from Caral to Teotihuacan had also been abandoned by this time, but these histories are not as well known.

From AD 50 onward, we have slowly evolved to once again being capable of building great cities, codifying laws, and at least not crucifying people in the street anymore. With the burst of the renaissance (when we went from the lowest age to the next highest age) we rediscovered many ancient technologies and began developing many new ones. At the same time we have brought back democracy from the Greeks, and are slowly but surely building a more civilized society. However, we have not even scratched the surface of human potential according to Yukteswar.

As he explains, when we are in the lowest age, mankind is only aware of the things he can perceive with his senses and has no knowledge of finer forces such as electricity or magnetism. Then, as consciousness progresses, mankind slowly becomes aware of these forces, as well as other subtle forces and subtle laws. Later in this current age (the Bronze or Dwapara Yuga) we are supposed to realize the energetic nature of reality and begin to see ourselves as energy beings (wearing physical bodies). If we are to trust our leading physicists in quantum mechanics (that say all matter is essentially vibrating strings of energy) then maybe such a concept is not so far-fetched.

In the next highest age, the Treta Yuga beginning in AD 4100, Paramahansa Yogananda, author of *Autobiography of a Yogi*, tells us we will return to a pre-Babel state of consciousness where "clairvoyance and telepathy are once again common knowledge." Supposedly then writing, as we know it, is no longer essential. Perhaps that is why it does not seem to come into being until the post Babel age, even though mankind was capable of great engineering projects and other works that would seem to demand detailed plans and written communication as a prerequisite.

After that, the cycle suggests most of humanity becomes so advanced that the earth returns to a Garden of Eden. It is said then that mankind overcomes the limitations of time and space and communes with the stars. If true, it would certainly cast some light on the meaning of some of the early hieroglyphs and pyramid texts that hint at such capabilities. These kinds of things sound fantastic and impossible to our

Swami Sri Yukteswar

present state of consciousness, but Yukteswar and other proponents of the cycle would simply say we do not yet have the capacity to understand. The many ancient tales of magic and mankind's becoming demigods or gods are nowadays deemed to be the gibberish of a primitive people— even though Christ himself once said "These things that I do ye shall do also and greater things." Perhaps we just can't believe it. But if 2,000 year-old stories of a heliocentric system were found to be true, maybe, just maybe, the Great Year might be discovered to have a basis in fact. If so, we have a glimpse of the future. ∽

~ ~ ~ ~ ~ ~ ~ ~ ~ ~ ~ ~ ~ ~ ~ ~

Magnetic Avebury

Almost 5,000 years ago, the largest henge in English history was erected just 30 miles down the road from Stonehenge. Avebury is roughly three times the size of its famous cousin and even contains an English village inside. The purpose of these henges, and other megalithic structures from the Neolithic period, has long been a mystery. The recent and startling findings of two international scientists, American John Burke and Dane Kaj Halberg, only increases the enigma. They spent a month at the site and took over 1,000 readings with their flux magnetometer: Of the 66 remaining upright stones at Avebury, all have their North Poles pointing towards the next stone in line!

This implies that the Neolithic architects and builders could somehow determine the polarity of the stones and had a purpose for the arrangement of the small degree of magnetism present in the stones at Avebury. Like lodestones, all stones have magnetic polarity stemming from the time they were first formed by the earth in relation to the North and South Poles. But with most, like the sarsen stones at Avebury, this polarity is so slight it is impossible to determine without the use of modern scientific equipment. Consequently, it is highly unusual to find anything but a random arrangement of the polarity of the stones at Avebury. The odds of this magnetic arrangement being accidental is equivalent to flipping a coin 66 times and having it come up heads every time. It is a statistical impossibility.

The configuration of the polarity is strangely similar to a modern particle accelerator like the Large Hadron Collider now coming on stream in Europe. No one is suggesting the ancients knew anything of such technologies, but the massive site and the unidirectional alignment of magnetic polarity must have had a purpose still to be discovered.

The henges of Avebury

Burke and Halberg have now taken an electrostatic voltmeter and magnetometer to over 80 ancient sites in Europe, North America, and South America. They have found many similar examples of highly knowledgeable use of naturally produced and harnessed electromagnetic forces. These are cataloged in their recently published book: *Seed of Knowledge, Stone of Plenty: Understanding the Lost Technology of the Ancient Megalith-Builders*. They believe that many of the ancient mounds and megaliths were created to boost agricultural yields by exposing seeds to certain natural occurring electromagnetic forces found at these sites. It is known science that seeds subjected to a mild electrostatic charge tend to propagate faster than seeds left unexposed. However, they are still puzzled by the strange arrangement of polarity at Avebury. —*Editor*

For more information about the science, mechanism, and mythology of the Great Year, please look for Walter Cruttenden's book, Lost Star of Myth and Time, *and DVD,* The Great Year, *narrated by James Earl Jones.*

God and Gold

*What's at the Heart of the Mystery
that Provokes Such Intense Pursuit?*

John White

I s money the root of all evil? No, quite the opposite. Interestingly, the origin of money arises from humanity's search for God from our perennial human concern with the divine.

Before monetary systems began in the third millennium B.C.E., wealth was simply the accumulation of material goods, livestock and other commodities. The basis of economics was simple barter: so many cattle for so much grain, etc. But when wealth began to be stored on a symbolic basis by using money, which has little or no utilitarian value, gold was the primary substance used. (Silver was the second most common substance.)

Gold, the king of metals, is universally prized and most precious. Why? Even today, gold has relatively few p--ctical applications. It is used primarily for jewelry and ornamentation, decoration, dentistry and sophisticated modern technology such as noncorroding electric circuitry in computers. You can't eat it, live in it or protect yourself from the elements with it. Gold can't be grown or reproduced only discovered, mined or smelted from ore. Despite that, throughout history people around the world have been attracted to it. Although it has little intrinsic usefulness for human survival, it nevertheless was sought and valued even before monetary systems arose and was considered as the ultimate form of wealth for kings, priests and merchants.

In fact, gold was considered a divine substance with divine properties. According to Jack Weatherford in *The History of Money* (Random House: New York, 1997), the ancient Egyptians believed that gold was sacred to Ra, the sun god, and they buried great quantities of it with the corpses of their divine pharaohs. Likewise, the people of ancient India considered gold to be the sacred semen of Agni, the fire god, and they donated gold for any service performed by Agni's priests. Among the Incas of South America, gold and silver represented the sweat of the sun and the moon, and they covered the walls of their temples with these precious metals. Gold is the first precious substance mentioned in the Bible. Gold artifacts and jewelry have been found that date back 6,000 years. Nothing else in history served to display wealth, power and prestige as did gold jewelry and adornments.

Ra, the Egyptian Sun God

The Origin of Money?

Why was gold selected for use as money? The origin of monetary systems is not clear. Three types of origin have been proposed: a sacred or religious origin, a social or state origin and a commercial or trading origin.

The latter is preferred by economists because gold's physical qualities are clear. It is the ultimate commodity to use as a medium of exchange for storing value, and has been universally accepted as such since Roman times. Pure gold is the most malleable and ductile of all the metals. It is unaffected by air, heat, moisture and most solvents. In short, it is durable (noncorroding, unchangeable and practically indestructible), convenient (easily portable), malleable (easily worked), easily divisible, easily recognizable, scarce, beautiful and universally acceptable (prized).

All that is true but not sufficient to explain the use of gold as money. In my opinion, the commercial theory must be merged with the sacred theory for a complete explanation, because there is a psycho-spiritual dimension that must be recognized as well. That is the fundamental aspect of gold, prior to the commercial aspect. Nothing else shines forever, as if indestructible and immortal.

According to Paul Einzig, in his book *Primitive Money*, "Primitive man was guided by non-economic considerations. Among these [was] the belief and fear of supernatural forces. The evolution of the economic system in general was itself largely influenced by the religious factor." (I quote Einzig from an article entitled "Money Systems of the World, How We Got Where We Are" by Stephen Zarlenga in The Barnes Review, June 1996.)

The earliest money was ingots of precious metals used in Mesopotamia about 2500 B.C.E. This gold and silver protomoney was called shekels or talents. When money systems of eastern Mediterranean societies began shifting from a cattle standard to a gold standard, between 1500 B.C.E. and 1000 B.C.E., the temples played a big role in monetizing gold. Prayer and sacrifice by the temple authorities on behalf of worshipers brought, at the outset, great quantities of consumables as fees for such services; temples became the earliest centers of trade and commerce. As gold began to replace livestock as a medium of exchange, temples accumulated a large proportion of the existing gold. Their abundance of gold was one reason for temple officials to monetize it. Another was their control of existing gold stores; it would be difficult for others to obtain it except through them and they could therefore create a value for it by accepting it for their services.

The Divine Nature of Gold

However, it was the "divine" nature of gold that brought it to palaces and temples in the first place. The value of gold includes its capacity to remind us of divinity. Think about that the next time you hear someone say, "Oh, what a divine necklace" or "What a heavenly ring" or "That jewelry is simply out of this world." There is greater wisdom in those words than the speaker probably understands.

The simple truth is that gold is precious and has ultimate appeal because early in human history it was regarded, like the sun, as a tangible symbol of a higher state of being, a domain beyond the physical that is characterized by radiance and permanence. (Jewels are also regarded that way, as Aldous Huxley pointed out in a talk entitled "Visionary Experience," which I collected in my 1972 anthology, *The Highest State of Consciousness*. I acknowledge his insight as the beginning of my own consideration of money in relation to God.) Because gold is so durable—one could almost say eternal—and because it seemed to come from a world of timelessness and light, it was, for early modern man, a reminder of paradise, a sparkle of spirit.

Gold still has that quality and we still experience it that way, although for most people the experience is subconscious. Nevertheless, gold and, more broadly, precious metals and gems and even sky-lighting fireworks is fundamentally a scintillating symbol of the Ultimate Reality from which creation springs. To wear it or jewels somehow increases a person's appearance of worthiness; somehow it apparently makes him or her a "better" person of "higher quality" than someone who has no gold or jewels.

Symbol of the divine right of kings

The Meaning of a Crown

Let's consider that further. Think about why royalty wear gold crowns. Why do they place a circle of gold and jewels upon their heads? The answer: It creates an effect reminiscent of a quality originally thought to be embodied in rulers and leaders, but which has been lost through the ages. Originally, that is, when civilization arose leaders and heads of state were quite literally considered to be god-kings or agents of divinity. There was no difference between a spiritual leader and a political leader. Those who led their people in either sphere of activity were one and the same.

The "divine right of kings" to rule meant, theoretically speaking, that monarchs were superior human beings with self-evident godliness, which qualified them as worthy to lead their people and as worthy of reverence. Addressing them as "Your majesty" or its equivalent was meant quite literally, as in "You transmit or reflect the majesty of God." That concept is still present in a theocracy, where a nation or religio-political organization is headed by someone who is regarded as divine or an elevated agent of divinity, such as the pope, the Dalai Lama, the Emperor of Japan, and the mullahs of Iran. In non-theocratic monarchies, the head of state is nevertheless usually the head of the state religion. It was thus quite natural in early history for temples and the priestly class to be associated with the royal household.

The Meaning of a Halo

Halos in Byzantine art

That quality of divine superiority is the same thing we see in the halos around saints and angels depicted in works of art. A halo, for saints, is the sign of holiness; a halo, for angels, is the sign of their membership in a divine order of creation beyond the human. However, even a halo is only a symbol of something else—something that the artist could not represent directly and realistically. What is that something?

A halo is an artistic stylization of the bright golden light that surrounds holy people and celestial beings, and is especially intense around the head. It is a clearly perceptible indication that the person is worthy of honor and reverence. It is the sign of extreme holiness or divinity.

Both halos and crowns, when we penetrate to their true meaning, are symbolic forms of what clairvoyants call the aura, the energy field or envelope of light surrounding a body, whether human or divine. The word, aura, is derived from the Latin aurum, meaning "gold," whose chemical symbol is Au. The color, intensity and shape of the aura are said to be indicators of a being's physical, mental and spiritual condition. A highly spiritual person, one who is deeply attuned to God or to the Divine Source of our existence, can be identified by his or her aura, it is said, because it is literally visible and has an unmistakable golden color. It shines and scintillates like sunlight, and it has its greatest dimension and intensity around the person's head, where it is called the corona, the same word for what is seen around the sun during an eclipse. When royalty is crowned, of course, it is called a coronation.

That is what crowns and halos represent, and they are associated by tradition only with royalty, holy people and supernatural beings such as angels and archangels. That is, it seems to me, what gold signifies. In the center of ourselves, we are always aware of God since we are one with God, but the ego creates the illusion of separation from God and habitually substitutes itself for God. And all the while we subconsciously long for removal of the illusion so that Reality is directly perceived. Gold, through its various properties and qualities, is linked to God in the minds of those who do not perceive God directly through the ascent of consciousness.

Thus, since that is the condition of most of humanity, gold is precious and has been associated since the rise of royal, priestly and mercantile classes at the onset of civilization with the human outreach for God. In the words of James Buchan, the meaning of money (to quote his recent book's title) is "frozen desire." Because money can fulfill any mortal purpose, Buchan says, for many people the pursuit of it becomes the point of life. However, I reply, the point of life is God-realization; that is the heart's deepest desire, and it is not a mortal desire but a immortal one.

Ego misplaces that divine desire onto false substitutes for God-realization, such as power, fame, prestige, honors, social status and, of course, wealth. Through its permanence and its beauty, gold subconsciously reminds us of the goal of life, but insofar as ego blocks perception of true God and attempts to install itself as God, gold will continue to be a false god, and greedy accumulation of it an empty form of self-worship.

In the mythic view of history, human life began in a Golden Age. People lived like gods, free from worry and fatigue, free from hardship and suffering. They grew happily into old age and died peacefully in their sleep. That mythic view, however, is a false one; it hearkens back, in retro-romantic fashion, to a condition that never existed in history. The true Golden Age is to be found not in time but in timelessness—the timeless but ever-present condition known as heaven or everlasting communion with God. The timeless-now exists eternally, but can only be attained via ascent to a state of consciousness beyond ego called God-realization, because ego is itself the source of time and temptation, sin and suffering.

The ego, not money, is the root of all evil. Satan personifies the ego-principle in humanity. Satan, wanting to replace true God with itself, projects its yearning for divinity onto things and situations that it ignorantly thinks can substitute for God. Gold is one of the oldest substitutes, but it is nevertheless inherently unsatisfying.

If the conquistadors in search of El Dorado had understood they were actually questing for El Dios, they would have become conquerors conquistadors of the ego. If the miners in the gold rushes of California, Alaska and elsewhere had realized their search for gold was really a search for God, they would have erected temples instead of banks. Bank vaults retain, even hoard, the shiny metal; temples nurture, even release, the sparkle of Spirit. God alone is our true treasure. Only when we awaken to that fact via enlightenment will we experience the true Golden Age.

ଔ

29.

Apollo Seated with a Lyre
(Naples Archaeological
Museum)

The Mystery of Music

*Have We Forgotten Secrets
that the Ancients Once Knew?*

Ron McVann

The universe hums like a great harp string resounding a mighty chord answering each thought by returning a thing from that place where all things are stored.

Sound is the principal medium by which the higher animals express and excite emotion, and music, or sound indulged in for its own attractiveness, far preceded man's creation of a spoken language. The Thrice Great Hermes is credited with designing the first musical lyre by stretching intestinal cords of sacrificial bulls over a tortoise shell. When his half brother Apollo heard its beautiful tones he traded Hermes his prized herd of cattle for the lyre, which became a very familiar trademark instrument attributed to Apollo in its latter perfected design. In the mysteries the lyre was regarded as the secret symbol of the human constitution, the body of the instrument representing the physical form, the strings the nerves, and the musician the spirit. Playing upon the nerves, the spirit thus created the harmonies of normal functioning, which, however, became discords if the nature of man were defiled.

It has long been held that no music ever played could compare to the music of Apollo's lyre. Later, Apollo's son Orpheus became renowned as a master musician in his own right. Hermes was also known to have created the Pipes of Pan. Pan's music was known to be so enchanting that anyone hearing it played could not resist it. Pan could lure his listeners deep into the woods and when they found themselves lost they would become anxious and fearful, and thus the word "panic" found its origin into the languages of Europe.

The Ionic lyre had become perfected early in the seventh century BCE by old Terpandros of Lesbos, "father of Greek music," who increased its strings to seven and "canonized the Heptachord." Pythagoras and his followers believed that "all things are numbers" and that every structural form is, in essence, a piece of "frozen music." (For scientific confirmation of this idea see the following article. Ed.) The realization between musical sound and form led Goethe to declare that "architecture is crystallized music." Aristotle would later write that "the elements of numbers are the elements of things and therefore things are numbers." The alchemist

Robert Fludd believed that most primitive music and the natural sounds of the world are in the minor key, because the creatures inhabiting the lower planes of life have not the spiritual intensity to produce or respond to the major key. Plato had stated that the music and poetry of ancient Egypt were of such an exalted and inspiring nature that only gods or god-like men could have composed them.

The great teachings of our heroic legends, gods and history were handed down from the lips of bards, rhapsodists and minstrels. Priests in turn relied heavily on the emotional effect of chants and ritual dances. It is well known now that music can control the human heart, raise the courage of men to battle, spiritual adepts to the divine, quench the fires of anger, even cool or excite erotic yearning.

Pythagoras of Samos has been credited with the discovery of the diatonic scale and the correct measurement of music intervals. He viewed the entire universe as a vast musical instrument and was believed to be the first human to hear and comprehend the Music of the Spheres. Harmony is the combination of tones into a chord, and the laws governing harmonic interval are the ones believed to have been discovered by Pythagoras. Unfortunately the records of the Pythagorean community were destroyed, and it is not known that any of the formulas of his musical philosophy survived.

"The vital experience of a positive life revealed through contact with important music strengthens man's realization of the reality of his internal, invisible, psychic being."

—Manly P. Hall

The ancient Greeks took their music very seriously and composers could be fined, even exiled from the state, if their compositions were considered to be detrimental to the public good. The modern societies of today could learn many valuable and intelligent lessons from the Greeks of old. The ancients were far more wise in the understanding of the negative effects of discordant music upon both the individual as well as society as a whole. We know now that the rhythm of an ordinary army of men marching in perfect unison across a bridge can act upon the molecular structure of that bridge and virtually collapse it.

Nikola Tesla proved to the world that with perfect oscillating rhythmic wave sound patterns he could split the entire earth in half if need be. The great opera tenor Enrico Caruso could shatter a glass with the proper high steady pitch of his voice. The poets and musicians of ancient societies were sometimes held in higher regard then the kings themselves, such as the Druids. They were believed to be closer to the gods than most other earthly men. *The Iliad* of Homer tells us how the heroes of the Trojan War kept their wives faithful at home by leaving them to the care of the right musicians. In today's times a musician is probably the last person you would want to leave your wife with.

Through the course of our lives we are constantly maturing in our taste of music. In our youth our hearts beat faster and we are more prone to wild beats and fast rhythms. As we get older we usually learn to appreciate the finer tastes in music. As a people we still remain slow to adjust to new sounds we are not familiar with. Many composers that inject a fresh musical genius of their own style are not always accepted at first.

Richard Wagner's compositions were thought to be somewhat barbarian by some critics when he first entered the world stage of music. The music of Brahms when first played in Boston repelled many concert goers. It was found at the time that signs mysteriously appeared over the doors of the concert auditorium reading "Exit in case of Brahms." Now of course we have all collectively come to appreciate the full beauty of both Wagner and Brahms music and others of unorthodox creative genius as well.

Wilhelm Richard Wagner
(1813–1883)

Johannes Brahms
(1833–1897)

Until we learn to escape the immediate inclination to judge musical values in terms of the familiar, we will never grasp the true power and influence of the arts in the life and growth of the human being. The ability to understand the difference between harmony and discord is a first major step. Music is music. Noise is noise.

In music, harmony is the total symbol of pure beauty, and it appeals directly to one's consciousness, which is itself composed of harmonic elements. If you have ever felt yourself swelling with emotion during a particular passage of music, it is that mathematical perfection of harmony that is reaching your emotional heartstrings. Sound creates moods and stirs emotions. The theory of music is mathematical; the practice of music is philosophical. Man is thus surrounded by a supersensible universe of which he knows nothing, because the centers of sense perception within himself have not been developed sufficiently to respond to the subtler rates of vibration of which that universe is composed.

> *"Music exalts each joy, allays each grief, expels diseases,*
> *softens every pain—and hence the Wise of Ancient Days*
> *adored one power of Psychic, Melody and song!"*

—Armstrong, Celtic Poet

The vibrations of music serve as a healing quality for both mind and body. Negative thoughts and destructive emotions only discourage, run down and deplete one's energy. Music, on the other hand, does just the opposite. Most have become aware at some point that singing while you work makes the work easier and the time goes faster. Music is the least intellectual but the most intelligent and powerful of all the arts.

> *"Music represents the great struggle of reaching the 'wholly other,'*
> *which it can never express. And insofar as religion also embodies*
> *man's efforts to reach or respond to, that same wholly other, then music*
> *has its given place; without it, man's quest would be immeasurably*
> *harder, and his pilgrimage immeasurably poorer."*

—G. Van der Leeuw

Both health and beauty are intimately related, and to preserve the first we must cultivate the second. Harmony is the only basis of all of life's successes and happiness, while absence of harmony lies at the root of every problem of the human race. Simply put, harmony generates harmony and attracts harmony; disharmony generates disharmony and attracts disharmony. This applies not only in music but in all and everything in the universe. Harmony is imposed as a rigid law upon the entire universe of existence, except humankind, which has its choice, by exercising free will, of "Harmony" or "Disharmony." Which, in your fleeting days of physical life upon earth, will be your choice?

If mankind would only take the time to study the simple law of harmony found in nature, number and sound, and adopt it as a code of life, there would be an instant miraculous transformation in the world, which up until now, has always relied upon force in all things. Force is the antithesis of harmony and the key reason why mankind is vastly self-destructing and destroying the very planet that provides us the only sustenance to survive as a living species.

Even the hospitals, which are supposed to heal people, do quite the opposite and use force in most all of their applications. If someone is ill then the immediate remedy is to cut and slash in the effort to do away with the body part in question. Other resources would be to bombard it with radiation or smother the patient in the use of costly, unnatural, oil-based, pharmaceutical drugs that most likely have ten or twenty dangerous side effects. Hospitals are butcher shops, which, just like every lawyer, know how to do at least one thing right, and that is to professionally and quickly relieve you of your life's savings and hard-earned money.

There are only two courses of life open to mankind at this time in history and they are diametrically opposites. One is founded upon harmony, knowledge and intelligence, and the other is founded upon force, discord and ignorance. Surely force has its time and place within the reality of our world. However, when it comes to the point of a virtual annihilation of the planet and millions if not all of the people upon it, that is where the high intelligence of harmony must intervene. Those who now have nuclear weapons obtained such out of either fear or lust for world control or both. Those who now hold nuclear arsenals swear that they will never use them …. only as a last resort. Those who know their history and/or the pride and arrogance of human nature, know that it does not take much pushing to reach that 'last resort.'

This planet and all the people upon it cannot afford another world war, of which this time no one may survive, and the ones that do survive may wish they had died. Harmony! Not Force! is the only hope for human survival left to mankind in the doomsday world of force he has created!

> *"Nature is the shape in which the man of higher cultures synthesizes*
> *and interprets the immediate impressions of his senses. History is*
> *that form which in relation to his own life, which he thereby invests*
> *with a deeper reality whether he is capable of creating these shapes,*
> *which of them it is that dominates his waking consciousness*
> *is a primordial problem of all human existence."*
>
> —Oswald Spengler ☙

30.

The Legendary
Hiram Abiff Holds
the Plan for Solomon's
Temple

The Lost Word and the Masonic Quest

*What Is the Key to the Ancient Secrets
of Temple Initiation?*

Mark Stavish

In classic Masonic initiation the candidate for initiation would be blindfolded for the greater part of the ritual, and only through intense listening to the words of the lodge officers know what was happening. This detail may sound insignificant to anyone who has not undergone the experience, but for those who have, even decades after their initiation, entire lines from it are memorable because of the concentration given to what is happening around them. The effects of the denial of the sense of sight, the organ wherefrom we receive nearly all of our information on a moment-to-moment basis, is only accentuated in modern media culture. To be blindfolded and led around a room where you know nothing of its design, contents, or the number of people present, is truly a matter of trust and one that heightens the senses—even if only temporarily—to an unusually sharpened pitch. One begins to listen within as much as they listen to without. In truth, the entire Masonic initiation can be conceived as an initiation wherein we are listening to the inner Master rather than to the Master of the Lodge.

Those who have found "the Lost Word," the masons believe, have heard the voice of their Inner Master, the God within, and can truly be called Master Masons in both essence and form. The Lost Word has been recovered and is the True Word. The Substitute Word (more on this later) is no longer needed. The Master Hiram Abiff, who is slain by three fellows of the craft, represents the desire for humans to have power or privilege that is unearned. It is the false sense of self, derived from identification with the material world that slays and cuts us off from communion with our true Inner Master, and as such, until we can humble ourselves at the Porch of the Temple, we cannot enter, nor receive the Word. Until then, a substitute word is given. This substitute is religion.

Religion comes from the root, relig- or to unite, and the goal of most religions is to unite the human consciousness with divinity in some fashion. However, most fall far short of this goal, and instead are mediums, inculcating moral and ethical virtues into their adherents through the process of ritual and collective work. As such, true uniting can only occur on an individual level, and in the privacy of one's own meditation chamber symbolized by Hiram's daily meditations in the Porch of the Temple.

Jewish Magic

Within Qabala, the possibilities of magic are performed through the use of divine names. However, magic was considered to be a rare event, only performed by a pious person in times of emergency, and at physical and spiritual risk to himself. While qabalistic writings have warnings against the use of magic, there are no universal condemnations of it. This is further complicated by the distinction made between purely physical or material magic, and inner or spiritual magic, when such distinctions in practice are not always clear cut.

Spanish schools of Qabala made a distinction between schools of practice that they received from the Lurianic tradition using the Tree of Life, and those they perceived as being derived from magical practices based on the Name, or "Masters of the Name." It is these practices of the "Masters of the Name" upon which much of medieval and later surviving magical practices is based, including German and Pennsylvania 'Dutch' folk magic.

The Judgment of Solomon (Nicolas Poussin)

Within the widespread diffusion of Jews across Europe and North Africa, Jewish magic also took on some of the practices of its neighbors, especially Arab demonology, and German and Slavic witchcraft. The idea of 'the Jew' being a powerful magician, capable of conjuring up angels and devils, amplified awe of practical Qabala, and anti-Semitic fears. The ba'al Shem or "Master of the Name" was the archetypal magus of the Medieval period, and whose imitation many Christians sought, despite direct prohibitions by the Roman Catholic Church against magical practices.

Magical Writing

The belief in special alphabets attributed to angelic or divine sources is a cornerstone of phonetic Jewish magic. It also influences those in which the creation of talismans and magical drawings are also used, in that many of these images were composed of carefully crafted constructions composed of Hebrew letters.

The earliest of these so-called 'magical alphabets' or kolmosin ("angelic pens") is attributed to Metatron, the Archangel of the Countenance. Additional alphabets exist, attributed to other angelic and archangelic beings, such as Raphael, Michael, Gabriel, in the same fashion that various magical texts are attributed to Hermes, Solomon, Moses, and other important figures.

Reuchlin and the Miraculous Name

Johannes Reuchlin (1455–1522) was born in Pforzheim, Germany, and received a doctorate in philosophy from the University of Basel in 1477, and a degree in law from Poitiers in 1481. He traveled to Rome as part of the diplomatic corps, before settling in Stuttgart. In 1492 Reuchlin learned Hebrew at the age of forty-seven. This was a difficult year for Jews, and the beginning of several pogroms. Under orders of the new Catholic king and queen, Ferdinand and Isabella, Jews were ordered to leave Spain, convert to Catholicism, or risk death.

Johannes Reuchlin

Reuchlin's knowledge of Hebrew allowed him to study qabala directly from the original texts, and within two years he had produced his principle work on the subject—De Verbo Mirifico. De Verbo became a sort of Bible on what would eventually be called 'Christian' qabala. In it, Reuchlin claimed to have reconstructed the 'true' name of Jesus in Hebrew by taking the Tetragrammaton, or 'Four Lettered Name' of God in Hebrew – Yod-Heh-Vau-Heh—and inserting the letter Shin in the middle—YHShVH.

This name was quickly adopted to show that the true mission of Jesus was that of Savior, but also to show that within qabala, there were many secrets that had been forgotten since the time of the first Christian churches. This attempt to 'Christianize' qabala made it a politically safer topic for Reuchlin and others to study.

The position of Jews in Christian Europe was always a precarious one. When Emperor Maxmilian I ordered all books in Hebrew burnt on August 15, 1509, few might have really been surprised. However, authorities did ask Reuchlin, in what might have been an effort at entrapment for his Jewish leaning sympathies, if he felt it just to burn all Jewish books while leaving them only the Torah. Reuchlin answered "No" and was ordered to appear before the Grand Inquisitor in Mainz to defend himself against charges of heresy. Fortunately for Reuchlin, he was a well-liked man. Representatives from 53 towns in the province of Swabia spoke up on his behalf. To thank him for the great risk he took in their defense, the rabbis of the town of Pforzheim supplied him with the documents he would later use in writing De Arte Cabalistica.

De Arte Cabalistica quickly became the 'bible' of Christian Cabala after its publication in 1516. It was dedicated to Pope Leo X who had an interest in Pythagorianism. The basic style of De Arte is that of a dialogue between a Pythagorean and a Muslim that is mediated by a Jew who explains how kabbalah contains the oldest of divine wisdom. This wisdom states that the sacred letters and names of things, in Hebrew of course, are not just symbols, but that they carry the very spiritual essence of the thing they are related to. To substantiate his claims, Reuchlin references the Zohar and the magical text, Sefer Raziel (Book of Raziel).

Magic and Mysticism

While magic was seen as filled with dangers, and used mainly for creating effects in the outer world, mysticism, which used many of the same principles, was seen as a means of increasing one's personal holiness and relationship to God. Through prayer and meditation, it was believed that the individual could ascend the celestial spheres and at-tain increasing knowledge, love, and wisdom. These spheres, or the Biblical version of Ezekiel's Vision, was later adapted in Lurianic qabala as "The Tree of Life."

The end goal of these prayers and meditations was complete absorption into the godhead. In doing so, the breach between God and humanity, symbolized by the 'fall,' was repaired, and God became accessible once again. This often revealed itself in the form of ecstasy, sometimes even contagious to those around the one praying, and heightened states of awareness, such as prophecy, healing, and clairvoyance. These phenomena, however, were regarded as side effects of the state and not a goal in themselves. They were viewed similarly to Paul's advice on the charismas of the early Christians. A sign of grace but not the act of grace.

The Mason Word

In several of the degrees in Scottish Rite and Royal Arch, also known as Capitulary Masonry, or Capstone Masonry, the Secret Word is revealed to the Master Masons present.

Prior to this revelation of the Lost Word the Master Mason is given a word, known as the Substitute Word. Unfortunately, the oral tradition of Masonry has meant that in the transmission of this important word of recognition that the pronunciation has been garbled giving rise to two actual words in use. One is predominant in continental Europe and the second in England, the United States, and other primarily English speaking countries. According to Mackey, the second word came into existence and use during the formation of the High Degrees and the influence of the exiled Stuarts on Freemasonry.

What is intriguing about this is that both words have come to have their own unique and specific meaning, making both still of value to the Mason on the path of illumination and not simply a card carrier. This value is in part from the essential Hebrew origin of both words, the other is from the simple meaning of a word, or spoken phrase in Freemasonry and esotericism in general as well. However, in some instances this meaning must be injected into the word, or that word that the sound most closely approximates, because so many Masons were ignorant of the ancient languages, their meaning and pronunciation.

While some Masons will object to 'revealing' the Master Mason's

Word, it must be pointed out that these words are easily found on the Internet as well as numerous books on Masonry. It is hoped that they will realize this, as well as that without knowing the additional means of identification, or which world belongs to which jurisdiction, simple knowledge of the sounds will not allow one to pass themselves off as a Master Mason.

The Substitute Word

The identification of the Master Mason's word as the Substitute Word is of critical significance to the Freemason who is paying attention. The ancient religious, philosophical, and esoteric notion of 'the Word' is that of divine truth, unquestionable and omnipotent power and authority to create. Thus, if the 'Word' is divine truth, then the Lost Word must be that truth either forgotten, ignored, or transformed in some manner during the act of its very expression—just as clay remains clay, but is still modified when it is turned into a piece of pottery.

The Substitute Word can be seen as two-fold, either as a failure to find the truth, as the fellow-craft who went in search of Hiram failed to find the Word; or as a temporary bridge to assist one on their search for truth. It is a comforter to aid them until the Word is found. The suggestion of a 'Substitute Word' is found in various rituals of the 18th century, but is not identified as such until later. If the Word is then divine truth, the search of this truth is the very reason for the existence of Freemasonry and that each Mason's obligation and work is to find that truth. While variations of the Word do not change its essential character, the idea of it is critical to the very existence of Masonry. Without the Word, Masonry is dead.

The Word

Each Mason is tasked with finding the Lost Word, lost when the Master Hiram was slain, and from which was tasked the 12 fellowcraft Masons who went in search of his body, to return and tell of the first sound they heard, as that would act as a substitute for the Lost Word.

The symbolism here is particularly subtle in that the Word is not heard without, only a substitute for it, just as the Word of man is only a substitute for that Inner Word, the Word of God, of the Cosmic, of The

Grand Architect of the Universe, that speaks to our heart. This inner voice of God within is the True Word. It is unfailing, ever guiding, and life affirming, not only in the symbolic sense, but literally as the power of creation itself.

The Egyptians had complete confidence in the divine origin and creative power of speech. All living beings, of the material or spiritual worlds, and objects had their origin in the utterance of sound. The entire universe was understood to be under the control of men and gods who knew the sacred speech. In sacred speech, there is complete harmony between the spoken and the incarnate, between the ideal and the material form. Iamblichus regarded the Egyptian language as closest to the original primordial language of the gods, even more so than his native Greek.

This belief in the power of names and words is carried over into Judaism, with the sacred four-lettered Name of God, often called the Tetragrammaton in Greek, as being whispered from mouth to ear of the initiate. If it were pronounced aloud, all of creation could be undone. The *Masonic Encyclopedia* states that the Lost Word is none other than the search for the true pronunciation of this name—Yod Heh Vau Heh.

Of course, this doctrine of sacred or esoteric speech finds some of its most sophisticated development in the works of the alchemists and qabalists respectively, often referring to it as the 'Green Language' or the 'Language of the Birds' of which Solomon was said to be able to understand. Given the symbolism of the color green for life and the well known use of various birds in Egyptian and Oriental mystical schools, and even Christianity, for the consciousness—or soul—this term is easily understood as meaning that Solomon understood the inner voice of his Being.

Such notions are radically foreign to modern thinking, but must be reconsidered if the esoteric aspects of Masonry are to be fully understood. It is a proven fact that the very miracles described in the scriptures are possible. They have been done, are being done today, and can be done and are in harmony with the known laws of modern physics.

This original language is all but lost, and it is the initiates' duty to restore it. Just as the 12 fellowcraft went in search of the Word and found it not, but brought back a Substitute Word, initiates also use a substitute language, or series of languages until this inner Word can be reestablished.

Given this meaning, the Biblical story of the Tower of Babel, and the

The Tower of Babel (Hendrik III van Cleve)

idea of the Lost Word in Masonry are more easily understood. In many ways, the Tower of Babel is a fitting story for Masonic study, as it more closely fit's the Masonic myth than does the Temple of Solomon, for the Temple was completed and destroyed twice.

The Tower of Babel, on the plains of Shinar, however, was not completed. For Masons, like humanity after the collapse of the Tower, are confined to speak many languages and as such, encounter difficulty in the world of matter. The unity that we originally had is a faint memory, and the desire to reestablish it is seen in the desire for various forms of cultural, racial, and linguistic purity. Masonry even has an injunction against 'babbling' or meaningless speech both inside and outside of the lodge.

The only way that this unity can be established is individually, in and through each of us. The working tool to rebuild this Tower is the same as the Temple—the trowel, for it spreads the cement of brotherly love and affection. Only love can open the door to the true sanctum sanctorum that each Freemason must build for himself.

Excerpted from Freemasonry–Rituals, Symbols and History of the Secret Society *by Bro. Mark Stavish, M.A., 32°. Copyright 2007 Llewellyn Worldwide, Ltd. 2143 Wooddale Drive, Woodbury, MN 55125-2989. All rights reserved, used by permission and best wishes of the publisher.*

CR   CR   CR

Contributing Authors

(in order of appearance)

William B. Stoecker 2

    William ('Ben') Stoecker, former Air Force Intelligence Officer was driven to seek the truth through a lifetime of thought and study. As a result, he can effectively challenge orthodoxy in many fields, including science, history, astronomy and more. He is author of The Atlantis Conspiracy. *(<u>UnexplainedMysteries.com</u>)*

Steven Sora **8, 140**

    A Long Island resident, Steve Sora published the widely read and frequently quoted Lost Treasure of the Knights Templar, *in 1999. Since then he has authored four more books and over 100 articles. He is a frequent guest in documentaries dealing with ancient mysteries and lost history. (<u>TemplarTreasure.com</u>)*

Frank Joseph **15, 62**

    Frank Joseph is a leading scholar on ancient mysteries, and the editor-in-chief of Ancient American magazine. He is the author of many books including, Atlantis and 2012, The Destruction of Atlantis, The Lost Civilization of Lemuria, Survivors of Atlantis, *and* The Lost Treasure of King Juba. *He lives in Minnesota. (<u>AncientAmerican.com</u>)*

John White **22, 210**

    John Warren White, M.A.T., is an internationally known author, educator and lecturer in the fields of consciousness research and higher human development. He is author of: The Meeting of Science and Spirit, Pole Shift, A Practical Guide to Death and Dying, Everything You Want to Know about TM. *He has also edited nearly a dozen anthologies, including* Frontiers of Consciousness, Psychic Exploration *and* What Is Enlightenment?. *(<u>Amazon.com</u>)*

Michael E. Tymn **30, 40, 87**

    A resident of Hawaii, Michael E. Tymn is vice-president of the Academy of Spirituality and Paranormal Studies, Inc., and is editor of the Academy's quarterly magazine, The Searchlight. *His articles on paranormal subjects have appeared in many publications and he is widely read and referenced on these topics. He is the author of* The Afterlife Revealed, The Articulate Dead, *and* Running on Third Wind. *(<u>WhiteCrowBooks.com/michaeltymn</u>)*

Contributing Authors

(in order of appearance)

Stephen Hawley Martin is the only two-time winner of the Writer's Digest Book Award. His latest release, A Witch in the Family, *is an award-winning finalist in the "Best Books 2006 Awards," sponsored by USA Book News.* (SHMartin.com)

While in the Air Force, Len Kasten experienced a UFO encounter that transformed on his life. Since then, he has been deeply involved in UFO research, life after death, sacred geometry, Atlantis, free energy, holistic health, and related subjects. Len had written numerous articles for Atlantis Rising. *Len was able to bring his extensive metaphysical background into the writing of* The Secret History of Extraterrestrials, *which achieves a depth of understanding of the phenomena not otherwise possible.* (Amazon.com)

A full-time faculty member at Boston University, Robert M. Schoch earned his Ph.D. in geology and geophysics at Yale University. He is best known for his re-dating of the Great Sphinx of Egypt featured in the Emmy-winning NBC production, The Mystery of the Sphinx. *He is a frequent guest on many top-rated talk shows. His latest book is* The Parapsychology Revolution. (RobertSchoch.com)

John Chambers is the critically acclaimed author of Conversations with Eternity: The Forgotten Masterpiece of Victor Hugo *and* The Secret Life of Genius: How 24 Great Men and Women Were Touched by Spiritual Worlds. *He lives in Redding, California.* (NewPara.com/johnchambers.htm)

Ralph Ellis is author of the recently published, Mary Magdalene: The Princess of Provence and The House of Orange, *paperback available from* Atlantis Rising; *e-books available for Kindle and the iPad iBookstore.* (Edfu-books.com)

Contributing Authors

(in order of appearance)

Philip Coppens **109, 117, 132**

Deceased in 2012, Philip Coppens was an author and investigative journalist, reporting on subjects from the world of politics to ancient history and mystery. He lectured extensively and appeared on numerous television and DVD documentaries, including Ancient Aliens: The Series (The History Channel). *He is the author of* The Stone Puzzle of Rosslyn Chapel, The Canopus Revelation, Land of the Gods, *and other books.* (PhilipCoppens.com)

Andrei Znamenski **124**

A Russian native, Andrei Znamenski has studied Shamanism, Western esotericism, and the indigenous religions of Siberia and North America. His field and archival research in Alaska and Southern Siberia resulted in the books, Shamanism and Christianity: Native Responses to Russian Missionaries *and* Through Orthodox Eyes: Russian Missionary Narratives of Travels to the Dena'ina and Ahtna. *His latest book is entitled* Red Shambhalla: Magic, Prophecy, and Geopolitics in the Heart of Asia. (QuestBooks.net)

Jeff Nisbet **147**

While researching his family's Scottish roots, Jeff Nisbet discovered that one of the historical luminaries of the Nisbet clan, Lord Nisbet of Dirleton, had been an early Grand Master of Scottish Freemasonry. His research into Scottish history, the Freemasons, and the Knights Templar has led to an upcoming book and various articles for Atlantis Rising *and other publications, and for his website.* (MythoMorph.com)

Patrick Marsolek **156, 179**

A Clinical Hypnotherapist, Patrick Marsolek is the director of Inner Workings Resources and is a reporter and scholar covering the growing consciousness movement and its scientific implications. He is the author of Transform Yourself: A Self-Hypnosis Manual, *and* A Joyful Intuition. (InnerWorkingsResources.com)

Freddy Silva **163, 171**

Freddy Silva is one of the world's leading researchers of sacred sites, ancient systems of knowledge and the interaction between temples and consciousness. He is best-selling author of First Templar Nation, *and* The Divine Blueprint. *His first book,* Secrets in the Fields: The Science and Mysticism of Crop Circles, *is critically acclaimed, published in four languages, and a thorough*

Contributing Authors
(in order of appearance)

appraisal of this much misunderstood phenomenon. He leads tours to Britain, France, Malta and Egypt. (InvisibleTemple.com)

Edward F. Malkowski is a historical researcher with a special interest in philosophy, ancient Egypt, and the development of religious beliefs from ancient to modern times. He is the author of: Ancient Egypt 39,000 BCE, Sons of God—Daughters of Men, Before the Pharaohs, *and* The Spiritual Technology of Ancient Egypt. *(InnerTraditions.com)*

Andrew Gough is Director of the Institute for the Study of Interdisciplinary Sciences (ISIS), and Chairman of the long running esoteric research society, The Rennes Group. He is currently working on a television documentary on the Sacred Bee. (AndrewGough.co.uk)

Theoretical archaeo-astronomer Walter Cruttenden is the author of the binary theory of precession. He is the writer-producer of The Great Year, *a PBS documentary that explores evidence of astronomical cycles of time. Most recently he wrote* Lost Star of Myth and Time, *a book that provides an alternative view of history based on the solar system's motion through space. (BinaryResearchInstitute.org)*

Ron McVan has written a plethora of esoteric literature based on Indo-European heritage, the Mysteries, and Aryan mythology. His consummate Wotanist manifesto, Creed of Iron—Wotansvolk Wisdom, *is in its second printing. His latest release is entitled* Temple of Wotan—Holy Book of the Aryan Tribes. *(Amazon.com)*

A frequent lecturer on ancient occult knowledge, Mark Stavish is the Founder of the Institute for Hermetic Studies and the author of numerous articles on Western esotericism. In 2001, he established the Louis Claude de St. Martin Fund, a non-profit dedicated to advancing the study and practice of Western Esotericism. (HermeticInstitute.org)